ROLFING®

Stories of Personal Empowerment

SECOND EDITION

ROLFING®

STORIES OF PERSONAL EMPOWERMENT

Second Edition

Briah Anson

For Terese—
Hope and healing come in
many forms. Thank you so
much for your support &
our shared mission to
help this world a better place.

love,
Briah
9/15/23

Heartland Personal Growth Press
Minneapolis

First edition 1991
Second printing 1992
Third printing 1998
Second edition 2023

The words Rolfing and Rolfer are Service Marks of the Dr. Ida Rolf Institute®
Permission has been given from Rolfing clients to publish their Before and After photos. All photos are by Briah Anson unless otherwise indicated. Publisher/author is solely responsible for acquiring permissions and copyright compliance.

Original cover illustration: Jillian Platt
Cover design: Diane Waller

ISBN: 978-0-9629385-7-3

Printed in the United States of America.

Dedication

This book is dedicated to the living memory of
Ida P. Rolf, founder and pioneer of Rolfing and
to those who strive to express their human potential.

Ida P. Rolf, PhD

Ron Thompson

Contents

Linda M., dancer and dance teacher
Kathryn M., actress
Karin R., dancer
Kathrerine W., professional photographer
Rose S., professional model

The view from 2023

When this book was first released in 1991, as a practicing Rolfer® my purpose was to introduce the public to the practical applications and the many benefits of Rolfing® Structural Integration.

There followed a second printing in 1992 (also by Heartland Personal Growth Press), and a third co-publishing printing in 1998 with North Atlantic Books.

My intent in this revised edition is to furnish the reader with a unique insight into the healing powers of Rolfing, providing equal parts of information and inspiration. Parents will learn how Rolfing can help their children, even infants. Athletes, dancers, and performing artists will discover how Rolfing can help them increase their performance levels. The elderly and those in chronic pain will find helpful healing alternatives to traditional medical and surgical practices, and readers will benefit from the concise, insightful discussion of the healing link between the body and the mind.

The voices of 104 people whose lives have been transformed by the Rolfing process echo through the pages of this book. These first-person accounts, from parents of babies to seniors in their nineties, provide a unique insight into the immediate healing powers of Rolfing: its part in creating long-term wellness, and its place in the continuum of the body-mind connection.

Since the first edition, there has been an explosion of interest in Rolfing as an outstanding therapy for chronic pain, stress, and the release of trauma. There has also been an expansion in acceptance of many other modalities of bodywork, such as massage, deep tissue work, myofascial release, craniosacral work, and chiropractic, as well as the development of a number of schools that offer training in Structural Integration. There has also been a rise in acceptance of many forms of energetic bodywork, from Healing Touch, Reiki, Qigong, Frequencies of Brilliance work, to countless other modalities that affect healing in the body-mind arena.

We have also witnessed tremendous growth in the fields of psychology and psychoneuroimmunology helping us to understand how stress and trauma are held in the body-mind. Research has demonstrated that

Rolfing helps to resolve trauma embedded in our physical and emotional systems.

Dr. Bessel Van Der Kolk (MD, Psychiatrist and Professor of Psychiatry at the Medical School of Boston University) for the last fifty years has been studying the effects of trauma. He claims that Rolfing Structural Integration was the most effective modality for releasing the trauma of the bombing he experienced during World War II as a young boy growing up in the Netherlands. In his book, *The Body Keeps the Score,* he writes that trauma robs people of the feeling that they are in charge of themselves, and that it is like a severe stress response that never stops. He states that Rolfing releases the varied forms of chronic stress and trauma and its negative physical effects.

Rolfers have also championed research on fascia for decades and, in fact, Dr. Ida P. Rolf was one of the first to do so. Many Rolfers are leaders in the field of fascia research. This research is now bringing understanding to the important role of fascia and how it impacts structure, movement, and performance in the body. We are now seeing great advancements which support the writings and discoveries of Dr. Rolf. She was the first to understand that this all-pervasive, intercommunicating fascia is the organ that interfaces with gravity and determines whether we live with ease or disease.

Research by Robert Schleip, PhD, shows that our central nervous system receives its greatest amount of sensory input from myofascial tissues. Fascia responds to everything we do, what we do, how we move, and how we feel emotionally. Researchers, in fact, now believe that fascia forms the basis for proprioception (perception of the position and movement of the body) and interoception (sensations we often refer to as our sixth sense or intuition).

Dr. Rolf was a scientist (PhD in biochemistry from Columbia University, 1920) and a researcher for fourteen years at the Rockefeller Institute, doing work in organic chemistry. She was a longtime and serious practitioner of Yoga since the 1920s. She explored the professions of chiropractic and osteopathy; and studied cranial osteopathy for two years. She explored various schools and systems of movement including Pilates, Feldenkrais, and the Alexander Technique, and was very interested in exploring how structure and function (i.e., movement education) needed to work together. She worked closely with Judith

Aston and others to develop methods to help people move in a more supported and flowing way.

She furthered her studies in Europe with the exploration of physics, and studied the Materia Medica of homeopathy. She was truly interested in energy medicine, and knew and interacted with other scientists who were working in the field of frequency and energy medicine.

Dr. Rolf pioneered and developed the system of Rolfing® Structural Integration. Rolfing literally sculpts the body's structure into an aligned relationship with gravity so that it supports us instead of pulls us out of shape.

Toward the end of her life in the late 1970s, Dr. Rolf wrote an open letter entitled "The Vertical: An Experiential Side to Human Potential" (*Journal of Humanistic Psychology*, Vol 18, No. 2, 1997). In it, she expresses her concern that people do not seem to understand her basic developments, purposes, and ideas around Rolfing. Dr. Rolf stated that even though Rolfers and their clients would tell of their "wonderful, unbelievable" symptom alleviation, the guiding purpose of her life and work was the exploration of human potential. She went on to say that "Human potential per se neither includes nor excludes the palliation of symptoms."

Her clear conclusion was that there is no difference between the body and the mind. The evidence demonstrated to her that good structural health and alignment in gravity was no different than excellent mental/emotional health. Her guiding question and lifelong exploration asked "What kind of organism will develop if these body parts are appropriately related?" She concluded that "The vertical in man's structure is the outcome of his proprioceptive, sensory appreciation of the gravity pull of the earth. Whether consciously or unconsciously, he feels this pull and responds to it. This is a subtle concept: the intellectual formulation arises out of the sensory awareness." Dr. Rolf in the same article went on to state, "You cannot change the energy field but you can change the man. . . . What will be the psychological characteristics, the behavior both of the individual and of a group composed of such individuals?"

She went on to say, "Is it perhaps too far-fetched to wonder whether the taproots of human aggression and its underlying fear may be the continuous sense of insecurity which random humans unconsciously feel with reference to their environment—the energy field?" She concluded by stating, "It is possible that we are seeing the first conscious attempt at evolution that any species has evidenced." (All quotes from Dr. Rolf above are from *Journal of Humanistic Psychology,* Vol 18, No. 2)

So, why would anyone want to go through the Rolfing series? I believe the following quote by Dr. Rolf best addresses this question. "Some individuals may perceive their losing fight with gravity as a sharp pain in their back, others as the unflattering contour of their body, others as a constant fatigue; yet others as an unrelenting threatening environment. Those over forty may call it old age. And yet all these signals may be pointing to a single problem so prominent in their own structure, as well as others, that it has been ignored: They are off balance. They are at war with gravity." *Rolfing: Structural Balance Opens Potential* (The Rolf Institute, 1987).

For more than four decades working passionately as a Rolfing practitioner, I have had the great gift and privilege of watching people's lives and bodies change, and evolve into greater health and vitality. I have been inspired, sustained, and moved by playing a part in their transformative journeys into health and wellbeing.

I am hoping with all the research and advances in the field of fascia and Rolfing, you the reader will be inspired to explore this wonderful transformational system of healing for your own health and wellness. Furthermore, I hope this book might inspire some of you to pursue training in Rolfing to help alleviate suffering in your families, loved ones, and your communities.

Briah Anson, MA, Certified Advanced Rolfer®
Minneapolis, Minnesota
2023

About this book

What motivated me to write this book was the realization that I have been privileged to be a part of the Rolfing process of literally hundreds of individuals. I wanted to find a vehicle for sharing these empowering journeys with others who could benefit from hearing their stories.

Most of these people came to Rolfing experiencing some sort of pain in their life: physical or emotional or both. They are people who had exhausted their search for wellness in the traditional medical fields or individuals who had moved beyond the search for curing the symptom to a broader meaning of wellness in their lives. Without exception, the common denominator was people wanting to alleviate their suffering.

Another motivating concern in attempting this project was to get beyond the "anatomy" of Rolfing and instead assemble a collective, personal awareness of the Rolfing process. The definition of Rolfing is shaped by those who have embarked upon its journey. My intention, then, was to compile personal accounts of the various people who had been Rolfed into a book accessible to the public. There are a number of excellent books written about Rolfing but none to date on the actual experience of the Rolfee as told by them.

I decided to hire a woman who had been Rolfed to interview people who had experienced the Rolfing process. She was very familiar with the results of Rolfing as she, her three children, and her husband had all been Rolfed. I purposely chose a person who was not a professional interviewer, but who had the skills of talking and listening in an honest down-to-earth way about peoples' Rolfing experiences. These interviews were taped, transcribed, and edited by another person. Over 125 people were interviewed. Not all of the interviews were used in the final edition. I reinterviewed about twenty-five people who represented a particular profession and gathered more in-depth material of a more technical nature that I thought would be of interest to readers.

Rolfing is an inherently individual endeavor. There is no typical Rolfing experience. This collection of actual experiences will illuminate this point by describing various perceptions and demonstrating the similarities and differences. You, the reader, can then become learners from those who have already completed the Rolfing series.

This book contains the experiences either photographically or narratively of about one hundred people. Clients are of all ages, from infants to ninety year olds, having different life styles and physical and emotional conditions. They have had different reasons for coming to Rolfing. This book is a collection of their experiences, both positive and negative. I have made every effort to preserve the integrity of their personal experiences.

My clients over the past twelve years have included infants, teenagers, children, elders, dancers, musicians, accountants, bankers, executives, carpenters, painters, secretaries, and athletes, to name a few. Many of these people were living with chronic or acute pain in their lives.

I spend a lot of time educating my clients about their bodies and how to use them efficiently. I help them see the connection between their physical and emotional states. The more a person becomes aware of their total being, the more their goals broaden, becoming more inclusive. I have tried to continue this educational process using the format of the book.

I wanted people to understand that Rolfing is not an experience you do to people but something you do with them. It is a collaborative process. l am a guide with certain knowledge, skills, and talents. They come with their needs, a certain expectation and openness, and their imagination and mind to facilitate the process.

There is a consistency to the progression and pattern in the Rolfing series. Yet each person's story or life, the collection of history that is embedded in each person's body, is so different. The unwinding and emerging of the self is such a unique and exciting process. Rolfing is different for each person and that is what is so surprising. If you know someone who has been Rolfed, you might ask them, "How will Rolfing affect me?" "What can I expect?" A book that shares people's experiences is the most direct way to communicate this to you. To me there's nothing more refreshing and truer than people telling their own stories. Then you can decide if Rolfing is an option you might want to experience.

My hope is that these stories will be a wonderful journey of exploration for each of the readers as it has been for me and for those who are sharing their stories with you.

Introduction

Three thousand years ago, healing was considered by most people as a spiritual art. Those who practiced it intuitively understood the principles of unity and balance in life. Their interactions with others, animals, plants, and the elements, were based on the belief that the whole being—spirit, body, and mind—could not be separated from the environment.

The truth of this basic principle of unity of self and environment was discovered by Siddhartha, among others, in his search for enlightenment. The spread of Buddhism and Hinduism greatly influenced the healing arts in India. The various Yogic practices incorporated physical, mental, and spiritual health and growth. Ayurvedic medicine also reflected these philosophical systems.

The Chinese developed complex and comprehensive approaches to healing such as acupuncture, herbal medicine, and a recognition of our connection with the spirit world and our ancestors. The doctor not only treated the body but the spirit as well.

In the Southwest, the Navajo Indians still make sand paintings and use dancing, the playing of drums and other instruments, and chants to enhance the effects of herbal treatments.

The dream life of the Senoi Indians became an essential part of their healing approaches. This tribe, living in the upper Malaysian Peninsula, taught their children how to live and act in the world of dreams and how to integrate this with their waking state. New inventions, ways of planting, the ability to live harmoniously, and many other practical problems of life were solved in their nightly dream journeys. They learned the principle of self-empowerment through dreams and lived it in their waking lives.

Many of these indigenous cultures continued and developed this type of healing until colonization and Westernization began the disruption of these societies. The Western tradition of healing dealt mainly with symptoms. It was far removed from any integrated philosophy and even further removed from the daily lives and responsibilities of the individual. Body and mind were viewed as separate entities. Western thought rejected the belief that the mind could affect the body and vice versa. The Age of Mind and the intellectual tradition superseded what was considered superstitious ignorance and paganism. Over the

We are all looking for a way to evoke human potential. We are all looking for a way to establish greater physical and mental vitality. —Ida Rolf

centuries, this tradition grew and developed from the Middle Ages to the Renaissance. Healers, midwives, or herbalists, were often suspected of witchcraft and a great many were put to death. The power to heal was removed from the realm of the spiritual and was now primarily in the realm of the scientific. It was clear that such power did not belong to individuals or to the common people.

Under the continued influence of Western culture, medicine developed a tradition and belief system which discounted earlier models of wholeness in pursuit of "science" and the quest of rationality. This approach to physical and mental health was linear, intellectual, practical, and compartmentalized. The split of the self into pieces and the disintegration of the self from the environment had effectively taken place, and it seemed as if the baby had been thrown out with the bath water. Medical professionals saw the body as a battlefield. There was an entrenched belief that we could win the war against pain, illness, and even death. Medicine had become an attempted conquest—a battle against symptoms. Many improvements and innovations were made. Superstition and erroneous understanding were corrected. Many life-saving approaches and wonderful healing innovations have been made. Recently I saw a TV program about children around the world who had been born with various types of birth defects, primarily facial. The plastic surgeons who were giving these children dignity and social acceptability with their surgical skills were generously sharing some parts of our medical heritage that is helpful and to be honored. There are many research scientists who are helping us understand the makeup of matter, tissue, and cells, unlocking the mysteries of DNA and other previously unknown realities.

However, something was lost by embracing the metaphor of conquest so completely. This loss is becoming more evident as these methods of treatment approach their limit, lacking the power to heal. We have only to look at the crisis of AIDS, cancer, and other "unconquered" diseases to see that people are turning to self-empowering modes of healing to aid them in their journey towards health and recovery. The popularity of Norman Cousins' books *The Anatomy of an Illness,* and *The Healing Heart,* and Bernie Siegel's *Love, Medicine, and Miracles* are an indication of people's desire to restore the missing ingredients of self-empowerment, spirituality, and wholeness to the healing circle.

Let's look back for a moment to the 1800s as a few pioneers in medicine attempted to recapture a holistic approach to medicine. Samuel Hahnemann, a European physician, formulated the system of healing called homeopathy based on the law of similars, that is, like cures like. Essentially, he believed that nature had within itself the power to heal whatever disease or disintegration had occurred. Hahnemann felt that disease was not just the malfunction of an organ, but a disturbance of the vital force of life or life energy that is responsible for the functioning of the whole organism. By finding remedies that temporarily increased the patient's symptoms until they climaxed in a healing crisis, many insidious, chronic diseases, and physical dysfunctions were cured. In some ways, this was similar to the dynamics of acupuncture where a practitioner inserts needles at certain points in the body to stimulate healing of various organs, as well as to restore balance, thus helping the body to heal itself. The intervention in homeopathy differs from acupuncture, but the basic theory is similar. If the body is restored to balance, it will heal itself.

An American physician Andrew Taylor Still incorporated this same principle in the development of osteopathy. The first osteopathic college was established in 1892 in Kirksville, Missouri.

This approach to healing dealt with the musculoskeletal system of the body and its important interrelationship with all other systems. It was based on the belief that dysfunctions in this system could cause disease symptoms which would affect the functioning of other parts of the body connected to the musculoskeletal system through nerves and the action of hormones. The osteopath uses massage and other types of manipulation to treat these disturbances and, like homeopathy and acupuncture, to restore balance and create a level of wellness that is stronger and more resistant to illness or dysfunction.

Dr. Ida P. Rolf, PhD, a biochemist trained in traditional Western methods at the College of Physicians and Surgeons, Columbia University, studied the history of early medicine and spiritual healing. She understood the importance of Yoga, homeopathy, and osteopathy and through this wisdom built a foundation for a new and visionary approach to healing. The birth of Rolfing was an organic process that developed as Dr. Rolf worked on different people, moving and rearranging the soft tissues in such a way that allowed the body to straighten and balance itself. This process establishes an order in the body that expresses itself physically, mentally, emotionally, and spiritually. Based on Dr. Rolf's knowledge of the myofascial system, the wholeness of the body, and the interrelatedness of all the parts, coupled with the law of gravity, the process evolved into a series of sessions. Like many strokes of genius, it looks deceptively simple but is quite profound and powerful. Dr. Rolf's hands-on work with the fascial tissue did what Yoga and osteopathy could address only in a limited way. The tissue was pliable, sculptable, and a series of Rolfing sessions could accomplish what years of Yoga might. While osteopathic adjustments could cause change, if the tissue was damaged or pulling the musculoskeletal structure back to old positions, the effect of the treatment was not permanent.

Somehow, the fascial tissue was the organ of communication that acted as a connector for the other systems of the body. Dr. Rolf's profound understanding of gravity was the most brilliant final touch to her work. She theorized that if the body were in better vertical alignment within the field of gravity, then gravity would continue to extend the body vertically, rather than push it down. In fact, this has been demonstrated to be true. Once the matrix of balance has been established in the body, it continues to get "straighter" or more upright as time goes on. More observable changes occur between the last session of Rolfing and say, a year later, than between the first and last session.

The most vital ingredient in Rolfing is what brings a person to this mode today, problems that can't be solved anywhere else, such as pain, a sense of frustration, perhaps desperation about a condition. The healing ingredients missing in Western medicine—knowledge of the relationship of the body to itself and its parts, and the relationship of the body to the environment—are contained in the Rolfing process.

Rolfing works! As demonstrated in all the stories you are about to read. Rolfing is an integral part of the circle of healing. The circle began with self-healing, and a spiritual awareness of the universe. Scientific exploration of the physical body and of the universe has given us keys to unknown worlds. With work like Rolfing, the integration of those worlds brings us to a new place in the circle of healing and our quest for wholeness.

—Jude La Claire, PhD, Psychotherapist

What is Rolfing?

The Rolfing technique, developed by Ida P. Rolf, PhD, is a system for integrating the human physical structure. It is a form of connective tissue (fascial) manipulation and education and is based on the fact that the body is "plastic" or changeable and/or malleable. This quality of plasticity enables the human body to be anatomically ordered, thus lengthened and centered along its vertical axis.

Visualize a plumb line dropped through your ear, shoulder, pelvis, and legs through the ankle bone. Your head thrust forward, for example (in this model), has no support other than its own muscular effort to prevent you from falling by the shoulder, the shoulder by the thorax, the thorax by the pelvis, and so forth. Then gravity can promote balance. Gravity, according to Dr. Rolf, is the major cause of stress on bodies when they are out of vertical alignment.

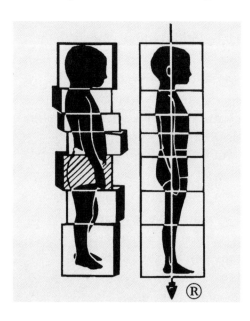

Vertical posture is not possible for the average person because the fascia (connective tissue) in the body has "set in place" and retains out-of-alignment holding patterns. Slumped positions are impossible to correct by simply "standing straight" after the person ceases to concentrate upon standing straight! This inability is caused through thickened fascia which sticks to itself in order to support the increased load on area muscles. These thickened areas remain after "slumping" or other causes of misalignment have long been forgotten. Physical injuries and chronic emotional states contribute to shortening and thickening of connective tissue.

They prevent the body from regaining its flow and freedom of movement. Thickening in one part of the body causes other parts to compensate.

Gluteal muscle separated showing fascial wrapping

Ron Thompson

1:1 ratio of fascia covering tibialis anterior

Fascia surrounds every muscle cell, controlling and guiding its function. It is a continuous wrapping that entwines all the muscle tissue in the body, as well as every bone, nerve, organ, ligament, joint, cartilage, and vessel.

Fascia can be broken down into three anatomical divisions:
1. Superficial fascia which is below the skin
2. Deep fascia, around muscle, bone, nerves, vessels, and organs
3. Deepest fascia, the dura of the craniosacral system
Fascia (from the Latin meaning bands) responds to trauma by tightening and shortening, creating a chain reaction with other parts of the body and, over time, pulling the body out of proper alignment.

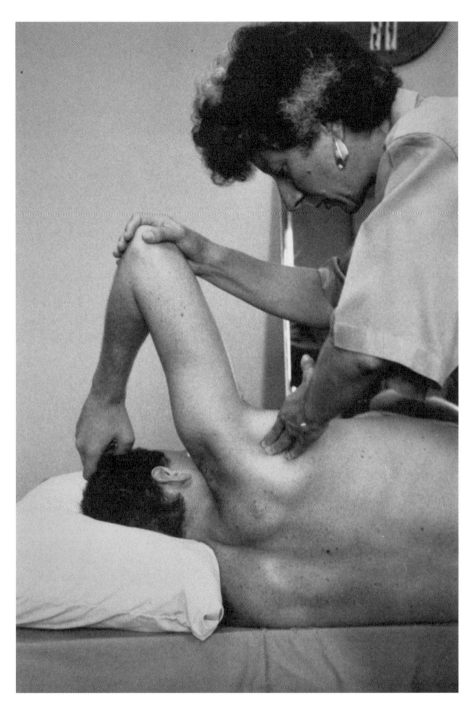

A key principle of Rolfing is that "the body is a plastic medium." The most immediate plastic component of the body that we can get our hands on, and physically alter in form and function, is fascia. Fascia gives form to the body; it is the most pervasive tissue.

Rolfing balances the fascial network by taking advantage of its ability to hold a shape induced by applied pressure. In a carefully developed sequence, the Rolfer reverses randomizing influences from the environment, moving tissue toward symmetry and balance that is called for so clearly by the architecture of the body. The process of Rolfing takes place in a series of ten sessions lasting about an hour each. Sessions are spaced in response to individual needs. Following the initial series, further Rolfing is available. This has sometimes been referred to as "advanced work" and may be undertaken after a suitable time has elapsed to allow for processing and owning new space.

What might you expect when you are Rolfed?

Rolfing practitioners are trained to see a body's structural organization. At the beginning of the session, the client is observed in his or her underwear, which is worn throughout the session. Then the person is photographed, usually front, back, and side views, to document the initial alignment before Rolfing begins.

The client lies on a cushioned surface while the Rolfer uses fingers, knuckles, and an occasional elbow to assist in movement and repositioning of tissue. There may be occasional discomfort associated with this stretching and loosening, but it does not persist after the tissue is released. Emotional release may accompany this process.

Subjective reports of the results of Rolfing vary from person to person. Generally speaking, a person feels a lift or lightness of the body as the head and chest go up, as the trunk lengthens, and the pelvis becomes more horizontally aligned. The knees and feet track more nearly forward; the soles of the feet meet the ground more squarely. Joints throughout the body regain freedom of movement, feeling as if "they were oiled." There is less pitching from side to side in walking and less raising of body weight with each step. Thus energy is conserved and is available for other purposes.

Many people who have completed ten sessions of Rolfing report psychological and emotional changes. The reports are as varied and complex as the people experiencing these changes. Some people report an enhanced and more positive self-image, new ease in interpersonal relationships, and increased self-confidence.

Briah's story

This being the twelfth anniversary (1991) of my becoming a Rolfer, I have spent much of the past year in a reflective mood. It's hard to believe the years have passed by so quickly. My excitement about the work is as fresh as ever. What a tremendous gift and benefit! I've had the chance to experience many modalities of body therapy, and I continue to believe most sincerely that Rolfing provides the best opportunity for me to help relieve people of their suffering. I would not trade my profession for any other. It has fulfilled my life-long dream. Growing up a natural athlete, I lived for the exhilaration of performing, competing, and experiencing my body to its fullest potential and form. I was junior golf champion of Costa Rica for several years, an avid equestrienne, swimmer, dancer, and tennis player. A day in bed felt like prison. One of my worst fears was of breaking an arm or leg or being disfigured in some way.

During my early teens I did volunteer work with physically and mentally handicapped children in Costa Rica. Many times I thought I couldn't bear to watch them one more minute. Simple tasks took them forever because their lives were so frightfully limited. The thought of ever becoming that limited terrified me, but along with that terror came a desire to help. In my mind's eye, I would sculpt the bodies of hunched-over old people, making them straight and tall again. I would change those handicapped children back to normal, healthy, beautifully functioning people. This was a vision of my mission in life. I never did break my bones, although I did have some interesting horseback and biking accidents. I fell out of a few trees, fell through cattle guards, and skidded down slick roads while bike riding. These physical bruises eventually took their toll on my body.

The first time I experienced a severe limitation was during my sophomore year in college. I was on the men's varsity tennis team and, halfway through the season, came down with a severe case of shin splints. It was crippling. I walked on crutches for weeks. I learned that my humbled body was not invincible. Years later I was working at the University of Minnesota-Morris as the Director of Residential Life, when a severe case of shin splints struck me again, and I had to navigate on snow and ice with crutches. About the same time, I was in a bad car accident and experienced severe trauma to both knees. Climbing stairs was painful. I was a practicing Buddhist, and kneeling was also painful. I suddenly started to feel older.

A few years later at a month-long professional development seminar in Estes Park, Colorado, I finally realized that I wanted a job that would integrate all my skills, abilities, and talents and enable me to use them to help facilitate growth in others. I knew somehow, in the core of my being, that becoming a Rolfer would satisfy that need. As a practicing Buddhist, I believed in the principle of the oneness of mind and body. Rolfing is a physical process of restructuring the body and aligning it within the gravitational and electromagnetic fields, which then allows the person's real being to emerge. It is, in a sense, a way of releasing the history that is stored in our bodies. It's amazing what happens when you bring a body to order within the vertical field. There are incredible changes that happen on every field, every plane. Regardless of the symptoms, Rolfing is a process that frees a person. It made total sense to me, and I decided I would make it my profession.

I went back to Minnesota, talked with the provost and gave a year's notice. When I told my parents they said, "But what about your benefits, your salary?" My parents had spent a lot of their hard-earned money to send me to college. It was a big sacrifice in their lives. And for me to go into a profession they had never heard of, something having to do with the body outside of the medical profession, was difficult for them to understand. At that time so few people knew about Rolfing. It was still the pioneering days.

In the meantime, I found a Rolfer about 150 miles away and began getting Rolfed myself. During my first Rolfing session, I felt like my rib cage had expanded several sizes. It felt incredibly wonderful to breathe. I had acute asthma in my childhood and occasionally in later years. If you haven't struggled with a great shortness of breath, it's hard to imagine what a full, effortless breath feels like.

After my first Rolfing session I went swimming; and I felt as though I could fly through the water. I had been a competitive swimmer, and I remember thinking, "What would it have been like to have been Rolfed as a young child or in college? No one could have caught me." The wheels of possibilities started turning in my head. The second Rolfing session dealt with my feet and legs. This session was very different from the first session, which was one huge rush. Everything the

Rolfer did felt awful. I thought, "This has to be worse than torture." It felt like sharp knives. I sat up to see what she was doing to my feet. I was sure she had a knife in her hand. I wore a AA shoe and had an extremely high arch; this was part of the structural problem with the extreme tightness I had in my shin bones and calves. My legs felt extremely tired, and the feeling seemed to last for days. I seemed to be reexperiencing many of the old aches and symptoms I used to have. Gradually my shoes started feeling funny, like they didn't belong to me. The bumps and curves were in the wrong place.

I was beginning to change form. My Rolfer would photograph me after each session, and we would study the photographs together. I was excited at how well I could see the changes, how unbelievable and yet perfectly natural it was. When I compare the After-Three photo to the Before-One photo, I noticed how much I looked like my mother in the Before-One photo. In the After-Three photo, that look of sadness and depression was gone. That was particularly significant for me. I realized the impact of this structural body work into the very fibers of my personality. A new connection was made—I could release many of the patterns that I had unconsciously taken on.

In theory, I had never doubted that our histories are anchored in our bodies, but to experience that reality with a whole new exterior look was really something! My chronic up-and-down emotional patterns seemed to be lessening. The cycles of depression were shorter. Something shifted again with sessions four and five. I experienced some old asthma coming out, even though it had been five years since my last asthma attack. It surprised me at first, but then I remembered the second session where we worked on my feet and how bad they felt for a few days. Later I suddenly had feet and legs that felt alive.

I was getting longer and younger looking, reversing the aging process. I began to realize that people who are not as straight seem to age faster. I seemed to be laughing and crying more. I had a lot of emotional release. It seemed as though I had a bottomless pit of sadness and grief.

And then we came to the seventh session. The Rolfer did some work inside of my mouth, along my gums. She seemed to hit one pocket of physical and emotional hurt after another. I relived all those times my braces would cut into my gums, endless visits to the dentist and orthodontist. I experienced all of it again and wanted the Rolfer to get the hell out of my mouth as fast as she went in there.

Then came some work inside my nose, which released sheer terror. I cried out, "No, please don't." The invasion seemed unreal beyond belief.

Each time she worked around my neck and head I felt quite panicky. Why did I keep thinking my head might just come off? I had a headache that lasted for days. She did some more work with me, and it seemed to help. During those days of pain, I think I felt every injury that had ever occurred. When I was 13, I had a collision on horseback with a herd of cows and had a pretty serious brain concussion. I was scared that those symptoms were back. I felt totally out of control, powerless and helpless in my body.

These events during my own Rolfing process became clear teachers regarding how events, physical or otherwise, are embedded in the body tissue. I learned l wasn't as invincible as I thought. Even a physically healthy, competitive athlete like myself could also be a wreck. I had spent the first thirty years of my life pushing the living daylights out of my body and thought I was in super shape.

Then I experienced the integrating sessions—eight, nine, and ten. I finally had some resolution to all these dramatic events that kept surfacing in my body. Another unexpected turn: I felt my whole body become very soft. It seemed as though my muscles had become too soft. I started having an identity crisis with my body. "Look what you're doing to me now," I raged at my Rolfer. "I'm pure mush." What surfaced for me were some real core identity issues. If I'm not my old body, then who am I, anyhow? This wasn't the image I had worked so hard to create. I had spent years developing my body, and I thought it was a pretty good one at that. I liked all those hard, well-defined muscles. Now it seemed I couldn't find them. I felt confusion. I didn't seem to be at home in this new body. I hated my body. I hated me.

There was no question that I objectively liked what I saw in my After-Ten photos. I looked years younger. I looked as though I had lost ten pounds at least, and yet I hadn't lost a pound. I had a longer waistline, a longer neck. I looked good! And yet I had all this awareness and feeling of self-hatred about how ugly and unathletic I felt.

My Rolfer explained that it was important to take a breather from Rolfing to give the body time to integrate all of the changes. "When am I going to get my body back?" I wondered. I would just have to hang in there with all these changes.

A few months later I enrolled at the Rolf Institute in Boulder, Colorado. I took a lot of prerequisites—movement sessions, anatomy, physiology, pre-med courses. And I became licensed in massage.

About five months after I had completed the initial Rolfing series, I realized I felt all connected. It felt as if those soft, mushy muscles suddenly had wonderful elastic tone. I felt well-put-together. Now I was beginning to understand what this spontaneous reorganization of the body was all about. The process of waiting for further Rolfing to allow the body to change is an important concept. It was as if my body took those first five months to reach that clear point of integration. This body of mine finally felt as though it was me—the "me" I dreamed of. I could finally see it and feel it. A whole new clarity came into my life.

I started learning about this unique process, about how each person is different; no two bodies ever look or feel the same. A body can feel very different from the left side to the right side, from front to back, top to bottom. A body can feel different one inch of the way to the next. It was difficult to predict what the Rolfee would experience. Rolfing became a journey of exploration, for both the client and for me. Together we could explore new possibilities, uncover new realities.

After my first phase of Rolfing training, I had a three-month integrating period. I discovered I had a lot of emotional issues that surfaced from the twenty or so Rolfing sessions I had experienced to that date. Childhood things, abandonment issues, cultural issues (I had been raised in Costa Rica until I was almost 18), feminist issues, authority issues, sexual issues—the list went on and on. How could I feel so weak and vulnerable? I had always had my act together!

According to Ida Rolf, a balanced structure creates a stronger person, a more secure person. Ironically, I felt as if I were falling apart. It was as though that stronger self could allow the old self to grieve and know that it wouldn't fall apart. This proved a crucial part of my education and helped me to understand the process with my clients. The discovery of a balanced structure allows many of the unresolved life experiences to have their completion. It was tremendously growthful therapy.

Rather than believing that therapy was for the screwed up or weak, my perspective changed. I discovered that therapy was a strong adjunctive process which could also accelerate my growth and empowerment. This was an important connection to learn for myself as well as my clients. I could open doors for my clients. Some people would choose to walk through and others would not. We each have many choices, alternatives, rates of change, and growth.

My own therapy and internal healing were becoming the impetus for me to be a truly more compassionate guide for my own clients. The better I dealt with my own pain, the easier it was for my clients to gain access to their own areas of work and feel safe. I began to understand that my own clarity, working through my own issues, translated directly into my touch. Why does the work of one Rolfer feel sharp and the work of another does not? How much of that process is theirs or mine? Tricky questions, but very real aspects of human touch and interaction.

In my ongoing training as a Rolfer, I continued to have Rolfing sessions on a regular basis and to explore ways to gain more clarity, definition, openness, and self reliance. I wanted to learn anything that would allow me to be fully present and available for my clients.

After completing my training at the Rolf Institute in 1979, I came to Kansas City, one of the most beautiful cities in the Midwest, I think. When I opened my practice here, few people had heard of Rolfing. I began with three or four clients who had attended workshops I had done in Minnesota. Since there was a Rolfer who used to travel from Aspen to Kansas City, there were, after all, some people in Kansas City who had prior knowledge of Rolfing. My practice grew as one person told another. For a number of years, I Rolfed clients who had some kind of severe physical problem and hadn't been able to get any relief from any of the established medical centers. I joked about how Rolfing was a last-ditch hope for many people.

I also seemed to attract clients who helped me face new challenges, new parts of myself, which I had not previously encountered. I learned that I could wear myself out trying to help my clients. While one would experience very dramatic results, the next would feel the results were subtle. So much depends on the client's ability to accept change, to accept wellness, and to have the capacity to be more of him or herself. I do my best for my clients and leave the rest to them.

Some similar characteristics underscore the clients who have walked through my office. They are ready for a quality life. They are ready to feel, to have their bodies working well, to move with more fluidity, to not be preoccupied with a nagging this-or-that. These are people who feel they deserve more out of life, that life can be pleasurable. They feel that at 40, they can be more pain-free than ever before, that their bodies can be flexible and fluid even at 40, 50, 60, or 70 years of age. These are people who believe a body can be sculpted to a new and better self.

Today I started Rolfing Mike, a 21-year-old carpenter. Three days ago I met with him to take his history and show him some photographs of people who have been Rolfed. This morning he said to me "You know, I had the best weekend. I was so happy. Everything seemed to go well for me. I haven't had a weekend like this since my car wreck seven months ago." Why? I felt a spirit of hope had been communicated to Mike through our interaction and my sharing those visual possibilities with him.

Today, as I gave him his first Rolfing session, he couldn't believe that just a few minutes of work on his left arm, which had been badly broken in the car accident, could make all the difference in the world. He could extend his arm fully, without a painful catch, without it hurting. He was simply amazed by the fact that his misshapen arm was beginning to look and feel normal. The hard knots now felt smooth and were beginning to disappear. This is only the start of his journey with Rolfing. It may be a long one because Mike is a young man who is lucky to be alive today. He had had several surgeries and many weeks of hospital stay, months of home care and physical therapy, just to be able to limp into my office. He understands the possibilities that lie in store for him, and he is excited and filled with hope.

As for me, what a gift to be able to help not only relieve Mike's suffering, but more importantly, help him regain his body and spirit. He told me that at the end of the first session he felt as if a huge fog had been lifted from him. He recognized that he had been depressed from having no energy. Hurting and feeling disfigured in his body, he had even quit dating because he felt so bad about how he looked. These are things that fairy tales speak of, so it's hard to believe. As client after client has remarked upon seeing Before and After photographs of Rolfed bodies, "It's almost too good to be true." The realization that it is possible to mold the physical, and often the emotional, self into a shape that looks and feels better is amazing and exciting. It is the birth of hope.

Thinking back on my own Rolfing, I can see that with the resolution of a lot of my personal issues, I was able to tap into other dimensions of space and time. I would experience myself living in different periods of history and in different parts of the world—Greek, Egyptian, Mayan, among others—that seemed to explain why I felt so drawn to certain types of art, motifs, time periods. I could literally feel my body as it was in a former lifetime. I could experience actual events and understand why I had certain fears or phobias. Gaining access to myself in this new dimension allowed me to work through some of these issues and resolve those fears and phobias.

After I had been Rolfing for three or four months, I had a body experience regarding the collective unconscious. It was the last session on a Friday afternoon and my client's first session. I worked up along her armpit and suddenly there was a very peculiar odor in the room and particularly in my hands. I must have washed my hands ten or twelve times that evening, but that smell would not leave. The odor was not familiar to me, and it was strong and unpleasant.

That night I woke in a cold sweat from a nightmare. I had seen burning bodies as if I were right there. I was horrified. I had never experienced a dream so vivid and real. Within minutes I was running a fever and was quite ill for a couple of days. I later found out that the parents of my Friday afternoon client had both survived Auschwitz as teenagers.

This information filled me with deep compassion, and I made another important connection. The body truly is the repository for our collective experience. We can and do pass on the unresolved experiences and traumas from one generation to another. I had believed in the collective unconscious, but experiencing it took me to a new dimension. A dimension that I could no longer just understand intellectually. Think of the therapeutic possibilities contained in this kind of experience!

I've experienced many types of body therapy, and there is nothing like a good Rolfing session. It's like being able to have your soul scrubbed clean. After a Rolfing session, I feel like a human being again. There is something very right about being able to feel free and effortless in your body, clean from any nagging. Over the course of twelve years, I have been privileged to embark on a process of discovery with my clients, as well as with myself. I have noticed that there always seem to be a set of "right conditions" that bring people to Rolfing. Almost from the start of my practice, it seemed that I had clients who fell into one category or another. They were in a major transition point in their lives—they came as a last-ditch effort for their lives—or they came sick and tired of the old patterns in their lives and wanted to bust through to a new, more expansive life. In essence, they were ready for a change. Clients were not only interested in a physical change, but they also wanted a new self, a self that not only felt better but could be and do more. They wanted a "Me" that was more of who they truly were. Through Rolfing, they could finally discover more of that person they knew was in there but couldn't quite reach. They could finally feel secure or confident enough to go out and do whatever they had always dreamed of doing. They were ready for a process that uncovered and released much of the pain, the victimization of life. They were ready to find a self that could stand up and take charge of life. A self that was okay with change. And, most importantly, a self that said clearly with every fiber of their body, "I am ready to rid myself of the pain I am lugging around." This is what the following stories, my own included, are all about.

Giving length and strength to the lower back

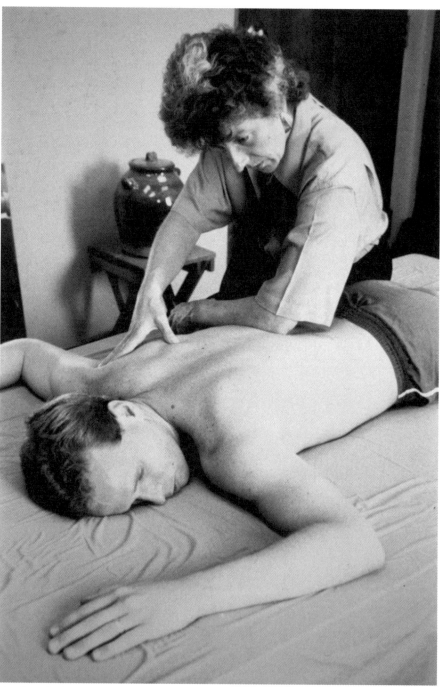

Briah with client

Rolfing Reflections

So many of my clients come in with back problems and want a "quick fix." They think you fix the part, when you really need to work on the whole structure. Their problem isn't just in their back, but in how the different segments of the body relate to one another.

Even as early as the second session, which deals with organizing the feet and legs, clients will begin to experience not only length in their back, but some relief from pain as well. There is a great deal of lengthening and untwisting going on. By giving lift to the upper body, we lift the torso off the pelvis and give space to the lumbar spine, resulting in less pressure from the upper body on the lower back.

This is one step in a sequence. In every step I am giving length and lift to the body with the direct goal of establishing a horizontal pelvis. As Ida Rolf taught, since bodies are still in the process of evolving toward the upright, the lumbar spine is an area where all bodies need more length and strength.

I can often tell just from looking at the client's foot how the rest of the body is going to be. Many body problems originate from a foundation that is out of alignment.

Basic support begins in the feet. It would be impossible for a Rolfer to fix a bad back without first balancing and organizing the structure of the feet and legs.

If you've ever broken a foot or sprained an ankle, and felt how it threw off the rest of your body, then you begin to understand the importance of basic foundation and balance over the center of your feet.

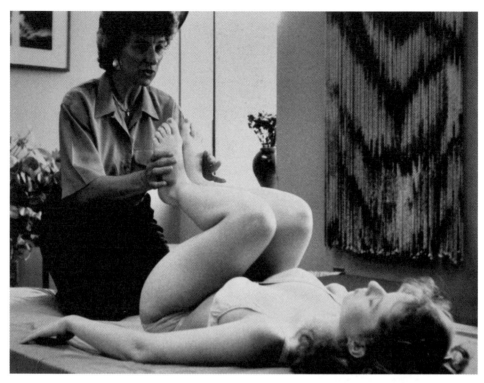

When you look at After pictures of people who have been Rolfed, you'll notice that they appear longer, lighter, and leaner. Almost all of my clients are taller after Rolfing, depending on how much curve they had in the their spines to begin with.

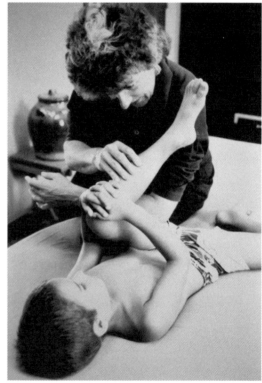

Rolfing Reflections

The goal of each session is to get the pelvis more horizontal, and the body more vertically lengthened and aligned. Putting the pelvis back in a normalized, horizontal position allows the stomach to fall back, creating a longer appearance, a flatter stomach, and a true front-to-back balance.

Sit-ups tighten and shorten abdominal muscles and aggravate chronic low back problems. Establishing soft tissue balance between abdominal muscles and muscles of the back provides an instant sense of relief and of lightness and slimness.

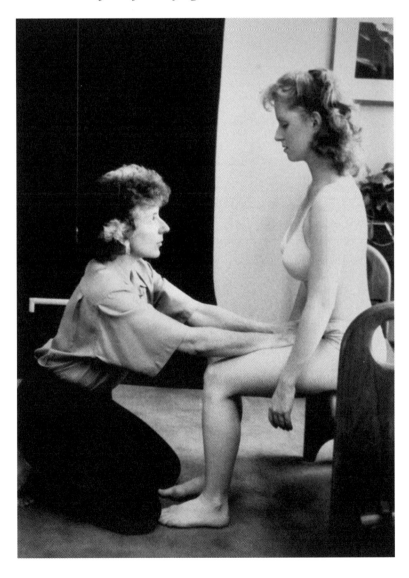

One of the problems with bodies is they need length. Every session of Rolfing concludes with special attention to the neck, back, and pelvis, as a way of integrating or tying together the individual Rolfing sessions.

One of my goals is to help people find their maximum vertical length, which extends out through the top of their head and neck.

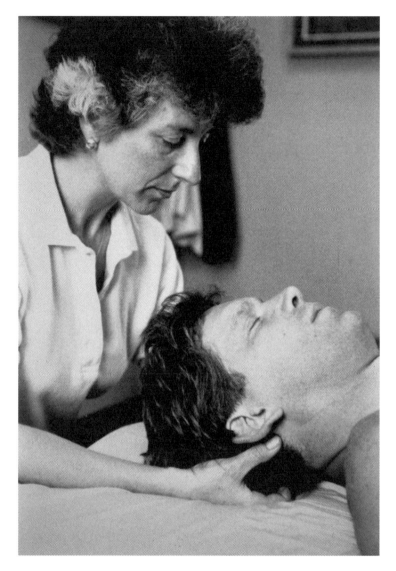

Neck problems are a common complaint. The neck and head also need to be balanced along a vertical line. Most people have a forward head posture or tilted head.

When this happens, the neck doesn't have the support it needs; the body isn't ultimately balanced. As the pelvis and lumbar spine are realigned, then the neck is in a position where it can be aligned. Body work which concentrates solely on the area of pain, ignoring the rest of an unbalanced body, offers only temporary solutions.

ROLFING ®

Stories of Personal Empowerment

SECOND EDITION

Chapter 1

Mothers, Babies, and Children

Christy A. and Katryna

A former abused wife and a very special child. "They couldn't even guarantee that she would live through the weekend."

Emily C.

"I have seen her blossom through the influence of Rolfing and plan to give her the benefit of continued Rolfing throughout her teenage years."

Lynne G. and Adrian

Can Rolfing affect fertility?
"I think Rolfing was the smartest thing we could have done for our child."

Robin M. and Kaitlin

"Rolfing was suggested to me by my therapist because I was having problems owning my body, feeling like it was part of me. I wanted to find peace with my body."

Jude L. and Maria

"As something is released, hidden and undeveloped strengths are uncovered and begin to grow and take shape."
Maria, Jude's adopted daughter, had many physical problems from the trauma of birth and abandonment.
How Rolfing helps babies born prematurely to "catch up."

Mimi

"It feels like metal turning to cotton. Rolfing is my favorite thing to do."

Pat T. and Erika

"I studied with a medicine man who said that many illnesses are caused by anger, and to get rid of the illness, we must get rid of the anger."

Erika

A child who'd suffered from Legg-Perthes says,
"Before, dancing was a dream. Now I'm taking dancing lessons."

Miryam R.

A massage therapist and Yoga teacher says, "I had the most wonderful sense of liberation, of just being freed from my mind."
Can Rolfing help us cope with early childhood trauma? How does Rolfing affect pregnancy?

Ted

"Rolfing was part of a multi-pronged approach to dealing with Ted's asthma."

Jamal

"Rolfing makes you not ache as much . . . and makes you feel much taller."

Nancy W. and Frankie

"I lived upstairs in the attic of my body."
Can Rolfing affect allergies?

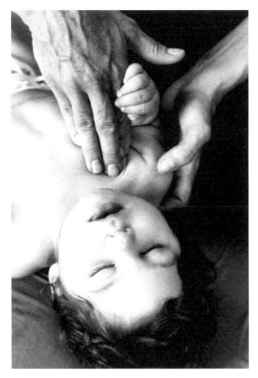

"Going through a birth canal is probably one of the most dramatic things that anyone will ever do," remarked a client. She was amazed at the immediate changes she saw when her newborn son was Rolfed.

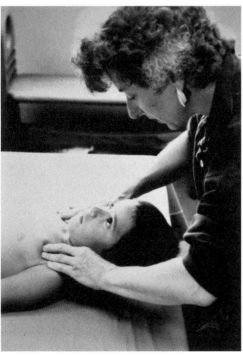

In small children, imperfect body patterns have not had a chance to be set. Everything is still developing and forming. You can make significant changes in a child—there's nothing subtle about it. Children respond beautifully to Rolfing. "I think Rolfing was one of the smartest things we could have done for our child," says another client.

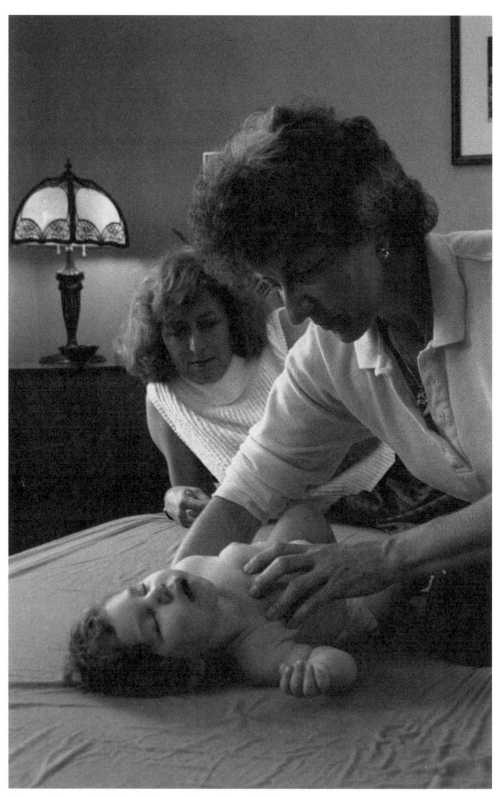

Katryna being Rolfed with her mother Christy looking on

Christy A. and Katryna

I first found out about Rolfing in 1981 from a very successful lawyer friend of mine. At the time I was going through a horrendous marriage. I had been beaten and was close to an emotional breakdown. My friends said that Rolfing would help stabilize me. So I went to a Rolfer named Nicholas French.

The benefits that I received from Rolfing were twofold. I had expected the physical benefits. As a result of a foot injury years ago, I had been putting 75 percent of my weight on my right foot to compensate for the injury. This caused me to throw my right hip out and become twisted and convoluted. I was so lopsided, I even asked for an emergency session because I was having such trouble walking. The Rolfing straightened me out.

The other benefit I had not anticipated was a spiritual-emotional one. I had quite a few revelations about my life while I was being Rolfed. They were major revelations about things that had controlled my life for years. I felt such a release in my body and in the emotions stored in my body. As the Rolfer worked on me, things came up to the conscious level. I had operated my entire life through a filter of not trusting men. This attitude was so deeply ingrained it colored my thought process, my life, everything.

After Rolfing I became healthier, more confident, and happier about life.

I was better able to face life. The insights, or "ahas" that I got were a definite release that helped me get out of this relationship with a clear head and a clear conscience. I walked away and was really honest and forthright about it.

When my daughter was born in 1988, I had a lot of emotional trauma connected with the pregnancy. Her father had abandoned me, and I was fired from my job because of the pregnancy. I was really hanging on to the thought that I would have this baby and life would be wonderful. It seemed as if everything else had forsaken me. It was a planned home birth, but everything didn't go according to plan. I was very scared and alone. My water broke about 4:30 in the morning, and I started into labor almost immediately. By 7:30 I was almost unconscious, and I still have no real memory of what happened. I dilated about 5:00 and assumed the baby would be born a few hours later, but she didn't come until 1:30 the next morning. Many times I wanted to give up, for I was truly tired, and I couldn't take it any longer.

When the baby was finally born, she was so still I thought she was dead. It was like a bad dream. She wasn't breathing. It was as if she was as exhausted as I was. She was resuscitated and taken by ambulance to the Emergency Room and put into isolation intensive care. She had a spinal tap within hours after her birth and massive amounts of medical intervention. She was poked with needles, had an EEG and a CAT scan, an IV, and monitors and tubes all over her. She was a tiny little baby with all these needles stuck in her.

The doctors wouldn't make a prognosis for two days. When they did come in, I could tell it wasn't going to be a good meeting. They said she had suffered a hypoxic insult (lack of oxygen), and they couldn't even guarantee that she would live through the weekend. Sometimes I think it was my very strong will that made her come and be with me, because I wasn't ready to give her up. But even though she was breathing, she wasn't quite all there for me. I spent as much time as I could with her in intensive care, talking and talking. I brought her some classical music, played at 60 beats per minute. I borrowed a tape recorder, and when I couldn't be there the nurses would play my voice. I sang songs to her.

She lived through the weekend, and the doctors had a final meeting to give me their definite prognosis. They said that Katryna had suffered extreme neurological damage and they doubted that she would be able to do much more than what she was doing right now. They cautioned me that she probably wouldn't live long because children that are immobile usually get a cold or virus, and the first infection they get kills them.

Devastation does not begin to describe the way I felt. But there was a part of me that said, "I understand you; I see the X-rays, and I still don't believe you. This child is not going to die." I just knew in my heart that she was not going to die.

Katryna was in ICU for about a month. She had many problems. She couldn't maintain her temperature, so they had to put her back in the heater several times. She also had a problem with the gland that regulates her kidney output. She came out of ICU scarred. To this day, her little heels are a mass of scar tissue because of all the blood pricks they had to take from her.

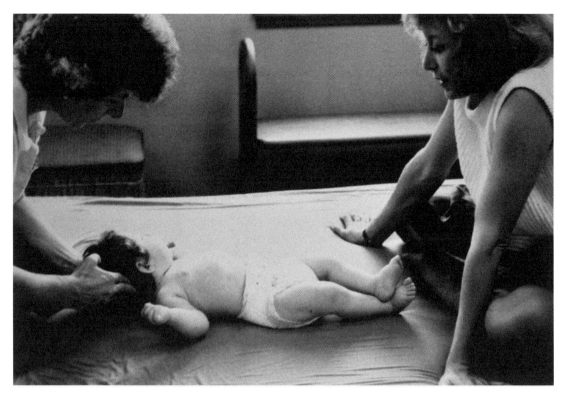

Katryna peacefully receiving her Rolfing session

Katryna had a very pronounced caput when she was born and looked as if she had come out slightly crooked. The caput is normally centered on the top of the head, but hers was slightly to the side. She had obviously had some trauma to her head. When she was finally stabilized, I was allowed to take her home. She was on phenobarbital for seizures, and she was an extremely fragile child.

Shortly after her release, I took Katryna to my Rolfer. She was not quite a month old, and had suffered so much. The Rolfing was very gentle, but I think she needed the gentleness because she was still so fragile and exhausted. I sensed that the Rolfing helped with centering, allowing her to feel needed and wanted, that it was okay to come into her body. Three days later I took her to Kansas City to live with my family.

We came to see Briah when Katryna was just three months old. From my experience, I knew that Rolfing wasn't going to hurt her, and would be very valuable for her. Just before her first session, we had been to see some neurosurgeons who said the X-rays and CAT scan showed that Katryna's skull bones were fusing prematurely and would make her head lopsided. The only answer, they said, was surgery. This made me want to have her Rolfed all the more.

During the first session, Briah worked inside Katryna's palate, smoothing and evening it out. Katryna had a very pronounced ridge on the top of her head caused by the bones overlapping. As Briah worked, the ridge went down and the palate was less arched. I don't remember when the ridge totally disappeared because she doesn't have it now. After the Rolfing session, I took Katryna back to the neurosurgeon. He said the bones had stopped fusing.

The first time Katryna was Rolfed she fought it a lot. It appeared to be painful for her, and she would seem tired afterwards. Each time I brought her in, Briah would say, "Well you should be prepared. She might get a little worse before she gets better." But I noticed that she got better almost immediately. She was more responsive. The Rolfing seemed to allow Katryna to come back into her body at her own rate. I remember one time during a session when the room was very still and the chimes on top of the table began to ring at the same time Katryna had a release of energy. That, for me, was earth shattering. I can't explain why, but it was very, very real.

Katryna has had five sessions so far. I always seemed to know when the time was right. For a five- or six-month period she had reflux, a condition that children have which causes stomach acids to back up into the esophagus. That was a real setback for her because she had to have surgery again, and she was very sick afterwards. By this time she was a little over a year old. It was taking me hours to feed her because she would put up such a fight. It was like a wrestling match and she was very strong. She would arch her back and neck and refuse to swallow. One occupational therapist suggested we have a stomach tube put directly into her abdominal wall to feed her, but I knew she didn't need it. Instead, I took her back for another Rolfing session.

Briah worked on Katryna's neck. She had a lot of problems with a stiff neck. She kept arching it when I tried to feed her. Katryna almost seemed to be leading Briah exactly to where she wanted to be touched. The next day I realized that it took only a half-hour to feed her, a dramatic difference. Since that time we have not had these problems—maybe a small wrestling match occasionally—but no more two-hour feedings.

I feel like those Rolfing sessions directly resolved Katryna's eating problems. After the first session, she lengthened noticeably. The doctors had just measured her, and she grew an inch by the following week. The Rolfing also helped her breathing. Her chest was a little constricted, and we opened it up and smoothed the ridge on top of her head. The plates can be manipulated just by rounding out the soft palate. Her chest used to be caved in. After Rolfing it became more spread out.

The first year of her birth, Katryna was hospitalized five times. This impeded some of the work we could have been doing with her as far as Rolfing was concerned. She was hospitalized for 21 days for her esophagus surgery. The second time she was hospitalized, they blew every blood vessel she had. They can prick your fingertips and toes three or four times, but Katryna had 80 pricks on her fingers, toes, heels, inside elbow, wrist, ankle, and groin. They used every blood vessel she had. She was under a lot of stress and strain.

During her next Rolfing session, Briah was extremely tender and loving with her, and I recall Katryna having a lot of release and coming back into her own. She is a real tough little girl, real strong.

The last time Briah worked on Katryna was a couple of weeks ago. I saw a lot of lengthening, strengthening, and stretching out. It was also a mystical experience because l definitely saw an aura, a green aura that became more intensified depending on what Briah was working on.

I know that Rolfing is beneficial. I don't always know that "A" happened, therefore "B" happened. But I know that Katryna exhibits reciprocal movement now. She can bicycle her legs instead of holding them together, as though they were connected by an invisible bar. That's an important milestone. She has also been creeping, getting up on her knees, and bearing weight on her arms, which she had not been able to do prior to Rolfing. I didn't tie it into the Rolfing session at first. It just happened. All this from a baby who was diagnosed as being in a vegetative state!

The neurologist who was on her case told me she had already doubled what he had initially expected. She grasps at my fingers, creeps and crawls, and is starting to make little noises. She talks, babbling a lot. This is her way of communicating. She's working on making non-vowel sounds. My intent is that she will walk, she will run, play, and feed herself. The doctors had said, "Take her home and she may die soon." But just look at what she's accomplished!

The last time Katryna was Rolfed she was much more present. She's coming back. I believe she is using these Rolfing sessions now and is very much engaged in the work. She would grab onto Briah's finger and not let go. She would move her arms, legs, or fingers as if being asked to make sophisticated movements. She's much more alert now. She still has problems with her sight and is considered cortically blind. However, the doctor says he feels that she will develop her sight. More and more she turns to bright lights.

The developmental pediatricians at Children's Mercy thought she was developing scoliosis or a potential problem with her back. They believed that one side of the muscle development was ahead of the other. I made an appointment with the orthopedic surgeons for July and had two Rolfing session for Katryna in between. She has no problems. Her hips are fine. Her back is fine.

She doesn't require any orthopedic inserts. She still has problems keeping her head upright and can't sit by herself, so we're working on getting her balance. Katryna progresses at a rate that's right for her. What I do is give her all the opportunities that I can. Rolfing is something we'll continue.

The fact that Katryna doesn't need any orthopedic braces, has no scoliosis, and doesn't have to be on medication for seizures is extremely significant and tells me that Rolfing is making a huge difference.

I'm still fearful because with a special child, you have to be prepared at all times to get slapped in the face with awful news. But I do feel that because of the Rolfing, Katryna has been able to come into her body at a correct pace.

Rolfing has really supported her growth and development. I cannot argue with an X-ray. If the X-ray shows an impairment, fine. But Katryna will have a quality of life that will enable her to experience life in a manner light years beyond what the medical doctors told me was possible. And she already has.

The doctors are amazed at her progress and can't believe how well she's doing based on some of her problems. Granted, she has problems, but the way she experiences life is going to be whole and complete. I share this Rolfing experience with other parents of special children. It's a non-traditional treatment. Parents may think I'm strange, but most of them have been through so much with their child. Their child is not typical, not normal, so they are quite clear about who their child is and consequently don't judge me. I'm always pleasantly surprised when other parents ask about Rolfing in a positive way.

These are the parents that have the sort of spunk and commitment I do and refuse to accept their situation easily. They have spirit and fire and are, therefore, more open to non-traditional types of therapy like Rolfing.

There is one thing that I've discovered. The minute you become complacent, you are accepting the limitations imposed by doctors. It's like the doctor has given you a road map, already set up for the child's eighteenth birthday. I will not accept that.

When Katryna was three months old, her doctor wrote a letter to the insurance company stating that she most probably would have cerebral palsy because there is a direct correlation between it and hypoxic insult. That is when we started Rolfing. Well, she does not have cerebral palsy. Maybe we averted the whole condition by working with her.

I don't ever defend Katryna because I'm just extremely proud of her. I think she's the prettiest baby I've ever seen and a wonderful, special human being, and I love to show her off. I've entered her in three baby contests, and she has won second place in one of them. I heard there's a girl with cerebral palsy who was in the Miss Teen U.S.A. contest recently. I feel so lucky to have Katryna at all that I want to share her with everyone.

Emily C.

Five years ago my son Ted went through the Rolfing series. I witnessed dramatic improvements in Ted's posture and asthmatic condition. I decided to give my daughter Emily the same opportunity even though she had no apparent physical weaknesses or illnesses. I knew that Rolfing would make Emily stronger, improve her alignment, and hopefully boost her self-confidence and self-esteem.

At the time Emily was seven years old. She had been swimming competitively for two years and had been involved in creative movement, tap, jazz, gymnastics, and stage performances since the age of three. Emily had the promise of natural poise and a desire to perform. Emily is a very quiet child and has always been very concerned about how she looked physically and how she projected herself.

Personally, I was very shy and self-conscious and I was very much motivated by these shortcomings to give Emily every possibility to feel good about herself.

I was also aware that Emily, a first grader, was already experiencing peer consciousness about every aspect of her appearance. This is a time when children are quick to point out the imperfections in each other's physical appearance and abilities. I knew that this behavior would only increase as Emily approached puberty.

Although intelligent and articulate when necessary, Emily is not a verbal communicator. She is quiet about her inner life, her feelings, and thoughts. She is reticent to share her opinions or wishes. Emily expresses herself with her physicality. Her body is her vehicle.

Given my own experience with Rolfing and knowing how much it helped me on the athletic level, I knew that Rolfing would hone Emily's physical tools of self-expression which were so contained.

Because the Rolfing had helped me achieve balance and added sensitivity, I was hoping for the same results with Emily. So we proceeded with the Rolfing series. Emily had weekly appointments which she went to quite willingly. Her Before and After photographs showed a lengthening of the torso. Her pelvis, previously tipped forward, was now horizontal. Her legs were under her and much straighter. She looked several inches taller.

Emily, age 11

Emily at age 15 after receiving a few sessions

Emily has returned once a year for a tune-up series of three sessions. Since Briah has documented photographically the results of each of these tune-up sessions, I have been able to observe continued lengthening of her body. All of her joints are horizontal and her neck and head continue to lengthen vertically. Her posture and alignment are incredible.

Last summer at the first swimming meet of the season, Emily, age 10, had just finished a three-session series of Rolfing. When she appeared in her swimming suit I was struck by how tall and graceful she looked. She stood out beautifully among all the other children around the pool. She had an inner glow of self-confidence. She looked poised and at ease with herself. Emily swam well the entire summer, improved her times, and placed in the championship meet in all of her events.

Emily also exhibits an excellent degree of endurance and strength in all of her physical activities. Her gym teacher has commented that she has very good upper body strength. When she was ten, she ran her first mile race at a track meet in 7 minutes, 29 seconds with no track experience. When she was eleven, she ran the mile in 7 minutes, 9 seconds, again with no training.

Emily has been in ballet for the past five years. At age seven she went to one class a week. Every year she has added another class per week. This past year she has gone to ballet class four times a week and progressed to point work. The instructor has mentioned that Emily has excellent "wind," her term for endurance. She withstands the rigors of the training well.

Point work is very difficult and demanding and many of her peers suffer from aches and pains. It is my opinion that her alignment is so good that she puts very little stress on her joints and body. The teacher also said when Emily went up on point that she had "steel feet" (i.e., her feet were strong and she didn't suffer like the other girls). In strength and stamina, Emily clearly excels.

I have seen her blossom through the influence of Rolfing and plan to give her the benefit of continued Rolfing throughout her teenage years. I know how Rolfing has already enriched her physically and emotionally, and I am going to continue to have both of my children Rolfed as long as they are open to it and a good Rolfer is available.

Emily swimming with dolphins

Lynne G. and Adrian

My husband gave me Rolfing sessions as a birthday present, and I could hardly wait to begin. I had known about it for quite a while and had several friends who had been Rolfed. I hoped it would help bring out my potential as a singer and improve my posture. As it turned out, Rolfing had an effect on my life that I had never considered.

I had been trying to get pregnant and was thinking of taking fertility pills, but Briah recommended that I hold off on that until after my Rolfing sessions. Rolfing, she explained, will often free up a person enough so that they are able to get pregnant after treatment.

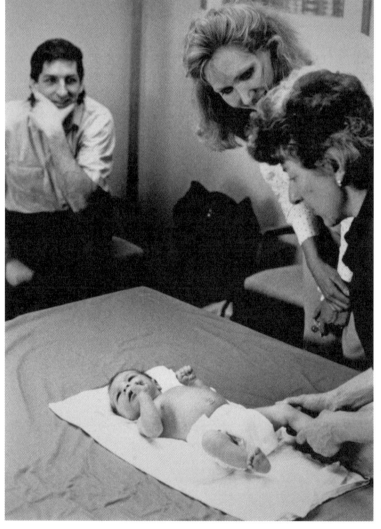

Adrian receiving his first session of Rolfing

Happy parents after Adrian's first session

I got pregnant almost immediately. Briah explained that, especially during the first trimester of pregnancy, it is best not to alter the pelvis or create changes that might affect my tenuous situation. So I postponed further Rolfing until after I had the baby.

To welcome our son into the world, Briah Rolfed him. What a great idea! Adrian was born in a posterior position, face down. This caused quite a bit of stress on his head and neck. His head was rather cone-shaped and bruised for a few days.

During the first three weeks of life, Adrian was very uncomfortable and cried constantly unless he was nursing or sleeping. When he was three weeks old, we had him Rolfed to release his birth traumas. During the first session, Adrian seemed to be in great pain whenever Briah touched his chest, neck, or head. But when she finished, the look on his face was incredible! He was totally relaxed and relieved.

Everywhere he went that night, people commented on what a bright-eyed baby he was. He didn't whimper or cry again and finally fell into a sound sleep.

After this session, Adrian started eating every three to four hours rather than every hour and-a-half. His neck and head were still very sensitive, and he seemed to be releasing a lot of toxins from his body. He cried if he yawned or moved his neck in any way and seemed to be ultra-sensitive to touch in these areas. When he was five weeks old, we took him for the second session and were amazed at his behavior. He seemed to know Briah and allowed her to work quietly on his body. When she came to his sensitive areas, he would cry out but sigh in relief as she released the area. He loved it and seemed to be relieved from pain and discomfort.

Now he cried for specific reasons, telling us what his needs were— if he were hungry, tired, or needed his diaper changed. His crying also became less intense.

Adrian is five months old now and already reaching his highest potential as a person. He is in the low 90th percentile for his age in weight and height. The pediatrician can't believe how big he is. He is very active and curious.

I can't let him out of my sight. And he is so happy. Everyone comments on how happy he is as he smiles and flirts with them.

Randy and I plan to have Adrian Rolfed again when he looks like he is ready to walk. I think Rolfing was one of the smartest things we could have done for our child. It definitely released a lot of tension from his tiny body. The struggle and trauma of childbirth cannot be an easy thing. The baby is literally pushed out into the world where he must learn to do everything. It's wonderful if we can help him become more comfortable and possibly ease his fear or physical pain through Rolfing.

Robin M. and Kaitlin

Robin's story

Rolfing was suggested to me by my therapist because l was having problems owning my body and feeling like it was a part of me.

When I told people that I was considering being Rolfed, I got a lot of different responses. People said, "Oh my God, I can't believe you're going to do that." "That's just weird." "It's really traumatic." "It's really violent." "It's really going to hurt." I don't know where they got these perceptions. I felt it was what I needed to do. I wanted to be at peace with my body.

I went ahead and had my first meeting with Briah, just to feel it out. I was very impressed with her and her explanation of Rolfing. I definitely felt comfortable with it and wanted to do it. After the first session I was hooked. It was wonderful.

Briah opened things up. I had an incredible rush of energy. My hands and feet were almost vibrating. There was so much electricity coming out of them. I had to literally ground myself, to put my feet on the floor to make it stop for a while. That was the most intense session of them all. I knew I had to come back and finish the series.

I started noticing actual physical changes after the second session. My back was a lot straighter. Walking was more comfortable, and I was lighter on my feet. I was less tired. My breathing was easier because the Rolfing opened up my chest. I do think my rib cage is actually wider now.

I'm not fighting my body anymore. There are still things I'd like to change: improvements, exercise, diet, things like that, but it's not a battle anymore. My last session was three weeks ago and I'm still continuing to change. I'm a school teacher, and I used to come home from school and take a nap. But I have so much energy now that I don't need the extra sleep, which is great because I have so much to do and now I feel like doing it.

The therapy and Rolfing worked beautifully together. It seemed that whatever I faced in therapy related to my next Rolfing session. It was just amazing how the mental and spiritual process worked with the physical process. My therapist feels that we worked through things much faster with the Rolfing.

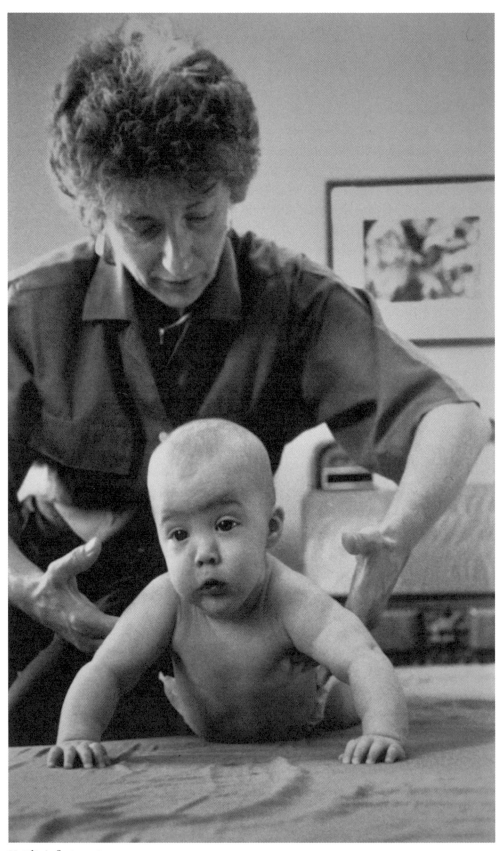

Kaitlin's first session

There was probably only one session where I felt stuck in the same place. Briah explained that this happens when things are coming out. It's there for a reason. That session was slow and difficult, but I think that was because things were working up and out. Another session brought up a lot of stuff in my throat area. It stuck with me for about three days. I coughed, gagged, constantly cleared my throat, and had difficulty breathing. When it was over, I felt a tremendous physical release.

At times I found myself becoming a little addicted to Rolfing. I would get a tiny crick or crimp and couldn't wait to go to Briah and get rid of it. It was like not wanting to leave your therapist even when everything has been worked out.

Rolfing enabled me to achieve a friendship with my body and the realization that I do have a responsibility to it. It helped me to live in the present, to be more grounded and functional. It's easier to work off stress. I feel stronger and more confident. All this contributes to a sense of well-being and wholeness.

People began to notice changes in my face and body. One friend said, "You look taller; have you lost weight?" Of course I hadn't. I told her I had been Rolfed and what she saw was the lift from the waist up. The planes in my face had also lengthened and so had my neck.

My friends who were so against Rolfing changed their minds when they saw what it had done for me. Now they want to be Rolfed, too. Sometimes people have such a difficult time investing in themselves. They'll invest in everything else, but the last thing they'll do is something for themselves. Rolfing was my investment in and my gift to myself.

Kaitlin's story

My husband and I awaited our daughter's first Rolfing session as eagerly as we awaited any of the other milestones in her development. We believed that Rolfing would promote a healthier beginning for her, physically and spiritually.

My first experience with Rolfing improved my relationship with my own body and enabled me to successfully carry a child. Traditional medicine had found no reason for my previous miscarriages, and Rolfing was suggested to me as a way to physically and spiritually prepare myself for childbearing. Within a month of my last session, I was pregnant with our daughter, Kaitlin.

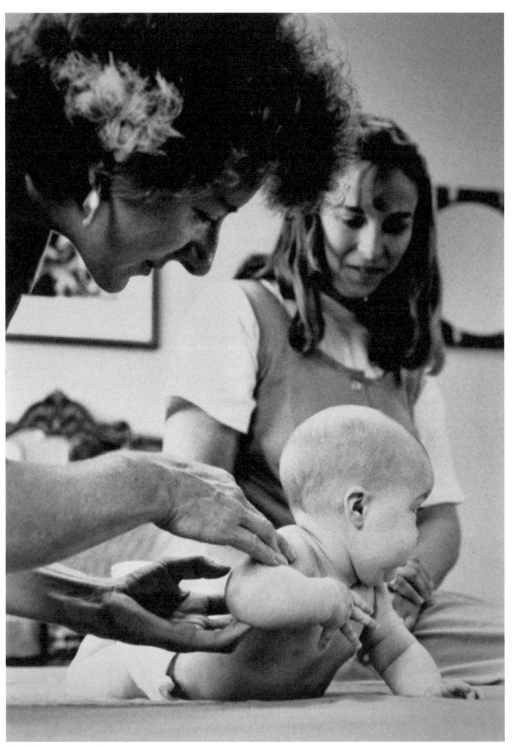

Kaitlin enjoying her session

I believe Rolfing also made pregnancy easier and more comfortable. My body adapted to the changes of pregnancy without difficulty, and I never became too awkward.

Kaitlin's birth was not the nurturing, natural experience we had hoped for. She was born six weeks premature by Cesarean section and spent two weeks in an incubator. Now the need for Rolfing was especially significant. We believed that the trauma of her birth experience could be lessened through the Rolfing sessions.

At her first session, Kaitlin was seven weeks old and weighed six pounds, one and one-half pounds more than her birth weight. During the session, she pushed and struggled as if making her way through the birth canal.

The significance of the work was evident in the weeks that followed. Her frail body rapidly filled out and became proportioned as a newborn's should. Her shallow breathing became stronger, and she gained three pounds in four weeks. Her next session was even more eventful. She cooed and babbled as Briah worked her legs and torso, but when Briah focused on her head, Kaitlin released an incredible amount of pent-up anger. It was as if she was expressing her feelings about separation and isolation after her birth. Noticeably, after that session she no longer kept her fists clenched as she had before.

Now Kaitlin is on schedule with full-term babies in growth and development. We had often been told that premature babies would take a year to catch up. We are thankful that we were able to provide Kaitlin with the benefits of Rolfing so that she could grow healthy in body and soul. Rolfing is a gift parents should be aware of and encouraged to give to promote the advantages of peaceful minds and healthy bodies.

—Robin and David Mesh

Jude L. and Maria

My beginning with Rolfing was like so many other journeys. It began with the personal and led to professional development. It may begin as a physical or emotional crisis. It is most often precipitated by pain in the here and now. The pain may seem insignificant and unrelated to any larger issues or aspects of one's life, but it becomes a search for wholeness.

The first time I learned about Rolfing was in 1973. I was in a Gestalt Training Group. Some of the group members were being Rolfed by a man who traveled from Colorado to Kansas City on a regular basis. I heard a presentation by him, and though I thought that Rolfing made sense, my Midwestern conservatism put up barriers. I felt this person was not clear about himself, and truthfully, being somewhat afraid of a new body process, I was surely not going to go be Rolfed just to be "one of the crowd." My pain wasn't sufficiently intense to push me beyond my fears and inhibitions at that time.

In 1977 I moved to Minneapolis, Minnesota. I was 35 and going through a major life transition. I had left a marriage, a thriving private practice, and family and friends in order to test myself in the unknown Northwest territory. I was searching, running, seeking. At the time I had some ideas about the object of this search, but looking back I can see now that I was in the throes of a transitional stage that was to cata-pult me into many new experiences and changes.

I was in chaos. Physical pain became more severe, which pushed me to a more daring frame of mind. My long-time sufferings with migraine headaches, allergies, and sinus problems as well as basic structural problems pushed at me painfully. On the advice of Briah Anson, who had just been Rolfed, I made my appointment with a local Rolfer for my first session.

I had watched my friend go through some fairly amazing emotional and physical changes after each session. All this happened without talking, no focus on emotional release, no analyzing or psychologizing. I was impressed.

As I went through Rolfing, emotional release occurred spontaneously, and my hips began to "even out." After my seventh session, which is on the head, I suffered a severe sinus infection and was releasing mucus from every orifice of my body. I was miserable. I went through several rounds of antibiotics after trying many home remedies. I recovered about six weeks later and since that time I have not had any chronic sinus infections. I still have some allergies and sinus problems. However, these are much more under control and require little, if any, medication.

I feel lighter, more balanced, energetic and much more in touch with my body. I can also see a change in my response time. Things that l used to only think of saying, I now voice more quickly. My feelings are closer to the surface and more fluid. It is as if a layer of physical and emotional defense has slipped away. The other more interesting part is that I have more sense of a core, an internal balance point that is stronger and clearer. I have seen this repeated many times with clients who have been Rolfed.

As defenses are dissolved, new patterns of movement, behavior, and expression are ready to emerge. As something is released, hidden and undeveloped strengths are uncovered and begin to grow and take shape.

When I completed my Rolfing, I decided to take my daughter, Maria, to be Rolfed. She was five at the time and she had quite a bit of physical constriction, especially in her neck, shoulders, and head. She is adopted and had experienced a stressful first six months of life. When I first saw her, at exactly six months old, her head was flush with her shoulders. She had no neck at all. Her hands were in tight fists and arms drawn into her body. Her toes were curled and legs drawn up like a very small infant. Her forehead was furrowed and her eyes were lowered. She made no sounds, neither cooing nor crying.

Very quickly after we took her home, she began to release her hands and arms, feet, and legs. She began smiling and making many sounds, including crying. But I noticed that when she was frightened, tired, or very emotional, the old constrictive patterns would return. She was shy by temperament. Her reticence, however, seemed to go beyond this natural disposition. I thought Rolfing would help her change some of this. She loved her Rolfing sessions and had decided by the end of her treatments that she wanted to be a Rolfer.

The session where the Rolfer worked on her neck and shoulders was particularly memorable. She screamed angrily while Judith was working on her neck and shoulders. The anger was of an intensity and type I had never seen her express. After the session, she jumped off the table and ran energetically around the room. What followed behaviorally was that she was more expressive of anger and limits and was more confident.

She lost a lot of the body constriction as well. Prior to the Rolfing, her feet turned in. She walked and ran pigeon-toed and occasionally stumbled because of it. One doctor suggested corrective shoes to address the condition. Others talked of hip braces, while another said to do nothing. Her condition was greatly improved through Rolfing. Her feet and legs straightened more. I could see the changes from the hips down.

Through the years she has continued to receive Rolfing as needed. She improved and evolved in all problem areas and continues to grow emotionally and behaviorally. Maria's physical and structural changes created emotional and behavioral growth.

I was hooked: Rolfing intrigued me. There was more here than met the eye. I needed to know more. This was the beginning of my quest to experience and understand Rolfing in the context of emotional and personal growth, and in the much larger picture of evolving the human person, not only physically and emotionally, but also spiritually.

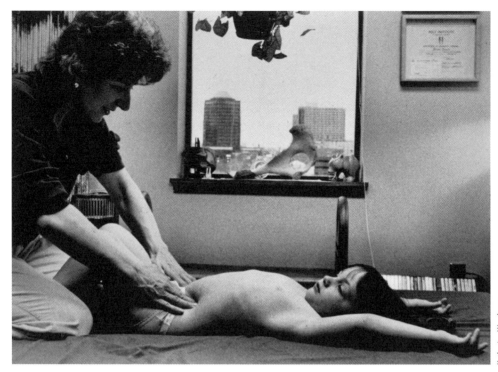

Katherine Weedman

Mimi enjoying her fifth session

Mimi

When asked what Rolfing feels like, four-year-old Mimi told her mother, "It feels like metal turning to cotton. Rolfing is my favorite thing to do."

"Within the first few days of being Rolfed, Mimi seems to have taken a huge step forward in her maturity level," says Mimi's mother. "It's amazing what's happening to her legs. She had the same twist in both her legs, and it's straightening out. She is not knock-kneed anymore. Rolfing set a course to break her out of a hereditary chain of a knee problem that has shown up in two generations."

"When I first started bringing her to Rolfing, the twist in her legs was obvious. Now it's very subtle. She's only had six sessions between the ages of two-and one-half and six."

Rolfing can help children get free of tension and injury patterns and even inherited body conditions before they become deeply ingrained. Rolfing is a skillful and purposeful releasing of old stress and trauma in the body. It's a hands-on technique of deep body manipulation. When the tissue is freed up, a new body becomes possible—one that is taller, straighter, more graceful ,and more centered. A new confidence becomes possible as the body becomes lighter, more relaxed, and more alive.

Pat T. and Erika

Pat's story

My daughter Erika was Rolfed when she was eleven. She had a bone disease in both hip joints called Legg-Perthes. The bones of people with the disease don't get nourishment and eventually disintegrate. Erika was on crutches for about four years while her bones built back up. After she got off the crutches, the orthopedic doctor couldn't do anything about her limp, and she was in a great deal of pain just shopping in the grocery store.

Chiropractic didn't help her so we turned to Rolfing. After four sessions, I noticed Erika was sitting at home cross-legged. She had never had enough mobility to sit cross-legged before. Erika didn't even realize she was doing it. I started screaming, "Erika, you're sitting cross-legged!" and she looked at me and said, "I am!" We both started dancing around. That was the first real dramatic change I saw.

Up to this point, Erika had a little baby face and baby body, and it seemed as if overnight she became a young woman. She lost her round belly. It became flat, and her toddler-walk became graceful. Her limp disappeared. When her face lost its baby fat, she became beautiful. She still had pain when she walked, but she only limped when she was very tired.

In her initial photographs, when Erika is trying to stand up straight, it looked as if her feet were crooked, like she is standing on the sides of her feet. One knee is way behind the other. After Rolfing, the end photographs show both of her legs in line and her feet flat. Her back is straight. It is an amazing change.

It's hard to see much on yourself, but on one of your children you can see it clearly. In a year, she had three advanced sessions. She's now on a volleyball team, which I never thought possible.

When I saw her sitting on the floor cross-legged for the first time, that was so wonderful. That was a biggie. She had never been able to participate in things the other kids did because of her crutches. She couldn't run and jump. It was just too painful for her. She had a lot of guts and courage. She pushed hard for what she wanted.

I think she was pretty excited about Rolfing because she thought that would help. I'd come home from a Rolfing session, and I'd be sore or tired and she never understood. She said, "I don't understand this, Mom. I never got tired or sore. It never bothered me." Of course, I have about twenty-eight years more accumulated injuries and abuse.

Erika had always been terribly dependent. After all the years on crutches, she had developed a behavior of letting everybody care for her. During the Rolfing, I noticed she started being less demanding and started giving a lot. Her attitude went from being a little girl to being a young woman taking responsibility for herself. The dramatic thing about her attitude change was that suddenly she had this graceful poise. She had always ignored adults, unless they could do something for her. Suddenly, she was having conversations with them—real adult conversations—and being very intelligent about it. She was thirteen going on twenty.

I was Rolfed about a year after Erika, after I saw what it did for her. I said as soon as I got the money I was going to do it. I had a neck problem from an accident. I would have to sit with a hot water bottle on my neck every night. The Rolfing helped that a lot. I still have pain. But I have a lot more movement, and it's not nearly as bad as it was before.

When Briah started to work on my neck, it was incredibly intense. I was frightened of her even touching me because I was so sore. I started crying. She asked why I was crying, and I said because it hurt. She said, "You don't normally cry when something hurts." I started feeling scared. I remembered the whole car accident like it had just happened, the sounds and smells, the intense horror.

That was very traumatic. Briah didn't even finish the session. She just patched me up and sent me home. During the rest of the sessions, there were some hard times. When she worked on my abdomen, it hurt a lot. I've had trouble with my abdomen all my life.

I had great damage from the car accident. I had a concussion, and several vertebrae were knocked out of place. Both my arms were in slings because of shoulder damage, and three ribs were out of place. I had a lot of intense anger. I had been in therapy about five years trying to get rid of this anger. I thought I had been doing a pretty good job. About halfway through my Rolfing, all this anger came out in a flood. I spent one whole night crying. The next day the anger was gone. I had once studied with a medicine man who said that many illnesses are caused by anger. To get rid of the illness we must get rid of the anger.

I don't know if this was coincidence or part of the Rolfing, but I was sick part of the time I was Rolfed because of a virus. I lost about ten pounds in a month. I know that my body was cleaning out a lot of toxins. I don't know if that caused the illness or just went along with the illness, but I felt a lot better.

It occurred to me, if great anger had happened to me, maybe it had happened to my daughter. Perhaps anger had also created her allergy problem. I know she's not an angry person anymore, and she doesn't have allergy problems. Somewhere along the line, she let go of a lot of anger and developed poise.

She had been angry at me and her dad for getting divorced. She was angry that this bone disease happened to her, that other kids got to run and play and she was on crutches. It made her angry at the world. I think anger gets stored in the body and it's really hard to eliminate because it's stored so deep. It's like poison in every cell.

I've noticed Erika's allergies aren't as bad as they used to be. She used to take allergy shots once a week, and if she didn't, she got severe ear infections. She was stopped up and sick to her stomach all the time. Now, even at the most severe times of the year, a little antihistamine and she's fine.

There is a movie with Burt Reynolds in which his character gets Rolfed. That was the first time I had ever heard about Rolfing. During the session the female Rolfer beat on him. The experience looked terribly painful. That was my first encounter with Rolfing.

I had several friends who had been Rolfed, and I had a great deal of confidence in one of them. I was pretty desperate. Erika was in a great deal of pain, the chiropractors weren't helping, and the orthopedic doctor wasn't helping. I was willing to fly to doctors in Peru or beyond.

Rolfing to me is incredible. You don't understand why this works, but it does. I guess it's not really important that I understand what it's doing to help, but I've heard many people say that it's really helped them live fuller lives.

Erika's story

I was Rolfed about two years ago when I was twelve. My mom and I decided that I should try it because of a bone disease I had. I developed Legg-Perthes, and when I was five, I had to be on crutches. The hip partially disintegrates so I had to be on crutches until the bone renewed. Then I had limited activity because I couldn't put too much weight on it, nor could I run or jump.

After I got off crutches, I was seven. I restricted my activity and got better. But when I was eight, it happened again in my other hip and I had to be on crutches until I was about ten. I couldn't sit cross legged, and I walked with a bad limp. Sometimes my hip would hurt. Every time I went to the mall or Worlds of Fun, it would start hurting. It would pulse with pain every time my heart beat.

At first, I didn't think Rolfing sounded too hot. It didn't really appeal to me. I thought it was weird, and it scared me because I didn't know much about it. Still, I was hopeful. Briah said it was like deep muscle massage that aligns your whole body. That took care of a lot of my fear. After the first session, I wasn't scared anymore.

I thought there might be something to it, so I went back again for the second and third sessions. I didn't even realize this, but one day I was sitting down watching television, and my mom walked in and said, "Erika, you're sitting cross-legged." And I thought, "Oh my gosh!" I hadn't been able to do that since I was about five. I still couldn't sit for very long periods of time. But after about ten sessions, I looked at the "Before" and "After" pictures. Before Rolfing, my body was all out of shape. I was not straight at all. But in the "After" picture I was straighter. I think I grew a couple of inches and became a little skinnier.

I'm on the volleyball team at school this year. I hadn't been able to participate in gym until last year when I was in the seventh grade, and then it was limited. But this year in eighth grade, I was able to do everything anybody else could do. I still couldn't run as fast or jump as high, but I could do everything.

I encourage other people to be Rolfed. I'll see somebody and think, "Oh, they need to be Rolfed." I know it works. My mom wants to be Rolfed.

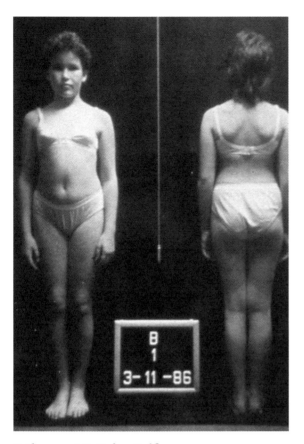

Erika, age 12, Before Rolfing

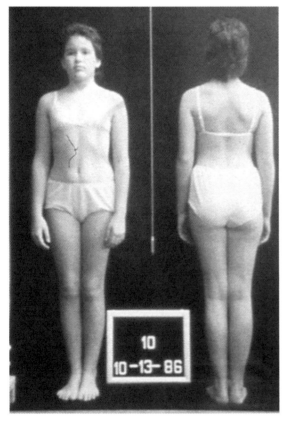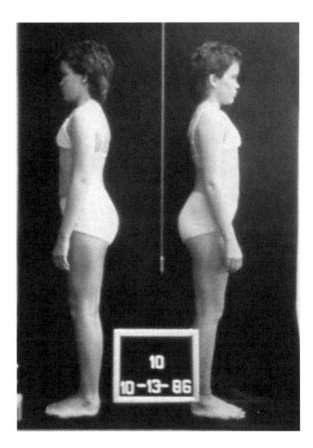

Erika, 7 months later, After 10 sessions

People told me I probably would have emotional things come up, but I didn't find anything much. I don't know if I didn't have stuff built up or what. After the sessions, I was really tired but also full of energy. I wanted to go home and go to bed, but in another way, I wanted to run out and have a good time.

I would have rather just laid on the Rolfing table and not worked. Briah pushed down hard on the deep muscles and that kind of hurt, but the pain was gone right after she finished.

We went to the doctor before I was Rolfed, and he encouraged it. Now, he doesn't think I'll ever have to come back again unless I have more problems. He was surprised that I hadn't been to see him in a year. I told him I was on the volleyball team. He said that I was healed and had much more movement.

I've had three advanced Rolfing sessions and can see some difference. My body is a little bit straighter. I wasn't really surprised about the differences because I didn't know what to expect. Before Rolfing, I went to Jefferson City with the Girl Scouts, and for two months after, I was in a wheelchair from all the walking. If we went to the mall, we could maybe be out twenty minutes.

Before Rolfing, dancing was my dream. Now I'm taking dance lessons.

Miryam R.

I am a massage therapist and, before being Rolfed, I had practiced Yoga for almost a year. While I was away studying massage, I became very aware of body alignment. I was also aware that our bodies are a manifestation of our inner lives, and so I knew that my body was storing a lot of memories.

While working on issues in therapy, I realized the benefits of body work in terms of helping those issues surface more quickly, and be felt rather than intellectualized. I trusted my instincts and felt that the Rolfing seemed right. My intuition said, "Do it."

I hoped Rolfing would deepen my integration process and, at the same time, provide me with a sort of container in which I could create a new body more representative of the person I was becoming.

The first session was exhilarating. I could actually feel my diaphragm working, and I experienced my breathing in a completely new way. When I got up to stand, my feet felt connected to the earth for the first time. It felt as if I were part of the Earth's energy, part of the force of the Earth.

After that first session, I couldn't wait to keep going. However, there was a two- or three-week interval between the sessions, and a lot of memories started coming up.

Throughout the sessions, I began to learn to allow my body to speak to me. I would ask it questions and find out what was coming up, what was happening. If I experienced any tenderness or soreness, I knew it was probably related to an experience or to things that I had put into my body.

I really began to trust that wisdom, to trust my body to teach me what I needed to see about myself and how to integrate the memories so they weren't hooked into my life any more.

I was physically abused as a child, and came from an alcoholic family. At the time that I was Rolfed, I wasn't yet conscious that I had been sexually abused. There had been dreams, meditation, and imagery of this abuse before Rolfing. I was beginning to put some pieces together.

Even through the Rolfing sessions, that memory never really came clearly to the surface, although there were other side issues leading in that direction. I could see the illusion I had created for myself. As a

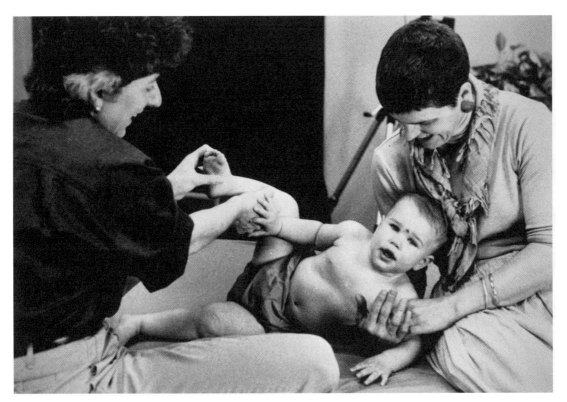

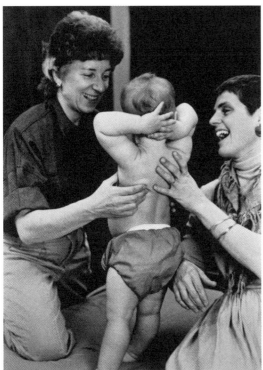
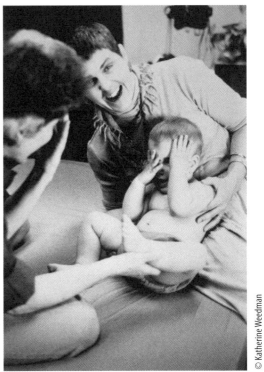

Miykaelah being Rolfed. Her mother, Miryam, helps with the session.

child, I had needed that illusion to survive. I blinded myself from the truth of what was really going on. I kept myself from understanding the dynamics of abuse and how it played itself out in other relationships in my life.

What the Rolfing did was help peel back the veils. I remember one time saying to Briah, "I feel like an onion." Each layer was coming off and revealing something new. And the revelation was one of beauty and awesome power, but at the same time of pain. It's like the two always went together. The pain wasn't so much physical pain, but memories and experiences.

I remember one particular session. It might have been the fourth or fifth. Briah was working in the pelvic area, around the buttocks and her hands hit this knot. I had an image and feeling of a rope that had been tied. The first time she hit it, I could experience that knot running all the way up and down my leg. So rather than saying to myself, "This is a painful experience, I am going to stop the process," I instead chose to say, "I'll take it on its own terms, and I will allow myself the free space not to make judgments about what is going to happen."

I had the most wonderful sense of liberation, of just being freed from my mind. I could have thought, "This is going to be painful" and clamped down. Instead, I chose a different path. It was very liberating. At that point, the work really seemed to flow a lot easier and my resistance wasn't there anymore.

In the process of being Rolfed, I lost about twelve pounds, simply weight I had put on myself for protection. Those "onion" layers just fell away without much effort on my part and a whole new life force began to flow through me. The first thing I noticed was the weight loss. It started coming off after the third or fourth session. When I look at the beginning photos, I'm very aware of how closed my chest is. It looks "S" shaped. I realized I was so out of line.

Then I became aware of my diet, of the effects different foods have on the body. I thought about refined sugar and how I felt after I ate an ice cream cone or a piece of cake. I had tapered off drinking wine and beer. I was fine while drinking a glass of wine, but within an hour my energy level would get heavy, and I wouldn't feel tuned-in. I haven't had alcohol since that Christmas and haven't missed it or felt the need to have any.

These changes have helped me tune into which foods seem to be helpful and which are harmful. I'm expecting my third child in two months. I would highly recommend to any woman who's thinking about getting pregnant to get Rolfed first, because this pregnancy has been a breeze. I've felt healthier and have more energy than ever before.

My other two children were, in a way, outward manifestations of my conscious level at that time. I had not yet experienced my own birth, so I lived through them a lot of my own subconscious fears and the traumas around my own coming into this world. I had developed problems out of my own lack of awareness. I put on considerably more weight during those pregnancies. I didn't feel good about myself and that definitely had an effect on my pregnancy. I didn't honor the rhythm of my body.

Now I will rest in the middle of the day. I do some guided imagery just before dinner, and Yoga and breathing exercises. I spend a lot of time on breathing. I don't pressure myself. I'm enjoying this process each day and what seems to be unfolding. My body is teaching me so much. It can grow and expand and hold another life within and then release it.

I'm really looking forward to the birth and how I can facilitate that process, really be in the process, be in that energy and power.

I feel like this is symbolic in terms of timing. I didn't think I wanted any more children because I knew I had a lot of my own work to do. I didn't want to pass along any more stuff. And yet, I feel now that this new person is a gift.

I became pregnant a month and a half after my last Rolfing session. Rolfing had a lot to do with how I feel about myself and how I feel in this pregnancy. I was in a good state of emotional and spiritual health to begin with. That was a great place out of which to become pregnant. It helped set the stage. In the beginning of my seventh month of pregnancy, Briah did two advanced sessions on my legs and pelvic area because I'm bearing a lot more weight and pressure on my legs. It helped with my circulation. I noticed one of my legs looked as if it were developing varicose veins. In the morning there was a lot of soreness in my calves. But since the Rolfing, that hasn't been happening at all. I feel that the work has given the baby more growing space. Briah is going to Rolf the baby after she is born.

What a difference between the first sessions and the advanced series! In the first sessions, I felt like I was very open and wasn't resisting, but I think on a deeper level I really did resist. The advanced work felt as if it went easily for me.

It felt as if all Briah had to do was touch me and things would move immediately in my body. I could sense the movement.

Briah's response was, "Oh yes, I always consider the first series like working through cosmic glue." I loved that image. That was my experience: that the glue has come unglued and now we can do whatever work needs to be done.

I am aware that my center of gravity is shifting dramatically, and I've been getting chiropractic adjustments on a regular basis which have helped establish a new center of comfortable balance. I was beginning to notice I had a lot of tension in my neck and shoulders and felt that the lengthening, stemming from the advanced Rolfing sessions, had made great improvement. I could start breathing again. Before Rolfing, I felt some restriction in my breathing and I wanted to breathe freely. Looking forward to the birthing process, I want to surrender as much as possible and relax through my entire body so it can be as open as possible for the birth of my child.

We worked a lot on movement—how to stand and how to walk. That has helped me a great deal. What I'm finding now is that when I walk I feel quite regal. Rather than hunching over, I feel very comfortable in my body.

I've listened to other women talk about being pregnant. I discovered I wasn't dealing with my feelings. I wasn't aware of what was going on inside of me emotionally. I didn't feel good about my pregnant body. There was a sense of losing control, of things being out of my hands. There are so many messages that come from the general culture suggesting that a woman's body is not beautiful when it's pregnant. What I've come to understand is that birth is a process, not just the labor and delivery. It's much more than that. It's a time for unfolding and a realization of possibilities. I find I have grown and deepened because I am open with myself now. It's a wonderful time for growth. That's how I'm approaching this time in my life, and it is feeding me. I feel nourished.

The body process is not linear, it's circular, always, it is circular. One thing goes awry, and the effects go on and on. A body is a web, connecting everything with everything.

—*Ida Rolf*

Ted

Ted was so active when he first came in to be Rolfed he couldn't stay in one place long enough to be photographed. This is why the sequence of photos starts after three sessions. Ted was brought in to be Rolfed because he had asthma. His mother tells the following story:

At age four, when Ted was first Rolfed, he looked like a little old man—with a sway back, stooped shoulders, and a concave chest. His neck and head also hung forward in front of his torso.

I felt that asthma had some postural implications that could be corrected—because the muscles of the chest and shoulders contracted as if in sympathy with the contraction of the bronchials.

Ted had been taken to the hospital emergency room on several occasions for adrenalin shots due to the severity of his condition.

Rolfing was part of a multi-pronged approach to dealing with Ted's asthma. There were changes made in his environment to assure the home was as allergen-free as possible. His diet was revised to include nutritional supplements, and he started an exercise program. By the time Ted was six years old, his asthma was much improved. He did not require regular medication.

He is now nine years old, and physically he continues to grow very straight. He does not have the characteristic rounding of the shoulders and concave chest that many asthmatics have.

I plan to continue to bring Ted in for annual Rolfing sessions as they have been so helpful to him, not only for his asthma but also to enhance his growth potential."

—Ted's mother (Sara)

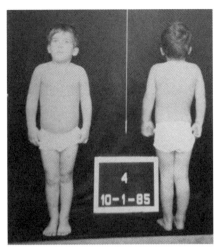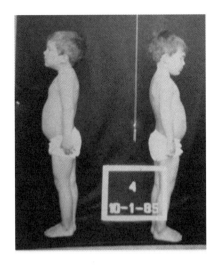

Ted, age 4, After 4 sessions

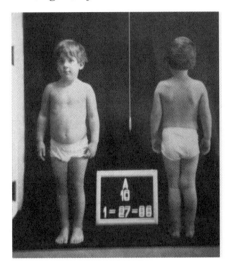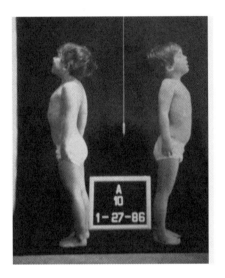

Ted, After 10 sessions

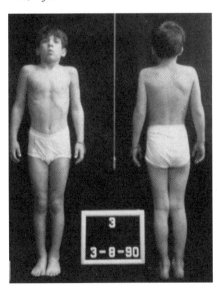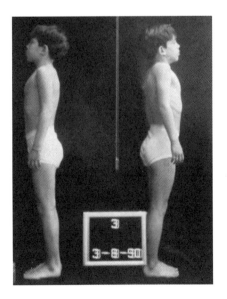

Ted, age 8, After Post-Ten work (4 years later)

Jamal

Jamal had his first Rolfing session when he was six weeks old, and his second session when he was getting ready to walk. In these After 5 sessions, Jamal, age 6, has lost a lot of the swayback posture so typical of small children. In the "Before" photos, you can see Jamal had a forward head posture, a round and rolled-forward stomach that seems to stick out, and he appears to be shyer and less confident than in his later photos.

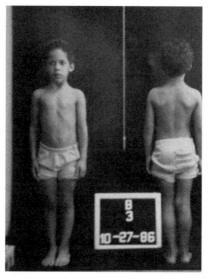
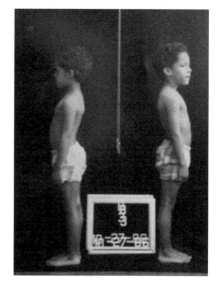

Jamal, age 6, Before 3 sessions

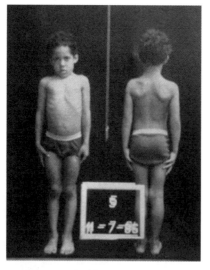
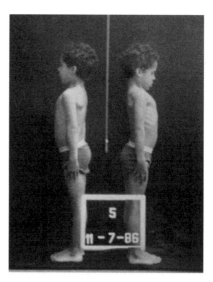

Jamal, age 6, After 5 sessions

Jamal is now 10 years old.

He looks strong and tall and confident, with very few traces of postural problems typically found in children. His outgoing personality has emerged. Jamal is becoming active in community plays and modeling.

According to his mother, "Jamal is pretty flexible physically and psychologically for a child his age. He is centered; he is himself, and I attribute that to Rolfing."

In Jamal's words, "Rolfing makes you not ache as much. It relaxes your muscles and makes you feel much taller. It's so relaxing, sometimes I fall asleep."

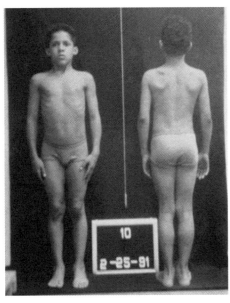
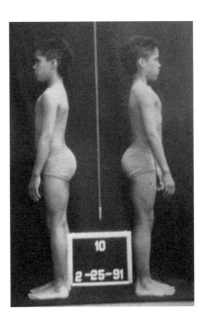

Jamal, age 10, After 10 sessions

Nancy W. and Frankie

Before Rolfing, I didn't really have a relationship with my body. I was very cerebral. I'd go to the beach and read a book. I escaped into my brain. I lived upstairs in the attic over my body.

The first ten sessions started me slowly reconnecting my mind and body. Now, maybe two years after I finished the first series of sessions, I still notice these changes. I'm more athletic. I walk, work out, or ride my bike every day.

One of the major issues I worked on in Rolfing was my neck problems. I was unwinding from my feet up through my mid-section. I'm in the advanced sessions now, continuing the work of unwinding and untwisting in my neck and shoulders.

I couldn't see all this torquing and twisting when I first started Rolfing. But looking at my last set of After pictures, taken after eight advanced sessions, I realized why my neck was causing me such problems. My shoulders had been tilted, and my chest was twisted and protectively hunched. I see things in my body I couldn't see before.

In addition to my neck problems, I also had back problems and a dead zone in my mid-section from two C-sections and a hysterectomy, all before I was 27 years old.

Once, Briah was working on my legs, and I felt it in my chest. Unbelievable! "I felt that in my chest," I exclaimed. Briah responded, "Well, they are connected, you know." But I had lost that connectedness, physically, and emotionally, after all that surgery.

I was disconnected from my emotions as well as from my body. I barricaded myself from fear, anger, and grief. I think I had been numbed out and depressed for several years without realizing it. I was in a job rut, a marriage rut, a life rut. I had been blocking myself from really experiencing life because I had been careful to shut out all "negative" emotions. I got a lot of anger out in these Rolfing sessions, which scared me.

After the tenth session, Briah suggested therapy, since it worked hand-in-hand with Rolfing for many of her clients. In my job as a management trainer, my company encouraged this kind of self-development. I thought, "Why not? Nothing will be too traumatic for me. I'm basically okay."

It took me about a year before I started dealing with things in therapy. I was still out of touch with my feelings in the same way I had been out of touch with my physical self.

During that year, I kept saying, "I'm fine," but deep down I knew I wasn't. This wasn't the body or self I wanted to have. I wanted to change physically, spiritually, and emotionally. But on the surface I was afraid. I wanted to avoid fear and conflict. Whenever I would do an important piece of work in therapy, I would wring my neck, roll it around. Whenever emotional issues would come up, my neck would hurt as I choked off fear and anger.

In the middle of therapy, I went to an Integrated Sound Workshop with a therapist and a Rolfer facilitating the workshop. It was a very physical and emotional experience. Emotions would bubble up, only to be stopped at my neck. Briah worked on my neck and helped release emotional blocks. But it was very significant to me to see that things would come up and I would manage to bottle them up in my neck, choke them back down. My neck was the shock absorber for my emotions.

After Rolfing, I began claiming back the right to all my emotions. I wasn't the "good girl" who went quietly along without making a fuss, without standing up for myself. I didn't have to hold back the floodgate of my emotions, fear, and pain from the hysterectomy and C-sections, hurt and grief from my childhood.

I left a job that was boring but safe and ventured out into a different job. That job didn't last long. However, I came out of that experience not just okay, but better than before. I started working for myself and went from a safe and unhappy job to a much freer, happier, and more creative lifestyle. I would never have done this if l hadn't had some sort of inner strength brought out from the Rolfing and therapy.

I was more willing to be afraid. I'd experienced fear in Rolfing, especially the head session. I'd been afraid when Briah worked on my scarred mid-section. I'd gotten used to being afraid, and it became easier and easier to take changes. If all else failed, I could still fall back on me.

I think change is a major theme of Rolfing. People change after they have been Rolfed because they go into Rolfing ready to change. People who aren't ready to change won't be Rolfed, or they will drop out during the first few sessions.

Courtesy of Nancy Wolfe

This is a picture of Nancy (LOWER RIGHT) when she was 13 years old. Note the rounded shoulders and caved in chest. Similar patterns can be seen in her son Frankie at age 9 in his "Before" Rolfing photographs.

"I was not poised or self-confident when I was growing up," says Nancy. This is pretty obvious in this picture of me. I'm the one hunched over on the far right. Rolfing helped give me physical poise and strength. It gave me a body I can be proud of, and the psychotherapy helped me grow into my body and into my more confident self."

To make Rolfing work, you must be ready for change and help it along by working with the Rolfer and taking control of your own change. Rolfing doesn't change you as much as you change yourself, using Rolfing as a tool or instrument of change. Therapy is another instrument of change.

I don't show my Rolfing pictures to many people, but I've shown Frankie's pictures, and people have been impressed. He is straighter and aligned. He looks healthier and stronger. He seems less constricted and closed-in, both physically and emotionally.

I was really motivated to have both my sons Rolfed. I didn't want them to inherit my body behaviors and posture problems.

I was so out of touch with my process, it was sometimes hard for me to see my sons' changes as well. Jeffrey, my youngest son, is currently finishing his first series, and Frankie has had a few advanced sessions.

My own process is very slow, very protected. And I'm glad it is because I don't have a lot of traumas forced on me. When I was Rolfed, things would come up, but they were never more than I could handle. I would flash on something that happened when I was a child. I would have lots of dreams. I went through periods when I cried or was in the dumps.

Part of me really regrets that I never saw any auras or had past life regressions. But I appreciate that my process is not to get too overloaded.

When the Rolfing would get painful, my first reaction was to tense up, which would actually make things hurt more. Usually the pain level was about that of a Jane Fonda aerobics workout. It took me awhile to learn to relax and let Briah work, and to work with her. I learned to take control of the process, and it became less painful because I wasn't tensing up.

For the first head session, I was scared. During the advanced head session, I realized that I trusted Briah not to shove a fingernail into my brain. I relaxed and worked with her—guiding her in a way—and the session felt fabulous.

Because I was in control of the process, I wanted to experience greater and greater releases. It sounds strange, but if l didn't have some area in my body where I felt I had done a great deal of work, I felt kind of cheated. Especially in the advanced work, I wanted to feel changes.

I notice that I'm more athletic now. I wear low-heeled shoes. I drink more water, eat less meat. I read books differently, holding them up in front of me like a shield rather than bending over to read the pages. My husband noticed great changes in my Before and After pictures. Usually people who haven't been Rolfed can't see all the significant but subtle changes. But Dennis noticed that my neck was much longer. I wasn't tucked in like a turtle in its shell. I had a waist for the first time. My stomach wasn't as big because my back wasn't as rolled forward.

Some of the changes happened because I'd lost 25 pounds, but I lost weight because I was more physically active. I was "in body" more.

The changes in my life over the past two years haven't been hard. It wasn't hard to lose weight. I used to feel like I "had" to lose weight.

I've "gotta" do something about my hair. I "oughta" exercise more. But it doesn't feel that way now. I haven't had to make myself do anything. My self-image is much better. I've even tried on swimming suits in the store before I bought them, and I don't look in the mirror and make terrible noises.

Gradually, over a period of time, things changed: my body; the way I dealt with my children; family relationships; and work relationships. There were multi-layered changes that have happened, but they've happened gently, over a period of time.

Frankie's story

Frankie, my oldest son, was Rolfed when he turned eight. Coincident-ally, I had been through some major traumas when I was eight, so there was synchronicity with his process and my reliving my experiences. My mother had been in the hospital for a long period of time when I was eight, and I dealt with "lost child" issues in therapy and Rolfing.

I could see the changes in Frankie more dramatically than I could see my changes. Once, Briah gave Frankie a crystal, and he used it to carve his initials on her door. Kids express their emotions much more overtly than adults.

The biggest issue for Frankie was taking responsibility for his own actions. This seemed to come to a head during Rolfing. He became angrier, moodier, more argumentative. He let feelings out. I had to deal with his changes as well as my own.

When one person in a family unit gets Rolfed, it affects the whole family. I think that is why some people don't want a close family member to be Rolfed. They know their family member will change. It's the same situation with therapy.

Before Rolfing, Frankie had allergies, a caved-in chest, a rolled-forward tummy, and generally a poor defense system. He was a slight, slender child. After Rolfing he filled out. He became more confident and aligned in his body.

I think when you change the vessel, you change the contents. We "decanted" Frankie. His shoulders went back straight and square, his chin went up, his chest became more open. He looked confident—he became confident.

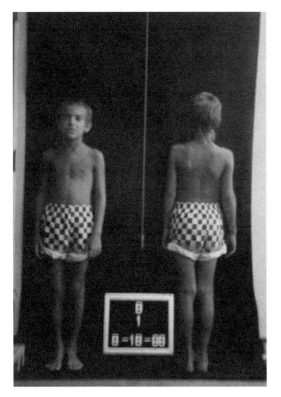
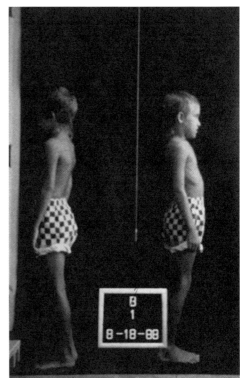

Frankie, age 9, Before Rolfing

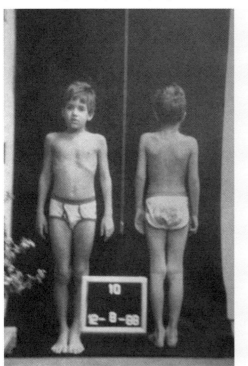
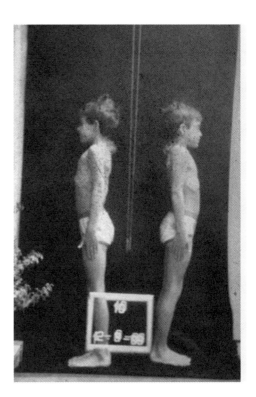

Frankie, 4 months later, After Rolfing

My husband didn't think a lot of Rolfing at the time, but when he saw the Before and After pictures of Frankie, he was astounded at the change. Frankie is a strapping young man now, whereas before he was rather weak, caved-in, and immature.

Frankie's allergies used to be severe. He would come in from playing in a field, and have black circles under his eyes. Once, we had to rush him to the emergency room because he wasn't getting enough oxygen. He doesn't have nearly the problems now that he used to have. Allergies just aren't something we think about because they haven't been a problem. The disappearance of allergies seemed to be a result of Frankie's physical changes as well as the emotional process of opening up.

Chapter 2

Teenagers Tell Their Stories

Ann G.

"I think many doctors treat the symptoms of a problem, not the cause."

Lucy

"She is now physically fit."

Adam

"Rolfing opened my whole body to let the energy flow through."

Ami

"I'm glad my mom realized the problems I had and had me Rolfed."

Lisa J.

"Basic self-esteem starts in the body."

Bill W.

"Rolfing really opened me up. I've changed a lot since I was Rolfed."

Ann G.

When I was in the eighth grade, my mom suggested Rolfing to me. She had been Rolfed and felt that it would help me with my back pain and other structural problems. Mom let me make my own choice about Rolfing. She didn't set it up for me; she let me do that. The purpose of my first series of sessions was to realign my body structure. I came back for more sessions to alleviate my back pain.

My parents are rather open minded, and I was exposed to many different points of view as I was growing up. Had I not been brought up that way, I would have thought Rolfing was pretty weird, and would have questioned whether or not it worked.

My mom said that the Rolfing would help me get rid of emotional stuff in different ways. During Rolfing, I didn't get angry or sad or break out. Instead, I became more in touch with my feelings. Because I was paying attention to how I felt and where I was at that time, I resolved a lot of problems with people. My dad and I are both independent and slightly bullheaded and tend to have a bit of conflict because of that. My morn, being a counselor, tends to analyze some of the things I do.

After Rolfing, I was able to take what I had been given and deal with situations and conflicts, rather than avoiding them. I changed a lot inside. A friend of mine who was Rolfed felt in touch with everything around him. He would have realizations as his energy was being released, and he was able to take in new insights around him. My changes were drastic for me, but no one said, "Oh Ann, you're so different now." I became more extroverted and realized that I was dealing with my problems in an entirely new way.

This probably accounts for the fact that I don't really have as many problems now as I did before Rolfing. I don't keep them inside anymore. I can now deal with them directly and get them over with. I've had the emotional release, and I don't want to let problems build back up again.

When I was 14 or 15 I had several advanced Rolfing sessions because of pain in my back. I was running track, and my legs were really tight. I was confident that Rolfing would help, and it did. I was also involved in gymnastics and ballet, and my body was able to move much easier. I was on the swim team, and as my endurance and lung capacity improved, I won more medals.

Rolfing is amazing. It hasn't hurt me at all. My mom said that it was like a deep massage, and she was right. I used to think really strong muscles are supposed to be tight. After I was Rolfed I was stronger, but my muscles were flexible and comfortable. I used to be prone to muscle spasms and would wake up with cramps in my legs. Rolfing relaxed my muscles and made them easier to use.

When Briah worked on my legs, which always felt tight, I would feel a muscle and experience discomfort, but no real pain. I found I drank a lot of water after a treatment. I would feel like I needed a nap after the sessions. It was more of a physical release than physical exhaustion.

I had been holding in a lot of my emotions and Rolfing helped me to let go of the tensions and feel more relaxed.

When I started Rolfing, I didn't realize the big physical changes that were taking place. They were happening gradually, but I was expecting a sudden dramatic change. When I look at the Before and After pictures, I can see that I am much more aligned now. I think many doctors treat the symptoms of a problem, but not the cause. Briah didn't just work on my legs and back. She worked on my entire body. That's what needed to be done. I had very poor posture (my entire family was swaybacked). My improper alignment caused bowleggedness and back pain. Briah helped solve the problems and not just the symptoms. I am satisfied with that.

I've told quite a few of my friends about Rolfing. They didn't know what it was, and I've had to explain it to them. My dad is being Rolfed now, and my sister is thinking about it as well. I'm glad I considered it and made the choice I did. I'm healthy now, physically and emotionally. I think I've grown through being Rolfed. Everything that happens is part of something else. Everything is connected. I think because of Rolfing I have been able to do more, achieve more.

Lucy

Lucy started having pains in her ankles, hips, and knees at age 7, followed by neck problems, headaches, and bouts of dizziness. By the time she came in to be Rolfed, she had been seeing a chiropractor regularly for a year. Her mother said Lucy often skipped recess because she was aching so much. Her pain limited her to such an extent that she would sometimes miss school.

Lucy's body was jammed through her joints, particularly through her midsection. Her legs were not connected through her pelvis, and she had a pelvis that was extremely tipped forward. There was no lower body support for the upper body.

These structural problems resulted in chronic discomfort in her joints—ankles, knees, elbows, and wrists. She also experienced a fair number of headaches and dizziness. She felt awkward in her body—not well coordinated.

"When Lucy was younger," says her mother, "We discovered she had a sensory motor lag; she wasn't as coordinated or athletic as other kids. She wasn't really perky as a young kid. Before 8th grade, she didn't have a lot of friends. Now she has lots of friends and is really social. Between discovering she was hypoglycemic and getting that corrected, and taking care of the structural problems through Rolfing, she has really turned around. Rolfing made it possible for her to exercise. Lucy has been very healthy since the last part of 4th grade. She is now physically fit."

In 5th grade, Lucy began jogging and running two to five miles at a time. She ran in 5K races in 6th grade without any problems. In 8th grade, she started skateboarding.

Now 16, Lucy is active physically and remains symptom free.

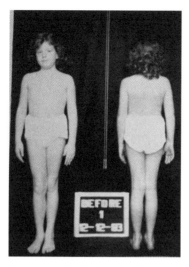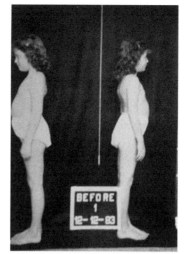

Lucy, age 9, Before Rolfing

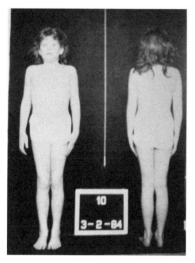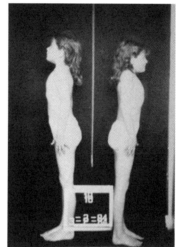

Lucy, 3 months later, After 10 sessions

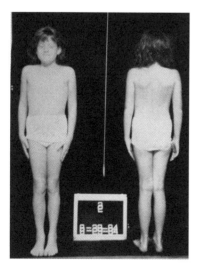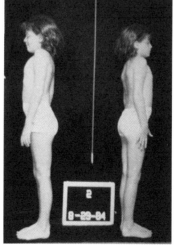

Lucy, After Rolfing, 2 more sessions, 5 months later

Lucy, now 16, has length, lift, and balance in her body.

Bodies need to lengthen and be balanced,
and a balanced body will give rise
to a better human being.

—*Ida Rolf*

Adam

The photos below show Adam before Rolfing. According to Adam's father, Adam had become "very shy and overly oriented to approval from peers; he seldom asserted himself." His parents hoped Rolfing would help Adam with his posture and breathing, make him more sure-footed, and improve his overall self-confidence.

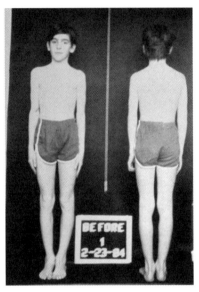 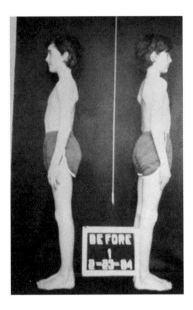

Adam, age 11, before Rolfing

After 7 sessions over a one-and-one-half year period

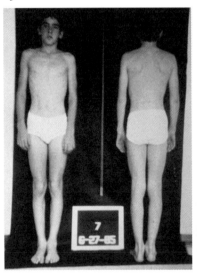 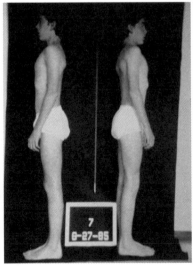

Rolfing Reflections

Adam's initial ten sessions were spread out over two-and one-half years, at a pace that was comfortable for Adam. The Rolfing work helped Adam grow into his body, and develop more self-confidence to go with his new-found body.

Since his initial Rolfing series, Adam has returned twice for tune-up sessions. He is now a freshman in college.

Rolfing "straightened me out," says Adam, "It opened my whole body, letting the energy flow through. When I come back now to get a session of Rolfing, I feel really relaxed and have more energy. I feel ready to go. I feel pretty coordinated in my body."

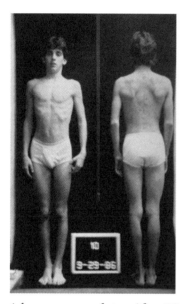 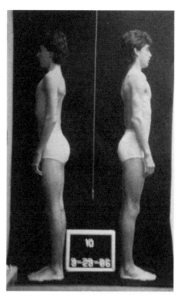

Adam, one year later, After 10 sessions

Adam, after 4 years, with one more session

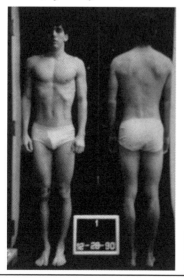 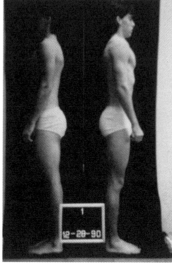

Ami

Eliminating "inherited" body patterns through Rolfing

Ami's mother had been Rolfed, and she began to notice that her daughter was carrying many of the same body patterns she had. She didn't want Ami to continue these patterns, so she brought her daughter in for the Rolfing series.

You can see that with a pelvis tipped this far forward, Ami would develop problems with her back, neck, and shoulders. After 10 sessions, notice the beautiful alignment in Ami. Although her legs are still not quite under her properly, she shows tremendous improvement. Her body has lengthened, her pelvis is more horizontal, and the swayback she had at the beginning disappeared.

"When you're young, you don't think about your body," Ami recalled. "I'm glad my mom realized the problems I had, and had me Rolfed before I became self-conscious about my body. If I had grown up without any professional help, I think I would have had problems with my self-confidence and self-esteem.

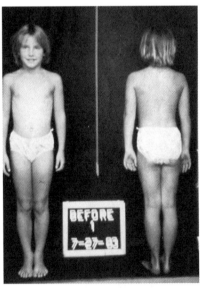 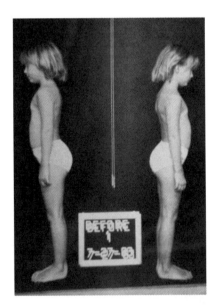

Ami, age 8, Before Rolfing

Rolfing Reflections

"I was in third grade at the time I started Rolfing. I remember a girl in class making fun of me because my butt stuck out. If that had continued through the years, I would have not felt okay about my body, and I would have been self-conscious."

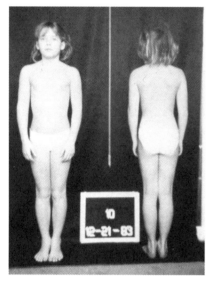 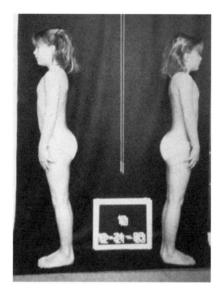

Ami, After 10 sessions

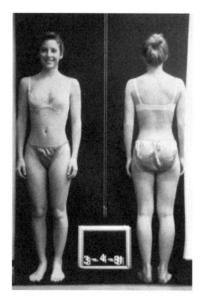 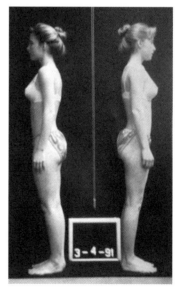

Ami, age 16, 8 years later with no additional Rolfing

Lisa J.

I was Rolfed when I was in the third grade. People thought I'd grown, but it wasn't that. I was standing taller. I used to trip a lot, but after Rolfing, I could walk better, and my gymnastics improved.

Prior to Rolfing, I had been terribly shy, clinging to my mom, hugging her leg and hiding behind her skirt. I would do anything to avoid interacting with people. After Rolfing, I was more self-confident and energetic.

After my eighth or ninth Rolfing session, I had to run a 600-yard dash. For little kids, that's a long way. But I knew my body could do it and that I would be able run faster than just about anybody. I had never been able to run like that before.

I had also been having a problem with my right eye. The muscle was fused to the bone and I had difficulty moving my eye up and down. I hadn't had an operation yet, and it was noticeable. During one of my sessions, while Briah was working on my neck, I was looking at a picture and all of a sudden I felt my eye move into place. It was like focusing a camera. In about a three-minute time period, I remember looking over at the picture and seeing it flat with just one eye and then seeing the whole thing.

I jumped up and ran over to the mirror and could see that my eye was moving around, following my other eye. It scared me at first, and then I thought, "This is neat." I was kind of sad when it reverted, but after surgery it did straighten out.

I remember walking out of Briah's office after my last session. My mom was so happy because she could see the difference Rolfing had made. I looked taller. My clothes didn't fit anymore, so l bought new ones and felt much better about the way I looked. I could breathe more deeply and felt healthier. School attendance records revealed another change—my attendance doubled.

I have a lot of friends that I think Rolfing would help, but l don't know how I could go up and say, "Hey, you need to be Rolfed." They would look at me and say, "I think you're nuts." But I know how much Rolfing helped me.

Basic self-esteem starts in the body

These photos are an excellent example of a young person who would be complaining of various aches and pains by the time she was a teenager. Notice how, in the Before picture at age 9, Lisa's body is at war with gravity.

The After Ten pictures show a body balanced and at ease. Lisa did not have additional Rolfing for nine years. She had an additional two-session tune-up when she was 17.

People often ask, "Will this Rolfing work last?" Rolfing gives the body a matrix of support around which they can continue to grow, balanced, and aligned.

As Ida Rolf said, "The purpose of Rolfing is to organize a body around a vertical line so that it can continue to receive support and healing from the gravitational field."

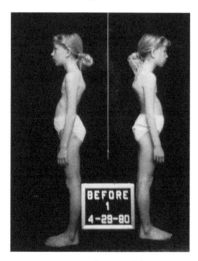

Lisa, age 9, Before Rolfing

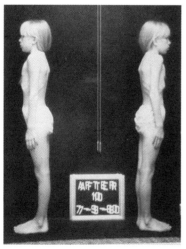

Lisa, After 10 sessions

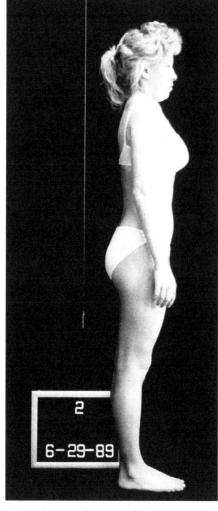

Lisa, 9 years later, with 2 more sessions

Bill W.

I was thirteen when I was first Rolfed. In a way, I didn't really decide. I didn't really think about it one way or another. My mother discussed it with Briah. She didn't get Rolfed, but I did. I thought at first that it was something like going to a chiropractor. I didn't really know what to expect.

While I was being Rolfed, my mom and I had lived with my grandparents, who are alcoholics. During the Rolfing, a lot changed, getting out of this alcoholic family and into a more stable place, so it relaxed me a lot.

I have a lot of allergies—to carrots, oranges, yeast, and airborne particles. I have asthma, too, but it's not as bad since I've been taking shots.

Rolfing really helped my nose. When Briah did the head session, it was strange, but I figured, "If it works . . ." It opened my nose up, made it seem bigger. I could tell the difference right away in my breathing.

They really said it would help with my allergies tremendously, that I wouldn't get sick all the time. I still get sick a lot and, well, that's kind of unfair. The allergies haven't been causing as many problems as before Rolfing, though.

Before I met Briah, I threw my lower back out twice skate boarding. I'd been to an osteopath and a chiropractor, but Rolfing topped both of them. Occasionally my back will be uncomfortable, but it's from something like sitting in an odd position for hours in the car.

I remember sitting in the car, kind of leaning back for four hours, and all of a sudden having my back hurt. It was fine once I stood up, it was just a strain. So I think the Rolfing helped a lot.

The worst session was when she Rolfed my neck and then she pushed her arms down on the back of my legs. When she worked on my back it didn't really hurt—it felt good. The only time I asked her to stop was on the back of my legs. That's the only time.

Growing up in an alcoholic family was very erratic, inconsistent. Rolfing really opened me up. I did learn to take care of myself, and I'm still working out those problems. But it's a lot better. I feel great. I go to Al-A-Teen. I've changed a lot since I was Rolfed.

As the structure of the superficial fascia
is changed, both the structure and
the function of the deeper-lying organ
will be influenced.

—*Ida Rolf*

Chapter 3

Mothers Discuss How Rolfing Affected the Whole Family

Eloise W.

> Eloise tells how four generations of her family were affected by Rolfing. "If it didn't do anything but improve my posture a little and release those steel bands of tension in my neck, I knew I'd be satisfied."

Charlotte O.

> "Before, I always functioned on the edge of myself. I was really detached, and the Rolfing allowed me to move back to my emotional center." Charlotte also discusses the Rolfing of her husband and their three children.

Eloise W.

After I hit 40, I became a dance instructor at an Arthur Murray dance studio. I had posture problems and had to try to keep up with people half my age. Being on my feet wasn't helping the situation at all, and since my supervisor was being Rolfed, I decided that it sounded just like what I needed.

I wasn't skeptical about the Rolfing. I had no apprehensions. If anything, I fought against thinking that it would do too much. I knew it wasn't a magic-wand type thing, but if it worked the way I thought it would, my expectations would not be too high. If it didn't do anything but improve my posture a little bit and release the steel bands of tension in my neck, I knew I'd be satisfied.

After my ten sessions, the bands were gone from my neck, and I experienced freedom of movement and relaxation. After childbearing, I felt like everything had dropped in one big heap right down to the lower part of my abdomen. I was having problems with involuntary release, incontinence ,and was considering having my bladder restrung, but the Rolfing corrected that. I used to have cramps every month, and that problem also disappeared.

Psychologically, I felt better than I had in years. My son came in to be Rolfed shortly after I did. He had just finished going through a divorce, and his circulation was so poor that halfway to St. Louis, when taking his little girl to see his ex-wife, his arms would go to sleep. After one session, his circulation was normal. He's been Rolfed five times and is going to go back for another five when he can afford it. He was stressed from the divorce and a lot of new problems as well. He had reconstructive knee surgery, and all of the ligaments and cartilage are gone from his right knee. He was wearing the heel right off of his shoe, so obviously one leg was shorter than the other. Now, his legs feel like a matched pair, and a lot of the stress and tension have gone out of them.

My whole family thinks Briah is a miracle worker. My mother had Alzheimer's disease and was living by herself. Before Rolfing she was not capable of being left alone; talking to her was like talking to a broken record. Information was not getting through and being processed. She follows conversations much better now, and her sense of well-being has improved. One shoulder used to hurt her so much she couldn't even hold a cup of coffee. Now she is back to using her arm a little bit and doesn't moan and groan with every move. Her sense of humor has come back. She still has memory problems. But there has been such a dramatic change. She is walking straighter. She used to have tingly sensations when she rode in the car for any length of time. That doesn't happen anymore, and her posture has improved as well as her overall circulation.

As my mother became more and more disoriented, she became reclusive and withdrawn. Now that Rolfing has improved her posture and sense of well-being, she is getting out of the house more and looking forward to starting back to church. Mother is taking an interest in life again. Before, it seemed that she was thinking, "All I do is ache and hurt, and I can't remember what the preacher says when I get there." That is the feeling she conveyed. If someone has been sick in bed for a long period of time, their memory isn't going to be as good as it was. They start to close down. The circulation slows, and therefore, everything else slows. As Mother's circulation improves, I think her memory does too, so she can follow conversations better and participate more. She is less withdrawn. I don't know whether Rolfing has helped the disease or not, but it has improved her quality of life.

My granddaughter has also been Rolfed. She's had three sessions and needs to have a few more before school starts. She carries her tension in her legs. Briah worked on her legs quite a bit, and, all of a sudden, her trousers were two inches too short. She also has a calmness about her that was not there before. I would tease her or give her a hard time, and she would say, "Now you know I'm busy, and you shouldn't be doing that to me so just leave me alone." It was like she went from being very immature to very mature. She still wants to be the center of things. She doesn't get nearly as frustrated and upset when you correct her or she can't have all the attention. She has better coordination and control. Her coloring used to be atrocious. It took a great deal of effort for her to stay within the lines. I noticed after a couple of sessions that her movements were smoother. She could stir pancake batter without the jerky movements like before.

My husband has had one Rolfing session and swears that if Briah worked on Saturdays he would take all of them, but what it comes down to is that he is not ready to change. And Briah has said that the people who are Rolfed are the people who are ready to change. I've been married to this man for 36 years, and I can push him and raise chaos, but if he doesn't want to change, it's money down a rat hole. He's a long-time smoker and has congestion and a cough that dramatically improved after just that one session. He walked around the house saying, "Wow, I feel good," and breathing deeply. Still, he's not willing to take the time off from work and drive in there in order to continue. Maybe he's afraid of making a big change.

Some people are afraid of new things. They're afraid that somebody is going to take advantage of them or laugh at them because they are doing this strange thing. People who have not heard of Rolfing think it must be unorthodox, and some of those who have heard of Rolfing say, "Pain! Pain!" But I'm saying, "No, strong discomfort, but not pain." Pain is having a nail driven through your hand, or a ruptured disc. Rolfing is not pain. It is strong discomfort, but it doesn't last long. The good that comes from it more than balances out the pain. Part of it is that Briah is releasing things, and even though you have made the decision to be Rolfed, the subconscious fights it to a certain extent. Especially if abuse has been buried for a lot of years. The subconscious does not want to let that come to the surface so you can face it and get rid of it.

I had some weird sensations during Rolfing. I don't know whether it was energy coming in or a deep-seated energy that was being released, but it was like those science fiction movies where there is a spiral with a light going out. It happened on a couple of occasions and was a strange but good feeling.

My energy level increases after each session because I think the release of tension gives me more energy for other things. I move with more energy now than people 20 years my junior, and I move with a sense of purpose. So many people—kids, young people—drag themselves along. They plod. And these are young people! Sometimes their shoulders are hunched, or they don't have a neck. Older people have a tendency to shrink. Before I was Rolfed, I had a physical and was a half-inch shorter than I had ever been before. After Rolfing I got my half-inch back and am planning to keep it. Part of that is my improved posture. I think rounded shoulders, slumping, and a dowager's hump are probably the first signs of osteoporosis. Working over a sewing machine or in the kitchen causes front muscles to shorten, and the first thing you know, you're shorter, your shoulders are round, and there's a hump on your back. During one session, Briah worked on my rib cage. I had one side lower than the other, and as she worked on this side, it sounded and felt like Saran Wrap pulling apart. That was the only time I really heard and felt the fascia releasing.

I walk on the center of my feet now, instead of the outside. My shoes used to fall over when I put them down, because I wore the outside of the heels off. Now they don't do that. They wear squarely down the middle because that's where I walk now.

Charlotte O.

My husband Ron used to have such severe back pains that he would be laid up in bed for days. He was depressed because he had always played softball and now his athletic activity was severely curtailed by pain. He was 36 years old and he felt much older. It was distressing to him, as well as to the whole family.

One of our friends, who used to have such a bad back that he would kneel down beside the table to eat, told us about the process of Rolfing and how much it had helped him. Ron was ready to try anything. We knew very little about Rolfing, but we were desperate. Ron went in, talked to Briah, and started the ten sessions. His back has gotten progressively stronger, he's resumed softball, and we've even gone skiing.

Ron does overdo things sometimes, and he'll have aches and pains. He sees Briah maybe two or three times a year for some tune-up work. The interesting thing is that Ron was much better after the initial ten sessions, but six or eight months later he came back for two advanced sessions and that's when we really noticed the bounce was back. The process took time; it wasn't like a quick fix thing. He had to give his body time to accommodate the changes.

After Ron went through the process, I was impressed and also relieved. I had been faced with the prospect of running our construction company by myself taking care of our three small children, and attending to a husband laid up from back surgery. Fortunately, Rolfing kept us from facing that.

About a year later I, too, was Rolfed. When I was ten, a horse fell on me and cracked a vertebra. I had severe neck and shoulder problems and could hardly use my right arm. I went to see Briah, and she wanted to know all my background information—injuries, childhood, what type of birth I had, if I had a C-section, if they used forceps, any birth traumas, things like that.

I really hurt, and by then I was ready to change because I was in such intense pain. Even though I had seen all the changes in Ron, it took a lot of pain to bring me in. It also took a lot of trust on my part. After three or four sessions, my pain was gone! It was like magic. I was telling everyone about Rolfing.

Then after three or four more sessions, my pain came back. I became angry, depressed, and disappointed. I'd had pain for so long I had become accustomed to it, but once it was gone, I realized how good I felt. When the pain came back, I didn't know if I could deal with it. I talked to Briah, and she explained that there was another level of work to do, and my body was actually getting better, even though it felt worse. I thought, "Oh god, I should have quit while I was ahead." But I went for additional sessions, and the pain went away.

After we finished Rolfing, I realized I was better physically, but a wreck emotionally. I plunged into a severe depression. I went to bed and couldn't move. That the body and emotions were related was a foreign concept to me. It was a total surprise that I experienced post-Rolfing depression. Prior to Rolfing, I had been in therapy and worked on childhood abuse issues. Talk therapy helped on a superficial level, but Rolfing opened me up. Rolfing dealt with the physical pain, so that I could go on to deal with a deeper pain—the chronic emotional pain.

I was referred to a therapist and was in a group for less than a year. I think the Rolfing opened me up to my emotions, and I worked through a lot of emotional issues in a very short time in group therapy. I recently had several advanced Rolfing sessions, and more emotional stuff has come up. I seem to be digging through different layers of stuff, and as these things are released, I can deal with them. Before, I always functioned on the periphery, on the edge of myself. I was really detached, and the Rolfing and the therapy allowed me to move back to my center.

Sometimes this is scary because you feel like you're finished. You'll come back in because you feel physically out of whack, you do some more body work and boom—the emotional things come up. The intervention place for work is physical. As I change physically, and my body moves to a new place, then my emotional self is not in the same place. It's like a ghost effect on TV—your body is one place and your emotions are that ghost-step behind.

Physical pain is a warning light for me, and I've learned to listen to my body more. Rolfing releases incredible amounts of stress. Rather than holding in things, I get Rolfed, and these stresses diminish.

During one session a few months ago, I felt like electricity was running down my arms and out my fingers. That feeling lasted for hours while the energy poured out, releasing the stress I had accumulated in my body. Rolfing has taught me there are signals that your mind and body put out. You have to pay attention to these signals and deal with them. I'm not afraid of them anymore. Fear had always been a big issue with me. It took awhile to learn to deal with my fears. And every time I go through the process of dealing with issues, with fears, I learn something new, I feel stronger. It's an unfolding process.

Rolfing makes you aware of your body. You want to take better care of it. For instance, beer doesn't taste good to me anymore. I drink a lot more iced water. Our family has been eating healthier. We put in a water filtration system. The Rolfing helped open me up to a new way of thinking about my body and my life.

I noticed it's the same for my three kids. After I was Rolfed, I realized my oldest son Jay, who is now 16, rolled his shoulders forward, and his head leaned forward. Jay was really introverted; he didn't interact well with other kids and spent a lot of time in his room. He was Rolfed and the physical changes were dramatic! We had a new kid. His posture became very straight, and he blossomed physically. He's started to lift weights because kids at school wanted to know what kind of weight training program he was on—and at that time, he hadn't been on one. He had just been Rolfed. With his body changing, suddenly his self-image changed, and he became a lot more self-confident, more outgoing. He now has a lot of friends and interacts with people. He and his sister get along a lot better, too.

Jamie, my daughter, was also Rolfed about the same time. She and Jay are developing a better rapport. It's made the teenage years easier. I think Rolfing disarms the defenses you put up against each other. Jay let go of his defenses, and he's a happier kid. He's very clear in his boundaries, and I've learned to accept his process and his boundaries.

Jamie blossomed from a little girl into a beautiful young lady. She hasn't gone through an awkward adolescent stage. She's fluid and graceful, and looks healthier. She used to be sick frequently with bronchitis and problems with her lungs. When we went on car trips, she always got sick. She used to throw a lot of tantrums but not anymore. She doesn't need to do that now. Somehow the Rolfing helped relieve her of internal pressure.

It was taking a lot of her energy just to handle day-to-day things, and she didn't have any edge to deal with additional school or family stress. Now she seems to have that extra margin to deal with things better.

Before she was Rolfed, Jamie's school sent home a note that said she had scoliosis—curvature of the spine. That freaked us out. We talked with an orthopedic person about a brace, exercises, and other types of intervention. We had these terrible visions of Jamie being all hunched over with severe problems. We brought her to Briah, and she told us that Rolfing could help that kind of curvature.

Briah assured us that the Rolfing process had already started helping her get better. It was really tough for us to trust that process. Here's a 12-year-old kid, and you want to correct her problem in the short time frame she has available before puberty. About four months ago at the end of school, we got a note that said the scoliosis was gone! I was surprised they were monitoring her at school, but it was nice to have that outside checkpoint. It wasn't just us saying she was okay.

The difference between Rolfing and traditional medicine is that with traditional medicine you give yourself to the doctors and the system. They have all the power and you don't have any input. With Rolfing you're an active partner. Rolfing isn't a quick-fix. It's a process that takes time. You have to move different parts of your body to incorporate the changes that Rolfing creates.

I had to step back and allow Jamie to take control of her own Rolfing process, empower her, let her say, "This is my body and these are my decisions."

And there's my son, Aaron. Aaron was eight when we first started talking about Rolfing. He came in for the first three sessions, and during the fourth session he came unglued. He was pissed off. He hated the Rolfing, he hated me, he hated everybody, and he didn't want to come back. I had learned that you cannot force someone to be Rolfed. It's not something you do to someone. You do it with them.

So we backed off. He wasn't ready. Then about a year later he was ready to try it again, so we started the sessions and got to session eight. Briah was working on the inside of his legs, and he came unglued again. He got mad at Briah. He was infuriated. Briah explained that the insides of his legs carried a lot of anger, and it just poured out of him.

When Aaron was a baby he had a lot of traumas, a lot of allergies. He has a low threshold of pain. He is very sensitive emotionally and that comes through physically. I've noticed his breathing is better now, and his allergies are not as intense.

Aaron has also had some craniosacral work. We've been in therapy with him. He has daily headaches that are severe and interfere with his concentration. We've gone on a diet of no artificial colors, additives, or preservatives. His allergies are much better now. Physically he is much straighter and stronger.

Aaron's process is very different from the rest of the family's. He is very much the extrovert. One of the benefits of Rolfing is that we're functioning a lot better as a family, a lot clearer and less embattled. Before Rolfing, we had five individuals busy building their defenses, creating little fortresses where they could function safely within the family. Now we're functioning much more as a family. It doesn't have to be perfect. But when there's a problem, we deal with it and go on. We don't have to store it all up and then have a big blowout.

Ron and I are changing at different speeds and that causes some conflicts. When one individual is changing at a different rate of speed from the other, there is an incongruency that develops. My processes move fast, so it's hard for me to be patient. I have to learn that I can't make someone else's process go at the same speed as mine.

Another shift I've seen is the relationship between Ron and me. He is a very sensitive person, and I think I gave up that part of myself. He took care of that part because he was so good at it, and I took over other parts. I was good at organization. So we traded things, and now we're in the process of owning those parts again. We used to let each other play out different parts of ourselves. Now each of us is a whole person.

I have friends who, I think, could be helped by Rolfing, but I've learned that when people are ready, they'll do it. I've seen the changes in myself and my family. We can tell our friends about Rolfing, we can even be models of it, but they won't choose it until they're really ready. If they're not ready, they'll probably quit in the middle, or find it's too painful.

I think Rolfing has been a real benefit to me, and it's been a gift that I've been able to offer my children.

Chapter 4

Is Rolfing too Late when You're Over Fifty?

Ula B.

Former child dance prodigy and an octogenarian discovers new vigor and vibrancy. "Rolfing was really responsible for getting my stamina back. My son William says it rejuvenated me."

Charlotte B.

"Hats have always been a part of who I am, and I'd worn them for years. I can't wear hats anymore, they just don't belong now."

Ernest M.

"The benefits I most appreciate from the Rolfing are strength and a feeling of initiative."

Bonnie N.

"You could spend many, many times the cost on doctors or drugs and still not get the results."

Phyllis P.

Can Rolfing alleviate chronic back pain even after surgery? "I don't think about getting up and down anymore, stepping off a curb or doing anything like that anymore."

Priscilla W.

Can Rolfing help someone with arthritis? "My grandmother and aunt both had a dowager's hump, and I thought 'I am not going to have that, so help me!'"

Dori G.

"I was hoping for a miracle and I got it!"

Ula B.

I've always said that I started dancing as soon as I could walk. If there was music playing, I suffered if I couldn't move with it. I was born dancing.

My father was a civil engineer, and we were living in the Philippines when I was around two or three. One night we went to Manila for dinner. I remember I didn't even want ice cream because the band was playing, and I wanted to dance. I couldn't stand it unless I could get down and move with it. The music was driving me crazy. So I asked my mother if I could get down, and she said yes, thinking that I would stay just at the table.

Instead, I gradually moved out into the center of the floor. As I broadened out, they began to move the tables and chairs back. That, as you might say, was my first dance appearance.

I had always been physically uncomfortable when music was playing and I couldn't express it. When I was four, we were in a hotel in Hong Kong. I was in the dining room and this lovely band was playing. A tall, leggy gentleman, who looked like the cartoon of Uncle Sam, danced with me and taught me the cake walk.

I traveled around the world before I was four. We were originally from Spring Hill, Kansas, about thirty minutes from Kansas City. When I was nine, my dad worked in South America on the Madeira Memorial Railway, and my mother and I lived in Kansas City. I took ballet lessons for a few years. My teacher trained the ballet for the Ringling Brothers Circus in the summer. He taught the good old Italian style, and he put me on my toes when I was only five years old. That is a bad thing to do to any child. I went ahead and danced, and had a marvelous career, but it really ruined my body. I spent the rest of my life undoing the damage done by this early training.

The teacher finally suggested that Mama take me to New York. In New York, we learned about a man in Philadelphia who did interesting shows and acts. That was in the days of vaudeville, and they would use children in these acts. The man was very enthusiastic, and he whipped up an act for me of three or four little dances.

In those days, they had a very strong Gary Society, which did not allow a child to sing or dance or play an instrument professionally if

Miss Ula Sharon, "The Talk of London,"
. . . she recently took London by storm as is shown by the following item from The Tatler: "The London theatre-going public, including the critics, without any exception, have exhausted their entire stock of adulatory epithets in speaking of this dainty little lady who has taken this town off its feet with her own."—The Blue Diamond, July 1928

they were under 16 years of age. Pennsylvania and Rhode Island were a few of the exceptions. From the time I was ten, I was booked in Pennsylvania.

That was 1914, the first year of the First World War. My father wrote us saying that he was going to Australia for a six-year contract to build railroads and that we should join him. My agent was quite sad, but the next day he called up and said, "Wouldn't you like to have your way paid to Australia and back?" We accepted a contract with the Tivoli circuit out of Australia. It turned out that Mama and I were on the ship when we received a cable from Dad saying his contract had fallen through and he wasn't coming to Australia. But by then Mama and I were on our way, and I had a three-month contract. I was ten years old at the time.

At that time, I was the highest paid child performer in Australia. After my contract ended, we returned to the States and spent the summer in Santa Monica. We then returned East, and I studied with a teacher in New York. By the time I was 14, I was a professional on stage in New York. Of course, I had to pass for 16 because of the Gary Society. I was starring with Burt Williams, one of the greatest comedians, and Eddie Cantor in Broadway Brevities. After about two weeks, they put my name in lights, which was quite exciting.

By the time I was 14, however, I had to find a chiropractor. I found a man to treat me, and he started me on a search to find out what went wrong with my body. On my back and every other place he touched me, I hurt. I was in such pain that I would walk the floor every night. My mother took me to a doctor in New York who suggested I take sleeping pills. That's the way they treated you back then because they didn't know what else to do. They didn't think of handling your body as a machine, seeing what was wrong with your parts or if it were aligned properly. That is where Rolfing comes in, because if the skeleton isn't aligned with the muscles, it will go right back to the old patterns.

Rolfing actually changes the muscle, puts it into the correct position to hold the bones the way they should be held. And after you are Rolfed and the muscles are back to where they should be, it releases all the energy that kept them out of place.

When I was 15, I went to London. I had always wanted to study with Cecchetti, considered to be the greatest ballet teacher ever known. I studied with him two classes a day for an entire summer. I returned

The Sketch,
October 27, 1926
One of the hits of the London
Hippodrome's latest success:
Miss Ula Sharon, the dancer
of Sunny.

to the States then and signed
with the Greenwich Village
Follies. At 18, I returned to
England to play in "Sunny," a musical comedy. I was asked to dance
for King George V and Queen Mary, a command performance at Drury
Lane Royal. A very special performance, it included Shakespearean
actors from all over England.

When I was 25, I again played Drury Lane in "Three Musketeers."
By then, I knew I was not well. Something was wrong, and I wanted to
be attended to on my home shores. We came back to Kansas City and I
had an appendectomy. I returned to Kansas City to get back into condition and train with Dorothy Perkins.

Dorothy was a very unusual person. She pioneered body mechanics
and was fascinated with the idea of the body as a machine. She believed
the laws of mechanics should apply to the body's movements. People
always think she was a dancer; she was not. If anything, she was a singer.

It had been predicted that I would be a wheelchair case by the
time I was grown. Doctors said that my muscles had been that badly
overtrained.

Ula

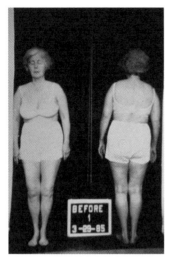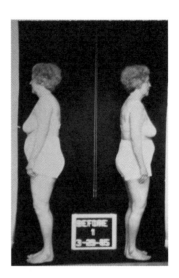

Ula, Before Rolfing

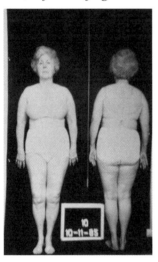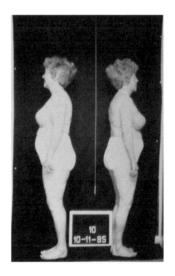

Ula, After 10 sessions

Ula remarked that after Rolfing she had a lot more length and lift. "Everything was going up instead of being pulled down."

"I don't know how much Rolfing contributes to my seeming young," she says, "But no one ever thinks I'm my age, which is 86."

My older clients report that Rolfing gives them a renewed semse of well-being and energy. They feel relief from the accumulation of aches and pains. They are surprised to find they don't have to live with these limitations. One client, whose mother is in her mid-70s, began "taking an interest in life again . . . it has improved her quality of life."

I was a skeleton, overtaxed and out of position. I had a very weak lower back. I was able to forget about dancing and appearances, and launched into trying to find out what was wrong with me. I worked with Dorothy Perkins for a tough year and, believe me, it hurt. It hurts to change things. We'd work every day. Dorothy had gone away for summer vacation and, when she returned, she was astounded at the progress I had made.

I began to work with youngsters, teaching small classes for Dorothy Perkins. Rosella Hightower, one of the greatest ballerinas today, was one of those youngsters. I taught in the attic of the house I was living in. As time went by, more and more people liked my work and my clientele grew.

I had small classes and was able to give each student more personal attention. I stressed body mechanics, as Dorothy Perkins had done with me. Holding the body correctly, doing things the way they should be done produces an effect quite elegant and beautiful. It looks light and effortless.

Children don't like to just take lessons. They like to show what they can do. So I began to put on some shows. As a child, I had always made up my own stories, so I made up my stories giving each child their own part. Some of the parents were involved with the Nelson Art Gallery and they arranged for us to put on these productions at different places. We appeared at the art gallery for the next ten years. Each year I made up a new story to show the new acquisitions of the art gallery. During a Mozart centennial, we took pages out of the life of Mozart.

In 1983 I developed colon cancer. The operation was successful, but it tore me apart psychologically. I was a nervous wreck for about three years afterwards.

A pupil and friend of mine introduced me to Briah Anson. My friend recognized the likeness between Briah's work, Rolfing, and my work with body mechanics, and she wanted to bring us together. It was a very fortunate incident and, at that time, I felt like I needed some work desperately.

Massage was too soft for me, almost like petting. I had excellent osteopaths, but none of them did the trick. None of them got in there and gave my heavily worked muscles what they needed. I thought about Briah and the fact that one of my own pet doctors said that she was so good. That gave me all the more reason to see her. I began working with Briah about a year after I had surgery.

I'm sure it was a tough workout for her with my over-trained muscles. My son first commented on the renewed energy I had. He says she brought energy back to me. I was bent over a little on one side—the scar tissue had pulled me down on the right side. Briah worked out these misalignments.

You have to work that out. Any osteopath can set the skeleton in a certain place, but you have to do more than that. Being misaligned, your muscles are tight and pull the skeletal mechanisms back. Briah commented that my legs were very, very tight, like steel cables. She used to say that my mid-back was set in concrete.

After we did about 18 sessions, Briah happened to show my photos to Stacy, her Rolfing teacher from Hawaii. She told Briah I looked 20 years younger. I did have a lot more length and lift through the front of my spine. Everything was going up, rather than being pulled down.

I don't know how much Rolfing contributes to my seeming young, but no one ever thinks I'm my age, which is going on 86. It's amazing. You can change your body, but there are so many things that are really just postural habits that many people think we're born with, stuck with—but we're not!

Rolfing brought me back to the condition that I should have been in originally. In fact, I had never been that way because of over-training. Rolfing has made a new life for me. My son, who has also been Rolfed, will testify to that. I encouraged my son to go, and I worked on getting many other people to consider being Rolfed. I usually come back every few months and have a few sessions.

My son, William, and I do a lot of traveling now. We took a trip to Florida and another trip to California. Then my energy seemed to have bounced back, so we packed up our three dogs and drove to Alaska in 1986. We were gone for about three months on our Alaska trip, and the Rolfing was really responsible for giving me back my stamina. William says that it rejuvenated me.

I think if I had discovered Rolfing earlier, it would have changed my whole life. My life would have been different. But better late than never!

Charlotte B.

I had heard a lot about Rolfing from friends, but I never did anything about it. I just didn't think I could give myself permission for that kind of luxury. I thought it was too much money to spend on myself.

Later, when the time was right and I was going through some inner changes, I thought about Rolfing again. I went for the spiritual, emotional changes more than the physical benefits. I tell everyone about my Rolfing experience. So many people are interested in doing it at some point, but I believe they have to be ready. Rolfing is a tool for growth and development that can only be used when the timing is right.

Rolfing gave me physical length, so much so that I had to move my seat farther back in the car because it was too uncomfortable using the old setting. Now I drive with the seat way back and I'm not that tall.

The remarkable thing is that it was not painful. That's not always the case. A friend of mine had a great deal of pain, but I experienced only some minor discomfort.

I came back for three advanced sessions this year because I had been through some traumatic experiences. I felt my body had collapsed, folding protectively in on itself. I couldn't sit up straight. After the first advanced session, I could straighten up. I could easily feel and see the difference. I had a lighter step and my breath seemed to fill my body. One day as I left Rolfing, I realized that I was actually listening to the music on the radio and was aware that I was hearing it differently. I wanted to listen to it.

I felt like dancing. I drove to the park, sat in the parked car and listened to the music. That was a very beautiful, vivid experience.
One other thing I remember, that is rather amusing, is that I kept leaving my hat in Briah's office. Hats have always been a part of who I am, and I'd worn them for years. But every week I would leave Briah's office without my hat. I've always loved my hats and felt that they set me apart from the rest of the world, but I no longer feel comfortable wearing one. I was talking to Briah about it and she said that energy comes out of our heads and a hat would contain and hold it down. I can't wear hats anymore. They just don't belong now.

Ernest M.

My husband has always lived his life with gusto. He teaches at the university, writes music, gardens, and has a very active social life. However, after two illnesses in the past year, I have been saddened to see this vital man losing his vigor. I heard the Surgeon General say that it is possible for people to die healthy in bed. I wanted that for my husband. My husband's doctor put him on pills to increase his utilization of oxygen. I reasoned that if he could breathe better his body would not be starving for oxygen. I had just begun Rolfing sessions and noticed how open my chest was. The Rolfer said Rolfing helps people of all ages. I was delighted to see my husband standing straighter and more open in his chest by the first session.

By the second session he had cut back on his oxygen utilization pills. A wound on the top of his head seemed to heal faster than previous such wounds. Most important to me, the bounce returned to his step and his twinkling eyes sparkled even brighter. So far, he has completed half of his Rolfing sessions.

I feel very fortunate that we were able to find Briah to be our Rolfer. I am convinced of the efficacy of Rolfing, but I also feel that Briah's strong belief in the healing powers of this technique and the resilience of the body are an essential ingredient in my husband's renewal.

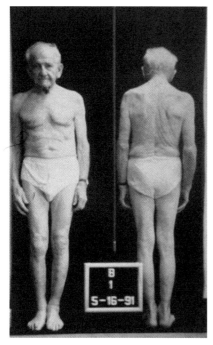

Ernest, age 91, Before Rolfing

"The benefits I most appreciate from the Rolfing are strength and a feeling of initiative," says Ernest.

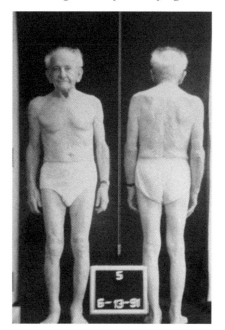

Ernest, After 5 sessions

Bonnie N.

I was in the hospital when my son was being Rolfed. I had a bad sinus infection which went into the lungs. My doctor had never seen this in his 25 years of practice. It's called Wegener's granulomatosis, and the doctor figured out that I probably had it for over 20 years.

I was in such pain that I couldn't bend my knees or elbows, sit by myself, turn over, or raise my arms over my head. My hemoglobin count, which should be around 50-something, was 8. This was caused by systemic vasculitis, an inflammation of the smallest blood vessels, which is a symptom of the Wegener's that caused every vein in my body to hurt.

At the same time, my mother was dying of cancer, and I was under incredible stress in my professional as well as personal life. I was taking Cytoxan, a chemotherapy drug they use to treat cancer patients, and I was beginning to recover from the systemic vasculitis when I came down with a urinary tract infection. My doctor said that was a common reaction to stress.

I was in the hospital for five days for that. When I came out, in the fall of 1985, I started my Rolfing with Briah. My son said it would help release things and that it is a cleansing process. I thought, "Oh great, I could go for that. My spiritual path is one for cleansing." I was ready to get into the dungeons of my mind and totally free everything stored there, getting the junk out of my mind as well as my body.

I knew I was a mess. One shoulder was so much higher than the other. My knees and hips were totally out of line. I wanted to get straightened out. I was in so much pain. Every session with Briah felt excruciating. I noticed one thing though. No matter how painful it was, when she stopped, usually the pain stopped. I'm still not totally pain-free. But after I was Rolfed, the degree of pain was greatly diminished.

My son David was right. Rolfing is a releasing and cleansing process. Everything starts in the mind and expresses itself through the body. But somehow the Rolfing releases things, opens all the doors. I would go home after these sessions and bawl and bawl and bawl. I didn't know why I was crying, but I let out so much sadness. It all came out. Then I would feel so good because I had gotten rid of all this excess baggage. Sometimes it was a delayed reaction.

I had three advanced sessions in September 1987 and later on in the fall, I started crying. I swear the sorrow came from the tip of my toes and every pair of shoes I wore hurt. David said he thought it was a reaction to the Rolfing, and I had another session with Briah. All the pain went out of my feet. At the end of the session, I felt wonderful. My shoes feel comfortable now, and I don't have any problems with my feet. My knees are straighter and I walk taller. My back feels great. My carriage has improved and I just feel better.

I had an inner conviction about Rolfing. I absolutely knew this was the right thing to do. And I had complete confidence that Briah was an excellent Rolfer. Everything always worked out. I could always keep my appointments. Just the fact that I was doing it made me feel better.

Briah opened up my sinuses as well. I could breathe better through my nose. I had done Yoga for a number of years and thought that I had learned to breathe deeply, but Rolfing gave me a depth of breathing I never thought possible.

One of my friends was Rolfed and found it very beneficial. Another friend who lives in Topeka is also planning to try it. I think everyone ought to be Rolfed. When I see women with their purse hanging on their shoulder and their body sagging I think, "Oh my dears, you need Rolfing." But I don't say that to them. Rolfing is really a very personal experience. It breaks up a lot of things: physically, mentally, and emotionally. You could spend many, many times the cost on doctors or drugs and still not get the same results.

Phyllis P.

I first heard about Rolfing three years ago when I was 52. A salesman who used to call on my husband told me about it. We used to compare notes on our back problems and surgeries. He had heard about Rolfing from another client and when he finally had it done, he would not leave me alone until I tried it. Every time he came to town, he would call me and say, "You've got to make an appointment." He really wasn't able to explain Rolfing to me, and I couldn't understand how it could possibly work. It sounded like a lot of hocus-pocus to me.

Finally, because I was having so much pain and discomfort, I decided, "What the heck." I was amazed at how it took the pain away and gave me so much freedom of movement.

I had thrown my back out of place and had gone to a chiropractor several times. Once as I was picking up one of my children, I threw my back out and couldn't stand up. Another time I was dusting a table, and I bent over and couldn't get up. I remember when I was about 33 years old, I picked up my youngest daughter when we were at the swimming pool, and I couldn't stand up again. Maybe every three years something like this would happen. I would go to the chiropractor and have a few treatments and I would be fine.

But then I was in an automobile accident. To avoid hitting the other car, I was practically standing on the brakes, and in doing so I took a blow to the top of my head. I had a headache off and on for two weeks and I was sure I'd suffered a mild concussion. Six weeks after the accident I woke up with my right leg hurting. We were going to Columbia, Missouri, for a football game. My leg didn't bother me too much during the middle of the day, but by dinnertime it really started hurting.

The next morning I couldn't get out of bed because of the pain. They brought my clothes to me, and I got dressed lying down. I said, "I'll go home and have my chiropractor cure me." Every day for a week my husband took me to a chiropractor. And every day I got worse.

The following Sunday I was so bad I called a neurosurgeon. He had me come in first thing the following morning. The pain was so bad I could not move my toes. It hurt all the way down my back and my leg. The neurosurgeon immediately sent me to the hospital for a myelogram. I found out I had a ruptured disc, and the doctor performed surgery the next morning.

I wasn't able to sit for about four weeks. I had to either lie down or stand up. Afterwards, I slowly resumed my normal activities, but I would have a lot of pain when I sat or got out of the chair.

The pain stayed with me. If I walked up a step even an inch high, I'd have pain. Any time one foot went higher than the other, I would have a muscle spasm.

It was also difficult to get comfortable at night. It would take forever to get straightened out. I always sleep on my left side and bring my right leg up, but I just didn't have the mobility to do that. I had to be really careful, or I would have these terrible muscle spasms.

I had played a lot of tennis before surgery, but afterwards I would play and then have to come home and lie in bed for three or four hours. Finally, I just quit playing because it hurt so much. It was very frustrating. I'd think, "Well, if I ever fall I'll really be in trouble."

I had taken some Yoga sessions around the Fourth of July in 1986, and the muscle spasms increased. My back was in bad shape. I could be standing up, sitting down, lying down, riding in a rough car, riding a boat when the waves were high and the pain was so bad I could hardly move.

I don't like to take cortisone shots or medicine. I won't even take aspirin. I figure the pain is my body's way of saying, "If you're hurting, don't do this." My husband really gets mad at me because we never have any medicine in the house.

I saw an orthopedic surgeon who told me I had arthritis in the area where I had the surgery. Finally, I decided to make an appointment with a Rolfer and have something done. I live in Springfield, and it was easy to come to Kansas City for the Rolfing and stay with my mother.

I was skeptical about Rolfing. I had had bad luck with trying different things. And there was no exact way of knowing what was going to happen. When I would try to tell someone about Rolfing, it was very difficult to explain. No one had ever heard of it in my town. I'd say, "Well, she rubs you." And they thought it was like massage or chiropractic. In my situation, I needed more than that. I'd had a chiropractor work on me before, and he told me the first week he couldn't help me.

After a couple of Rolfing sessions, I was hurting and taking Epsom salt baths. I remember being concerned after about three sessions, and Briah gave me the names of some people that had similar back problems and similar reactions with their first few sessions. I called one and talked to her for quite a while. She said she had the same experience and had left the first few sessions and didn't think she would be able to make it to the car.

Release from pain happened after about the fourth session. My muscle spasms almost disappeared. It was amazing! I started feeling great. After that I would have a muscle spasm maybe a time or two, but it was an unusual occurrence towards the end. I never have them now.

As I was going through Rolfing, it felt like a sculpting process. I felt lighter. I changed the way I walked. I led more with my legs. I couldn't believe the muscles that I had in my pelvic area. I had no abdominal muscles before Rolfing, and all of a sudden the appearance of my outer body changed because these muscles tightened up. The first two weeks I gained half an inch, and then an inch, and now I'd say I have about three inches of muscle girdle across the lower abdomen. That is most amazing to me because I had always worn a girdle. I had no muscle tone in that area. Well, I stopped wearing girdles and now just wear control top support hose. My biggest figure problem was my poochy tummy.

These muscles have pulled my tummy up, and now my waist looks bigger around. When you get Rolfed, your body is reshaped and becomes more proportional.

After surgery, my right leg had been weaker and now it has gotten stronger. I walk at least three times a week and always walk at least three miles. I can walk up and down hills in my neighborhood—3.2 miles in about fifty minutes. Before Rolfing, it would have taken me at least an hour and twenty minutes. I can walk so much faster now.

I have much more energy. My leg would get tired before. I've never been any good at sitting around doing nothing, but when my leg got really tired, I would have to sit down and rest it. Now I never think about my leg being tired, and the only time I ever think about my back hurting is in times of extreme stress. But that doesn't happen very often. The pain did come back last year, and I had some additional Rolfing sessions. I felt like my posture was getting a little bad, and I wasn't standing as straight as I wanted to. So I came back and had some post-ten work. I am so mad at myself. I need to pay attention to my posture. I don't want to end up an old lady with a big hump in my back.

My mother was also Rolfed. She is 77 years old and it gave her a lot of mobility. It also gave her an incentive to diet. She was really thick in the chest and abdominal area. She had some back trouble, too, and was hunched over.

Losing the weight and being Rolfed has made her feel so much better. She is active now. She feels good. She always says, "I can't believe I'm this age and feeling so good." She used to tell me she had arthritis in her back because my dad had bad arthritis as a young man. He died when he was 58, an invalid. Mom would say, "I know I'm getting arthritis like your dad." She was getting to be immobile because she wasn't exercising and she was overweight. She'd say, "Well, it's arthritis so I'll quit." She used to bowl, but she had been in an auto accident several years ago and had broken a lot of bones. She never did bowl or do anything after that. The Rolfing made her feel better, and it gave her the desire to take off weight. Now she goes bowling.

People ask, "What is Rolfing?" I say that it's a technique to improve my posture and regain mobility. My friends began noticing that when I sat down, I wouldn't grimace. They would say, "Oh, I can't believe you did this or that." I didn't realize I had been making such a to-do about the pain I was having. But the people I am with all the time had noticed it, and they noticed the difference Rolfing made immediately. They notice that I can sit on a low stool now or get out of a chair quickly instead of very slowly.

I don't worry anymore about getting up and down, stepping off a curb. That worry and the pain is all gone; that's the great thing about Rolfing.

Priscilla W.

Our 32-year-old son dates a woman who does all kinds of unusual things. She even went off and cooked for a crew on a ship once. One day, we asked him what Kate was doing and he said, "Well, she's thinking about getting trained as a Rolfer." And I said, "That's tremendous. I'm in the middle of getting Rolfed." He couldn't believe that I'd even heard of Rolfing, let alone was having it done. In the 70s, I began to have some arthritis creep up, particularly in my neck and shoulders. I got concerned because I had known people who had become terribly crippled from it.

I didn't mind the pain, but I didn't want to be crippled. So I went to an arthritis specialist in Chicago, and he gave me a prescription and told me to keep exercising. At the age of fifty, I swam fifty miles a week and did a lot of back exercises daily.

A couple of years ago, the arthritis flared up in my hip. I kept thinking I'd do something about it but didn't know who to contact. I went through quite a search and ended up with Briah's name. I called her, made an appointment, and went in to see her.

She explained what went on and ten sessions certainly seemed worth it. I had become very aware of older women who have a dowager's hump. My grandmother and an aunt both developed a bad hump. And I thought, "I am not going to have that, so help me!" I believed Rolfing would help.

During the Rolfing I could actually feel things moving. My breathing capacity—almost any capacity you want to name—improved, and I can still see improvement.

I do think that Rolfing and Yoga together have been important, partly because the Yoga is stretching and partly because it's a meditation exercise. I was already doing back exercises, which obviously weren't doing anything in terms of stretching.

Because of Rolfing, I have experienced many positive physical changes and have had all kinds of people tell me they see a difference. These are people who are not necessarily prone to handing out compliments. I firmly believe that Rolfing will keep me younger.

Priscilla playing tennis with beautiful form. She is able to lengthen and follow through with ease.

Dori G.

In 1985 I was in an accident that left me with a broken back. I was taken to the Mayo clinic and had Harrington rods put in my back. The doctor said that I might have to leave them in all my life, but they caused such excruciating pain that I eventually had them taken out. Without the rods I could move better, but I still experienced pain.

I had also suffered a collapsed lung and required a trachea tube for about a year and a half. After seven laser surgeries to remove the scar tissue from the trachea, I was left with only 40 to 50 percent breathing capacity.

I came to Briah through my massage therapist's recommendation and immediately after the first session experienced an opening in my throat and an improvement in my breathing. It was suddenly as if my chest was open, and I could grasp all the air that was available. It was such a miraculous feeling that I went home and just cried.

I had other wonderful experiences as well. My face filled out as Briah helped me realign my jaw, open my sinuses, and enlarge my forehead. I could see the changes and could tell my skin was softening like a new baby's.

The pain subsided and I could stretch. By lengthening and loosening my muscles and tissues, I was able to move without pain. My posture improved. I was able to walk longer and breathe better. One worked into the other.

While I was going through the Rolfing, I shared my experiences with Briah, and she assured me that any pain I had was a good sign because it meant the muscle or tissue was waking up and getting accustomed to being used again. Even now, when I stretch or move a certain way, I can feel the conditioning and healing still going on in my lower back. My body always seemed to know when it was time to be Rolfed. I would get tight, but then when I walked out of the office, I was a new person—taller and for the most part, free of pain. My emotional and physical outlooks were improved—a great experience.

During one session, I was having a bad taste in my mouth, and it turned out that Briah was experiencing the same thing. She said it could be the anesthesia or the medicine coming out. It's funny how your body finds ways to release things.

I believe Rolfing brings out the good in a person physically, emotionally, spiritually, and mentally. I feel very centered now. My whole being is in balance with nature and the rest of the world. I used to be uptight about my abilities and what other people thought. I'd struggle to do my best.

Now my best comes more naturally. I feel like I have found myself, and my attitude has changed for the better. I'm much more perceptive. I've even had some premonitions.

I didn't expect a complete cleansing of the soul, spirit, and body. All I wanted was to alleviate the pain. These other benefits were a special bonus. I've had so many people say, "What's happened to you!" They knew about the accident and the scars and can see the changes brought about by Rolfing.

My friends all ask about it. They want to know how to spell it and exactly what it does physically. They don't usually ask about the other personal experiences because they don't realize there are any.

I believe Rolfing helps people integrate and enjoy life. I am convinced that we are here for a purpose. People who stumble through life may manage to do some good, but they could do so much more if they were really centered and had a true sense of purpose. I feel like I'm operating from a center position now, not functioning from the periphery.

I don't think anyone realizes what beautiful, marvelous changes can take place along with physical improvements. My accident was bad, but I didn't let it keep me down. It helped me reevaluate my life.

Before I was Rolfed, I had consulted with a plastic surgeon about a cosmetic face lift. After completing my sessions, I went back to the doctor. He could see the changes in my face and said that surgery was no longer necessary.

I went into Rolfing wanting something more than a band-aid approach. I was hoping for a miracle, and I got it.

My husband was overseas at the time I was being Rolfed. When he came home at Christmas, he couldn't believe the changes in me. He thought I looked marvelous. Our relationship and our friendship improved. Because my attitude had changed, we became compatible. I knew it had a lot to do with the Rolfing.

My husband was so impressed with the new me that he's planning on being Rolfed himself. You see, when he was a boy, he broke his neck. I've told him some of my experiences with Rolfing but not too many because I want him to have his own.

I tell people Briah helped put me back together again. But she really created a new person.

All we are doing is directing the flow
of gravity by virtue of organizing the
body as though it were an electric wire
so that gravity can flow through it.

—*Ida Rolf*

Chapter 5

Learning to Ask for Help

Don Elbel

Attorney and businessman

Don Elbel

I first went to Briah Anson hoping to achieve relief from some upper back pain that felt like a pinched nerve and had been troubling me for several years. Previously, I had been working with a chiropractor who finally said, quite candidly, that he did not think he could help me anymore because my problem seemed to stem from the muscular or soft tissue rather than bone. He recommended Briah. I had heard good things about her from several other sources, including my wife. So I set up an appointment with her. I had also heard some troubling things about Rolfing in general, such as it was harsh, harmful, or dangerous, but the good recommendations were sufficient to get me to try the process.

The decision to seek help for my physical ailments rather than try self-help or simply "live with the problem" was central to the benefits, physical, and psychological, that I received. I want to discuss this point further, but, first, I want to summarize my personal experience with Briah's Rolfing.

I not only received considerable help in relieving my upper back pain, but perhaps more importantly, Briah helped me realize that I had not been aware of the connection between my mind and my body. In part this stemmed from being brought up to value a skillful mind far more than a strong, healthy, or dynamic body. Moreover, in the process of becoming an attorney and businessman, I had trained my mind far more than I had worked with my body. Thus, I had accumulated a lot of tense, contracted, disconnected, and almost stagnant areas in my physical being. Not only did I feel a tremendous amount of reawakening in the dozen weeks of the Rolfing process, but in the months that have gone by since, the process is building upon itself. The more I appreciate my physical being, the more I am encouraged to further enhance and enjoy my physical self.

Rolfing has been a step in a gradual process of becoming more comfortable with my physical body. It has been going on for a number of years, but the acceleration in the process that came as a result of the Rolfing was explosive—a fast leap, rather than slow or small steps.

During the very first Rolfing session, I experienced intense feelings, essentially tingling sorts of feelings much like you get after your foot has been "asleep" and you then move it. Several times I felt quite dizzy and somewhat anxious. I was experiencing physical sensations that I had not had for many years, and it was exciting but uncomfortable.

However, by the second or third session, I began to actually experience the connections between various small pains that I had had from time to time in my body and the more pronounced back pain that had originally sent me to Briah's office. I realized that the tension in my neck, the pain between my right shoulder blade and spine, the discomfort in my hips, the tightness in back of my thighs, and pains in my right foot were all connected. In fact, I began to recognize that the whole right side of my body was somewhat twisted; so much so that while my left leg and foot pointed forward, my right leg and foot pointed out to the side at a considerable angle.

Briah and I discussed the possibility that this twist might have stemmed from falling from a jungle gym when I was about five years old. I broke my arm, but my parents, being Christian Scientists, did not take me to the hospital or to a doctor and simply tried to realign the bones and let them heal "naturally." I have some vague recollection of the incident, but I think the pain was sufficient at that time that most of it has been blocked from my conscious memory. However, I had so much confirmation of the incident from family members that I have no doubt of the injury's severity.

I also have little doubt that this twistedness has been with me for as long as I can remember. I have clear recall of the fact that my right foot pointed outward and my left foot pointed straight ahead from far back into my early childhood. So, while I cannot exactly identify the cause, I can clearly identify that this problem was deeply ingrained into my body structure.

Not too surprisingly, as my right side began to release, straighten, and stretch during the sessions, I became aware of a somewhat countervailing tightness on the left side. Interestingly, it is my left side that is now showing more inclination to open up in this adjustment period after the Rolfing therapy, while it was the right side which responded the most to the Rolfing itself.

During the process, I could feel my body stretching, expanding, and lengthening. In fact, on physician's scales, I was able to confirm that my height had increased approximately one-half inch. That did not totally surprise me since a person is considerably taller at the beginning of the day than they are at the end of the day as a result of the spine compressing. So while this stretching was going on, it seemed perfectly possible to me that there would be some enhanced length to the body, especially in the spine area. I find it most interesting, however, that the lengthening has not retracted.

I do not feel that the process is finished yet. But Briah, as a result of her experience, has encouraged me to wait six months or so after the completion of the first set of therapies so that we can see what changes occur essentially as a rippling effect of the original work. Then we can see whether I have sufficiently absorbed and integrated the original sessions to go on to any further work. I believe each person has their own pace of change, the amount of change they can handle at one time, and I like the idea of additional sessions to continue the gradual process.

A very pleasant ripple effect that is not entirely the result of the Rolfing, but has certainly been enhanced by the Rolfing, is that I seem to be having much less difficulty controlling my weight. At this point, of course, I have no way of knowing whether this is a permanent effect or a temporary one. But along with other work I have done, the Rolfing has improved my self image, especially my physical self image. My awareness of my entire body has been enhanced (rather than a highly conscious sense of my mind and a rather unconscious awareness of my body which was my former state of being). The process has helped me get my physical shape more in line with what I want. I think what may be happening as a result of this increased connectedness (consciousness) is that I am adjusting my psychological "set point" for my weight and body shape. It remains to be seen how much of these changes will be permanent and how much merely temporary, but it has been an exciting and fascinating process to date.

I plan on continuing the Rolfing process with Briah after allowing a few more months to pass because I want to see how far we can go.

For example, for the last few years, I have had arthritic feelings in my hands, feet, and knees, from which I experienced enormous relief during the weeks of the Rolfing and continue to feel substantial relief. With Briah's help, I believe I can even further reduce this arthritic-like stiffness. It seems clear to me that this stiffness has been the result of a gradually increasing tension and contraction in my body tissue which, when expanded through the Rolfing process, was dramatically relieved.

It felt as if there was enhanced circulation, and there was almost none of the morning stiffness which I had come to expect as a regular problem. When I see the bent-over and constricted position that many older people who experience arthritis have, it does not surprise me to hear that when their bodies have been lengthened and relieved from this constricted tension, they too have experienced dramatic relief from the arthritic sensations.

As much as I have enjoyed the Rolfing benefits, I am aware of the difficulty that many of us have with seeking and accepting help from others. Whether we are going to see a doctor, a lawyer, a mechanic, or a Rolfer, as a society we are highly skeptical that we will get help that is worth the cost (or even get help at all). In today's world, self-help books, courses, tapes, and the like are all the rage. That is because of our society-wide fear of dependence on others. As a society we almost worship independence.

It is a sad shortcoming of our society that we so overvalue self-help and undervalue good help from others. We often cannot bring ourselves to get the help we need, and if we do finally go for help, we often have such difficulty in trusting the helper that we never fully give them a chance to do their job. In those instances where the help is indeed not good, we take that as a confirmation that all help is not worth the financial or personal price. And perhaps most sadly of all, our exaggerated fears of dependence on other people lead many of us to dependence on substances such as pills, alcohol, cigarettes, drugs, etc. Thus, while we worship independence, our lack of internal self-development leads us to unhealthy dependencies.

While it is true that Rolfing is much like Yoga and that many of the benefits received from Rolfing can also be achieved through the self-help of Yoga, it is clear to me that the process is greatly speeded up by allowing a professional Rolfer to assist. In certain ways, progress is achieved with assistance that simply could not be achieved alone. For example, I have practiced Yoga for some time, but the deep tissue movements in my back were extremely difficult (if not impossible) to achieve through Yoga, and yet they were relatively easy for Briah to accomplish. Healthy dependence on capable others can often be better than independence or self-help, and it is clearly better than dependence on destructive substances. My own observations lead me to believe that we "over-parent," meaning that we make too many decisions for our children, too often trying to protect them from problems and fears and failures.

I think this parenting mistake happens quite frequently. I know it happened in my household, in spite of the fact that both my parents had the best of intentions. As in many families, this problem is passed down from generation to generation. To break this cycle, we must come to realize how to provide emotional "help." First, of course, we often have to seek emotional help for ourselves. Ida Rolf, the founder of Rolfing, recommended emotional therapy along with Rolfing whenever possible. The Rolfing process not only relieves physical stresses and tensions but also releases certain feelings and emotions that have been tightly suppressed for years. Once I learned to accept all of my own feelings and emotions, I no longer felt the need to hide or repress my emotional self. I could rapidly mature.

Rolfing is an active process. The benefits we obtain are closely tied to the efforts we make to absorb, use, and integrate the help. The physical corrections are thoroughly interconnected with emotional and mental changes. How much change we allow or sustain is fundamentally up to us as clients, not the Rolfer.

In my own experience, I overcame the childlike view that there were only two choices, do it myself or let someone else control me and make my decisions for me. I could get the help I needed without giving up genuine personal freedom and independence. In this way we can not only get help with achieving a healthy physical connectedness through disciplines like Rolfing, but also achieve a more integrated, satisfying inner connectedness.

Chapter 6

In Search of Wholeness

Nece B.

> "I realized that in order to release the emotional energy needed to solve my problems, I would need to find the means to release some of that physical energy that was blocked."

Sherry W.

> "I felt like someone had opened my entire life and exposed all the books and recordings of everything that had ever happened to me."

Sally M.

> "I did a lot of work in my therapy that might not have been done without Rolfing. That is to say, if I hadn't felt something first in my body."

Carol K.

> "Before Rolfing I kept myself closed down like a tortoise in the shell. Now I am able to open up and face life."

Penny

Michael S.

> "I found out through Rolfing where I store my anxiety and tension. I feel more aware of my body; I live in it more."

Leiola H.

> "Something very strange happened. I saw my aura. There was a glow all around me."

Kim B.

"Sloughing off the limitations of the past."

Becky S.

"Rolfing gave me greater inner strength."

Barbara M.

"Moving through space is more fun. I'm a hiker and I noticed after my seventh session my step was lighter."

Connie H.

"Rolfing has been as important as anything I've ever done for myself."

Betty B.

"I use Rolfing to release blocks, whether old or new, and to create a better whole life integration experience."

Susan T.

"Rolfing really puts the boundaries in place. It puts people back in their own skin."

Dean

Nece B.

I had been in therapy for seven or eight months and was starting to feel totally disconnected from my body. As I dealt with my emotional problems, allowing them to surface so that I could deal with them, I noticed the different ways my body would react to certain situations. I realized that in order to release the emotional energy needed to solve my problems, I would need to find the means to release some of that physical energy that was blocked. I believed that Rolfing was the way to accomplish this and decided to try it. After my first two sessions I began to loosen up. By the third and fourth sessions, I found that I was having vivid dreams and was able to write them down in the journal I was keeping. I had never actually remembered my dreams before and it was a big deal for me.

The most powerful experience I had while being Rolfed occurred in the fifth session, which dealt with my chest. My whole body suddenly went into paralysis. What I felt like and the image that kept coming to me was that of an old Indian woman. For almost an hour, I felt old and I talked and was unable to move. It frightened me at first because I wasn't sure what it was all about; but even though I was crying, I tried to pay attention to what this old woman wanted to say to me. I realized that she was telling me about my own rigidity and inflexibility, the parts of me that were probably very old and stuck.

I believe this was the beginning of physical freedom. In my therapy, I'm continuing on an inner journey and going back to find the child within myself. Whenever I've been able to return to painful places, I feel an emptiness in my chest. That's my dark spot. The parts of me that have been wounded the most are in the heart chakra.

Physically and emotionally, it all ties in together. Understanding that, my biggest benefit has come from being able to be more open in my chest area. Now as I work in therapy, I can actually physically feel my chest expanding.

I think being Rolfed was the first time I became aware of being rigid in my chest, and that the area could be opened. It was the most powerful physical experience I have ever had in terms of seeing my body in a whole new way, seeing that my body really does carry rigidity, flexibility, and fear. At the end of the session, I had to get on all fours and crawl across the floor to get my feeling back, to have the numbness go away.

After my experience during the fifth session of Rolfing, I really looked forward to the next session. I thought, "What else is going to happen? What else am I going to discover?"

The biggest area of change I've noticed has been the expansion of my chest and shoulders. I used to be round-shouldered. I still struggle with that. But it's easier to hold my shoulders back now. I feel more aligned, less closed in.

I noticed in the pictures Briah took before she began the Rolfing that I have a fighter's stance. I can see it in my right arm, where I've always carried out my anger. That's the part of me that wants to strike out when I feel someone is going to hurt me. As I've worked in therapy, I've noticed a release of pain through my arm, and through Rolfing, my arm has gotten longer. It's not as tight or bound up.

Someone pointed out to me that we connect with people through our arms. I've always tried to keep people at a distance. Now that I've let go of some of that tension, I've been able to allow people to get closer.

I'm aware of being more vulnerable and trusting and seem to be taking more risks. At the same time, I can see that I have fears about making those changes. I think it's that awareness that allows me to take risks that I might not have taken before. Another issue that came up as I was being Rolfed was that of letting go. I was fighting that in order to keep my control. When Briah was working with the tissues in my arms and finding so much resistance, she would say, "Let go." And I would say, "What do you want me to do? I don't know what that means. I don't know what you want me to do."

Our bodies truly carry messages that dictate the way we react. I don't think I would have believed that before, but after Rolfing, I'm much more aware of it.

I know I'm ready for some changes. That scares me because I've become used to being stuck and don't like to think about other possibilities. I think Rolfing will help me recognize the areas I'm stuck in. It certainly isn't something that takes place in a verbal way. My experiencing of paralysis wasn't something that someone could have told me about. I had to experience it with my body before I could start to make choices. "Do I want to stay stuck? Do I like being rigid?

What are things I can do to change?" One of the things I've continued to do since being Rolfed is to get a regular, twice monthly massage. I needed a physical release for my issues. I feel as if I don't have to carry things with me as much as I used to. I never used to know that I could let go of them because I didn't know how to do that physically. Now I have opportunities to do that. I have pain or tension, but I also know that I have options to relieve them. I know that pain doesn't have to be there. Rolfing isn't bandaid treatment. It's being able to open up to new possibilities and then integrate and use them in your daily life.

Now that I'm learning to release pain and tension, I'm also beginning to experience memories that are joyful. One day after being Rolfed, I wrote a piece called "River" because I realized that all my life I've been like a hot whirlpool. It's too artificial. It stirs the water quickly and gets so hot that you have to get out. I realized that I wanted my life be like a river, which is natural, deep, flowing from within, not just moving on the surface. Rolfing taught me to allow my own energy to flow, to be able to see and develop the river within my own life.

Sherry W.

My boyfriend Rocky had been Rolfed. One day he was watching me doing dishes and said, "I really wish you could be Rolfed. You look so scrunched up." He said it looked as if I were headed for problems down the road, and it would be nice if I could catch everything before it got too far. I had conflicting input about what Rolfing was about. My sister had been Rolfed, and it was more of a mystical experience for her. Rocky was Rolfed, and he didn't see it as a mind trip at all. His experience was physical and grounded.

I had mixed emotions about being Rolfed. When I came to Briah, I was apprehensive, but I wanted to let myself experience as much as possible. I tried to be both physically and mentally present while she was working on me. Rolfing was similar to massage, a form of "laying on of hands," but it was much more involved than a massage. I found myself telling Briah a lot of things that came to mind while she was Rolfing me. Sometimes they would be current memories; sometimes they were dredged up from the deep past.

Rocky didn't share a lot of his experiences with Rolfing. He wanted me to have my own Rolfing experience rather than relive his, so he didn't tell me every detail about what happened. He told me he would have a real revelation after one of his sessions, but he didn't want me to be influenced by what he felt or thought. I'm glad he didn't because I didn't have a lot of expectations when I walked in. I had a lot of questions but not a lot of expectations.

At our first session, Briah gave me a diary and asked me to write down my experiences as I was Rolfed. I did this faithfully the first four sessions. I didn't have a lot of emotional tie-ups until the fifth and sixth sessions. After that, it started being more of a mental and emotional experience than a physical one. After the seventh session, I felt like someone had opened my entire life and exposed all the books and recordings of everything that had happened to me. I felt raw and emotional. Rocky had been waiting for something like this to happen because I had been coming home so happy after each session. After the seventh session, I stopped writing in the diary. Things started blending together for me. I was being Rolfed every Monday, and every Monday it rained. I wondered if there was any significance to that.

A few times when I was being Rolfed, the mobile hanging in Briah's office would start ringing. It wouldn't be moving, but it would ring. She told me to just observe as I continued to be Rolfed and see what other things happened. I noticed the lights would change in intensity and asked Briah if she noticed it too, but she wouldn't have noticed. About the fifth session, I decided these things were happening, and I just wouldn't write about them anymore.

I'd had a chronic eye problem since I was a child, and it had been getting a lot worse. I had a lot of eye infections and would go to the doctor and get drops to clear them up for a while, but they would come back within nine months. I had been seeing an eye specialist more and more frequently, and she had opened my tear ducts with a hypodermic needle and injected medicine into them. It's called irrigating the tear duct. About the fifth session, my eyes flared up badly, and the doctor said I was probably allergic to cottonwood and gave me medicine and eye drops to use. The doctor told me the next step was an operation.

The next session Briah noticed my eye problem and worked on my face. I thought, "Oh, God, she's going to keep poking on my face for the rest of the day." I felt so plugged up. That session really bothered me. The next day I got up, and something came out of my tear ducts, little hard matter. My eyes have not bothered me since.

When I finished my ten sessions, I was rather sorry that it was over. Briah told me to look at it as a beginning because it takes your body some time to adjust to the benefits of Rolfing. It took thirty-three years to get this way, and after ten or twelve weeks, I wasn't going to come out as this wonderful healed person. It would take time for more subtle changes. I have noticed a renewed feeling. My body doesn't feel those little aches and pains which I thought were a process of getting older. Mentally it opened up some new doors for me and I'm able to look a little bit deeper at things. I want to find out more and I'm more inquisitive. I have a fluidity of motion I didn't have before, as if my body were connected to a continuous string that moved in conjunction with the rest of my body.

Sally M.

I've been Rolfed twice: two ten-session sequences.

The first time I was Rolfed was about three years ago. I was real depressed, and I stayed pretty sad the whole time because I was working on some real crises.

The second series was done within the past year. I felt completely energized with each and every session. I'd come out feeling great. I was Rolfed in part to help me through my therapy. I wanted to get further along with my process, which I did.

The first time I was Rolfed, I could see differences in that I looked longer and I wasn't crooked. My shoulders were more even and my back and hips were more upright.

The second time, I felt and saw more difference immediately. I felt that it didn't hurt as much as the first time. I felt more relaxed after each session, and I did not feel like I'd been put through a wringer, which is what I'd felt like the first time. I was drained each and every time the first time I was Rolfed. The second series I was real relaxed, and I was much more energized and in a much better spot.

My thighs and my legs have definitely slimmed down. They're not as clumpy as they used to be. During most of the sessions, I was pretty much the same weight, but I could feel my legs slimming down. My thighs and hips were more in proportion.

It's like my weight shifted or evened out. I think I got more mobility in my neck and more freeing-up. My neck has always been pretty stiff.

When Briah touched my chest it was like my core emptying. It was a scary, dark, horrible space. That's where I center and I protect myself. My mother died when I was thirteen, and the Rolfing opened up a lot of stuff about never having been nurtured and about being left—the things that happened in my childhood that I dealt with in therapy.

I remember the resistance, hitting the wall. Then saying okay, I have to give this up, because I didn't want to feel that pain again. But each and every time she touched me, I felt that pain in the bony part of my chest. What it did, it opened me up. I could breathe better, and I could walk more upright. I didn't feel so hunched over.

I could feel lengthening in my entire body, so I know I became more upright. I could feel lengthening in my rib cage and particularly from my knee to my hip.

My feet changed as well. This was a real gradual change. It took about a year to change. But something within the arch on my right foot really hurt after about a year. I came back to Briah and she had it fixed within a day.

I think it's just the gradual shift because I could feel it again occasionally. So I think my whole body is still adjusting. My toes are flatter now, and they used to be more curled. I think the Rolfing straightened them out. She worked on my feet and did a lot of stretching. I used to have sharp shooting pains up through my arch and thought I had broken my foot. But I never went and had it X-rayed. When she did the Rolfing, it was gone—just like that. I loved the end of the sessions. Every single time it was like, "Take my head and twist it around, please." I used to have stiff necks a lot. We would work side to side and back and up and out on my neck. Then she would go down my back. I felt as if I could just melt into the table. I loved the ending of every single session. I wanted her to stretch me more. I used to have bad cramps and now they're better. I think that's connected to the releasing I've done throughout my body and especially my thighs.

I go to malls now and watch people. I can see the damage and the hurt and the emotional pain they have suffered in their bodies. There are a lot of times in group that I'll watch what people are doing and then I'll do the same body posturing myself to check out how they are feeling. Your body just speaks to you. It goes on and on about how terrible something is and how protective you have become.

Rolfing helped me energize and free some of my emotions rather than take them in. Several friends of mine have been Rolfed, and many of them had no emotional response whatsoever. I found that very hard to believe because my Rolfing was so emotional.

Carol K.

I felt trepidation going into Rolfing. I was certain that I would never leave the table alive. This fear stemmed from an experience I had four or five years ago. I was having a massage and suddenly my legs began to hurt. I felt like I couldn't get away. I giggled, went into sobs, and then it was over. It was not a pleasant experience, so I was not extremely eager to try Rolfing until I found out that I had an ovarian cyst and would need surgery. I knew enough about Rolfing to believe that it would open my body and help promote the healing that was going to be necessary. So, in spite of my fear of having to go into this room with a table and take off my clothes, I decided to give it a try.

The first meeting was just to get a history. That was interesting because it was not what I had expected. Briah asked what I remembered my mother saying about her pregnancy with me or my birth. I had no information about it—nothing!

I had never realized that the physical self starts long before birth because family history has so much influence on what a person will be like. There's quite a history of physical problems in my family. My father had a colostomy, and his father committed suicide. When I listed these things aloud, it occurred to me that I was probably not only holding my own problems in my body but those of my parents and grandparents as well.

I was aware of all this as I started my first session. I was curious, excited, and open for positive experiences. And I had them.

While Briah was working on my lower body, my entire upper body immediately kicked out an incredible amount of heat. Suddenly I was just drenched, and I knew that the heat was a direct result of whatever she had done.

Towards the end of the session, one of my hands wanted to curl under and the other to curl back. It was as if I had lost my muscle control. I said something to Briah and she had me shake them out.

When I got up, my whole body felt different. Even my eyes seemed to be focusing in ways they had not focused before. I knew that we had accomplished a lot. It was an intense, exciting session.

In subsequent Rolfing sessions, the most profound thing that happened was my understanding of who I was and what I was going through. I was looking at the cyst on a whole new level. Why was it a cyst in my ovary? Why had my body chosen that site? I was doing vast amounts of thinking and growing. Rolfing was integrating various parts of my physical body and causing things to happen that made me consider other facets in my life that were out of alignment.

I went into the hospital with an excellent attitude. I determined that I was going to be well quickly and went through the surgery with flying colors.

I think that it would have been more difficult to be Rolfed with someone less considerate and tuned-in. Briah's understanding of all things being connected helped me realize that the problems I have in my body and the problems I'm having with the world are interrelated. I had a lot of revelations on the Rolfing table. One of them was a willingness to take risks. Before Rolfing I had kept myself closed down like a tortoise in a shell. Now I am able to open up and face life.

Rolfing is not primarily a psychotherapeutic approach to the problems of humans, but the effect it has had on the human psyche has been so noteworthy that many people insist on so regarding it. Rolfing is an approach to the personality through the myofascial collagen components of the physical body. It integrates and balances the so-called 'other bodies' of man, metaphysically described as astral and etheric, now more modernly designated as the psychological, emotional, mental, and spiritual aspects.

—*Ida Rolf*

Physical health and mental health:
it's the same thing.

—*Ida Rolf*

Penny

Look at the dramatic results in Penny, a client in her 40s, after only five sessions of Rolfing.

Penny traveled from out-of-state. She received one or two sessions of Rolfing at a time, spread out over several months. After the fifth session, Penny was amazed at her new-found energy and vitality. She felt like she had a totally different body; she felt great relief from her chronic aches and pains, and she felt she was well on her way to a life of more activity.

Notice how, in her "Before" profile photos, Penny's upper body is sagging into her pelvis, causing her abdomen to jut out and giving her the appearance of a woman much older than her years. She looks tired and worn down.

Because of the strains of pregnancy, many women are prone to this kind of posture, particularly because carrying a child throws the pelvis out of alignment. It is difficult to reestablish that intrinsic balance of all the layers of the abdominal muscles. Exercise alone will not reorganize the tissue. Exercise tightens and contracts muscles. What the body also needs is length and balance, especially balance between the muscles in the front of the body and the muscles in the back of the body.

Before Rolfing, Penny's shoulders were slumped, rolled forward and down, causing her neck to feel tight and resulting in a forward head posture. Her abdomen looks pulled to the right. Her head is also off center, and you can see the twist in her neck. Less obvious is the major torque in her pelvis, which further aggravates the twist throughout her whole body.

Penny eventually finished her Rolfing series with a Rolfer who moved to her home state. She has returned to see me yearly for some additional "tune-up" work.

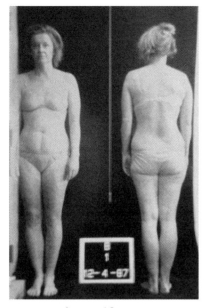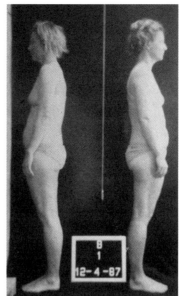

Penny, Before Rolfing

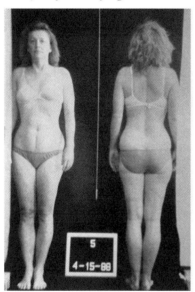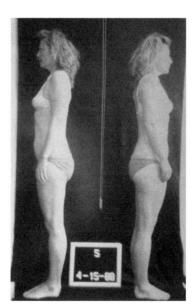

Penny, After 5 sessions—halfway through the series

"Some individuals may experience their losing fight with gravity as a sharp pain in their back, others as the unflattering contour of their body, others as a constant fatigue, yet others as an unrelenting threatening environment. Those over 40 may call it old age. And yet all these signals may be pointing to a single problem, so prominent in their own structure, and in the structures of others, that it has been ignored; they are off balance. They are at war with gravity." —Ida Rolf

Michael S.

Rolfing is one step of the process I have been going through to get more in touch with myself, with my personal power, my personality, who I am, and what I am. Having completed my sessions, I feel better and project a difference. It has been a continuing process and a great experience opening up my body. I am more aware of and more in touch with myself.

I began Rolfing when I turned forty. I had been having some problem with pain in my left leg. For years I had been walking with my left foot out at an angle. I didn't actually register pain, yet I was hoping for relief.

I was afraid Rolfing would overwhelm me at first. I discussed this with Briah, and she reassured me that we could handle whatever came up. Nothing that happened proved overwhelming. I had heard about muscle memory that some people experience from Rolfing. I had a traumatic childhood. I was emotionally beat up and was scared that some dark, long-buried trauma would come out and knock me flat. I was expecting to be assaulted with ten thousand forgotten traumas.

This didn't occur. Memories came forward, but didn't swamp me. It was more, "Oh, I'd forgotten about that." As a matter of fact, it was easier to handle these traumas because I was feeling more open, breathing better, and walking better.

Assessing my gait after Rolfing, my left leg and hip have become adjusted, diminishing the angle of my foot. My hip is less tilted.

Rolfing also changed the shape of my chest. Once rather caved in, my shoulder squared and my chest came forward, making it easier to breathe.

I felt more energized. There is more energy to tap, and I believe the reason is because the muscles are being placed back in their proper positions, so it takes less energy to run the body.

Rolfing, along with the other steps in my life, brought my personal power, confidence, and sincerity to the forefront. The Rolfing was a mode of transportation into another area. The group therapy was also another mode of transportation. When I told my therapy group I was going to be Rolfed, they were overjoyed. My individual therapist, who had also been Rolfed, said it was terrific to do it at this time in my process. It worked exceedingly well in conjunction with therapy. They complement each other.

I also found out through Rolfing where I store anxiety and tension. When I am suppressing things, I have a tendency to put them in my shoulders and hip area. If I had a week that was particularly stressful, my storage area was tighter and more aggravated. It was helpful to learn where I'm holding things in. It kicks the hell out of denial, because now I have to deal actively with my problems. It feels really, really good. I can't say that Rolfing was entirely pain-free because it wasn't. If you have a sore muscle in your arm and someone comes along and presses on the muscle, it won't be pleasant. That's how it was with Rolfing my hip. But the soreness left, and the end result was wonderful.

I had spinal meningitis when I was a kid, which caused some trouble with my back over the years. At the end of each session, Briah would have me sit on the edge of the table while she ran her elbows up my back. There would always be a little catch there. That was the most traumatic part of the session for me.

Also at the end of the session she would take a photograph. I thought, "What are you going to do? You're not going to show them to your grandchildren, now, are you?" But the more sessions I had, the happier I was she was taking them. The changes in the photos are subtle but dramatic over time. The photographs don't quite do justice to the way I felt because they couldn't show how much better I can breathe or how energized I feel. They do show that my shoulder is back in place, squared out, and they show the changes in my hip. I can see where I was and how far I've come.

I'm continuing to improve because I've gotten everything freed.

Things are still in the process of getting aligned properly. The adjustment period after Rolfing can go on for six months to a year, I've been told.

I feel as though I live in my body now rather than on an intellectual plane. Now, with the therapy and Rolfing, I feel more aware of my body. I'm living in it more. I've moved out of the attic and into the house.

Leiola H.

I began Rolfing for a couple of reasons. First, I was encouraged by other people who'd been Rolfed. Second, I "physicalized" emotional things. At a point in therapy, my therapist thought Rolfing would help me get through problems on a physical level that I had been working through on an emotional level. I had also been going to chiropractors for quite a while for problems with my neck, shoulders, and lower back. And I had really bad, debilitating cramps.

Before starting Rolfing, I was frightened that it would hurt. By the time we got to the end of ten sessions, I had let go of a lot of physical pain and released some of the emotions causing me to feel uncomfortable. Rolfing never hurt beyond my tolerance and never very often. Surprisingly, it usually felt really good.

During the first session, a song came on the radio that caused me to weep uncontrollably. It touched a place in me. I'd heard that a lot of people experienced distinct memories during sessions and I thought "Oh, that's great, but it won't happen to me." But it did, more than once.

I remember once as Briah was working on my rib cage and back, I had a very clear memory of my honeymoon. I remembered going into the hotel lobby in Aspen. I remembered the smell, what everything looked like. And that my husband and I went upstairs to our room and had a huge, horrible argument that seemed to last forever.

I wasn't remembering this in my mind. I was recalling it through one of my senses. The whole experience came to the surface. Briah asked me what was going on, and we talked about it. She said that when people get hurt they close down and physically pull in. The Rolfing was pushing my hurt out.

At the end of one of the sessions, Briah had me stand in front of a full length mirror. I always liked that because I liked the way I looked after I was Rolfed. This time something very strange happened—I saw my aura. I had never seen an aura before, but there was a glow all around me. I just stood there. I didn't want to move or blink or think about it for fear it would go away. So I looked at it for a long time. It was a wonderful experience. As I was coming back to this plane, becoming more conscious of my surroundings, the wind chimes moved. They rang even though there was no heater, no air motion to move them. Briah said that my energy moved the wind chimes. I thought that was really neat. Nothing like that had ever happened before. I felt like I had a real treat.

I've had so many people tell me that my posture has changed—that I hold myself erect. I think other things are tied into that. Rolfing was the first bodywork I experienced. I've since added massage and some cranial work and have continued to process through bodywork. Before I was Rolfed, I would always do my processing intellectually and emotionally. Rolfing has allowed me to be in touch with myself and, therefore, in touch with other people.

Kim B.

I first heard of Rolfing about five years ago. I had just started exploring what I would call "right brain" health. I cleaned up my diet, started taking a Yoga class, and began trying to develop my spirituality. Unfortunately, the block I had to bodywork was money, and when I found out about the cost of Rolfing, I thought I would never be able to afford it.

I did see a chiropractor because it was covered by insurance, but I felt that I needed something more. I had read an article on bodywork in Yoga Journal which helped me understand more about how our bodies are such an integral part of ourselves. I remember the section on Rolfing very clearly, because it seemed reasonable to me that human beings store memories and emotions in their bodies. The golden voice inside of me that speaks up when it hears truth told me I needed to be Rolfed in order to find out what was really going on in my life.

I had come to this first step of awareness through two things: one was a burning need for health, a very buried, very small seed that instinctively knew what was right; the other a personal history that involved both denial and pain. I didn't tie all of my history together until later. I am by nature an intuitive, sensitive person, an airy sort of dreamer. I was born into a family that, although loving, was wrestling with many unexposed and painful conflicts. Having a rather porous psyche and a weak body (I weighed only 4 pounds, 5 ounces when I was born), I absorbed all the negative energy around me.

The result was that at about 18 months of age, my health seriously declined. I was asthmatic, had ear infections and fevers, and was on antibiotics constantly. I weighed only 17 pounds when I was four years old. At that time my tonsils were removed which helped somewhat.

But a pattern of poor health continued. I was diagnosed as having a nervous stomach when I was nine. I had disorders in my bowels and my urinary tract. In addition, I became very near-sighted starting at about five years old.

These physical problems were chronic reminders of a weak body, but my body didn't really break until my last year of college, when I injured my left hip in a dance class. The injury started off as a groin pull and escalated to tendinitis in my hip. It weakened both knees and strained my other hip joint. I had ultrasound treatments and chiropractic care, but these didn't help very much. I could barely walk for nine months, and after that any physical exertion would irritate my hip again. This injury made my body feel very unstable, a condition which was indicative of my life at the time.

I know now that all of these physical problems were manifestations of emotions I had. My problem was that I always felt as if l were "inside out."

I don't think my parents ever knew I was a walking emotional wreck until I told them when I was 25 years old. I seemed to be living with my feet off the ground, denying my emotions and running around in circles in my head.

Of course, these patterns caused problems in my personal life, which sent me on a spiritual search for help. I began this quest in 1985 and discovered Buddhism.

Buddhism has been the main engine in my advancement toward health and a balanced life. I met Briah through this practice. As my district leader, she helped me in my practice and in my life. In addition, I met many people who had been Rolfed, which made it seem financially feasible. Also precipitating Rolfing was counseling. I realized that I was ready to change the patterns I had since I was a child.

After five months of counseling, I came out of my emotional denial and really began to see my life for what it was and scheduled myself to begin Rolfing. Three months later I had my first appointment. Two days before my first session, I had a very significant dream that helped release some of the emotions I would be purging during Rolfing. In fact, my most life-changing dreams happened right before an intense Rolfing session or before a series of sessions. Somehow, my psyche was already leading my body.

My first two sessions of Rolfing helped to open up my chest and facilitate my breathing. I realized that I had never before been able to "take a deep breath." My breathing has always been very shallow, just at the midsection of my rib cage. Although I didn't mention the details of being Rolfed to my parents, they noticed that I looked stronger and more solid in my chest. In fact for the first time, I was able to wear a strapless dress and look good in it!

After each session I would feel more connected to myself and more grounded. I would also feel emotionally vulnerable, but would allow my boyfriend to nurture and care for me, something I had never previously experienced. This vulnerability turned out to be the foundation for a healthy marriage.

As I approached my fifth session, when the work becomes deeper and centers on the stomach area, I began to experience overwhelming feelings of fear. I had to confront deep fears of abandonment and of being unloved. Again, my Buddhist practice, counseling and Rolfing dovetailed to help me resolve these feelings, which I am sure were the root of many of my obstacles in life.

The week after I finished my tenth session of Rolfing, I went on a canoe trip in Canada. We were out in the wilderness for five days. Before being Rolfed, I don't think my body could have handled the rigor of that trip as well as it did. I felt balanced and found that I could use my body in more ways than I had thought possible.

I felt more grounded after being Rolfed. I sensed that I had always tried to move with my head and had a natural inclination to put as little surface area of my feet on the ground as possible. After Rolfing my feet were more firmly planted, and using my whole foot as a basis of support helped heal my old hip injury and straightened my posture.

I went back for more Rolfing eight months later, in early Spring, so that I would be in good shape for my wedding in June. Briah concentrated on my legs and feet, straightening them even more and improving my ability to stay grounded. The ensuing few months were hell on my body. A wedding, the bachelorette parties, a driving honeymoon, and numerous other weekend trips in the car left me all knotted up. I continued to seek chiropractic care, which helped temporarily. Finally, a cranial session grounded me on my feet again, and it seemed to stimulate the effects I had from Rolfing.

Three or four months later, I went in for another session because my hip injury had been aggravated by driving a new car with a stiff clutch. Not surprisingly, this irritation coincided with preparing for a move to a different city. After this one session, I felt better than I ever had after the ten-session series. I believed that I was ready for an even greater change, ready to take all of the changes I had made and create a more whole, integrated self. I had been released from counseling the week before and reached a point in my Buddhist practice where I could say that I had gotten truly tangible results.

I now feel as though I am finishing the best segment I have had so far in my life, and I am moving on to pursue my dreams in a practical, grounded way. I am healthier and have much clarity and understanding of my own process of growth. Rolfing has been an important part of this growth. For me, Rolfing is a holistic, integrative process with the body as its point of entry. Using Rolfing with other such processes that have different points of entry helps make the integration complete.

I am more sensitive to poor posture and misalignments in my body now, even though I am much healthier and sturdier. This reflects in my ability to make significant changes in my life and stay centered. I am also more self-directed than I was before. But the work is not over. This new shining self could be straighter, more balanced, and healthier. For this reason, I will continue to use Rolfing as a tool for growth.

My husband has had seven sessions of Rolfing. I will encourage him to continue, and we'll take our future babies to be Rolfed as well.

I have already recommended Rolfing to several people, and as friends continue to confide in me about any physical or emotional problems, I will continue to recommend it. I believe Rolfing is a good form of healing for anyone.

Becky S.

During one of my first Rolfing sessions, Briah was working on my legs when suddenly I recalled my first bike marathon. The route included 103 hills. I hadn't been prepared for it and got hurt. Now I was feeling those hills again. They were still in my legs! I felt the memory of how much it hurt to go up and down those hills, my first experience with bodyrecall, an extreme event that the body memorizes and holds on to.

I had read the materials Briah provides her clients, detailing how the body might recall events subconsciously and deliver them to the conscious mind. The following story illustrates my experience with "body memory" during Rolfing.

In the seventh session, Briah was working on my back, from the bottom to the top of the spine, when I had a vision of a portion of a recurring bad dream.

In the dream, I'm walking by people in a grandstand watching the sea come in and close on a little baby. I wonder why no one is doing anything, so I run out to save this baby, which opens up its mouth to reveal rows and rows of barracuda teeth. It's glad to see me because it's going to kill me. I try to save something that's little and sweet, and it doesn't turn out to be innocent. My bad dreams have always been involved with that little kid.

One time when I had that dream, I was screaming "let me out" in the dream, but in reality I was also pounding my fist through a window. I woke up and had slashed my wrist and had to go to the hospital. Seeing I was disturbed, Briah stopped and asked me what was happening. I cried as I told her the story. She offered that maybe the image was a part of me that was always in there, maybe that was also part of that kid. That was a "dead" part of me that she Rolfed out. That day I walked out of the office really, really dizzy. A big feeling of loss came over me. I don't fully understand or explain the "dead part," but it was released. and I've felt a lot better since that day.

Today, I look in the mirror and see a lot of changes in my face. It's more relaxed. My neck is more relaxed, too. Stress problems in my back, including a failing disc, have released greatly. I feel better than I ever have.

I know what I'm going to be when I get out of chiropractic school. I'm going to be a Rolfer. I'll be forty years old, but who cares. What's another $20,000? That's my main goal, to get out of chiropractic school and get into Rolfing. I have three years to go. I always wanted to do something related to the body, something to help people. Chiropractic work is really great, but Rolfing is something special. I get love from seeing real healing—physical, spiritual, and mental—process with Rolfing.

Before my seventh session, I carried a feeling of dread. I was debilitated. I couldn't even move. Just recently, I went through a second bout of dread. I had several bad things happen: In a two-week period, one of my puppies died, and my car was wrecked. I was a little glazed donut. Had it not been for Rolfing, I couldn't have handled it. Rolfing helped a lot. It gave me greater inner strength.

Barbara M.

When I was in California ten years ago, I overheard the following conversation while standing before the Aquarium in Golden Gate Park:

> "Brian's being Rolfed."
> "Oh my God!"
> "Yeah, I know. The therapist pulls his muscle layers apart."
> "Really? The way l heard it, the muscles are pulled away from the
>   bone."
> "Something like that."
> "Poor old dog."
> "Naw, Brian says it's worth every scream."

Given such an introduction, I wasn't likely to begin a quest for the first Rolfer in sight. Besides, Rolfing was probably just one more indulgence for wealthy Californians. For the next seven years, I never gave this strange business another thought. So the matter might have stayed if I hadn't dropped in on my friend Sandra a few minutes after she'd been Rolfed.

Even though I was in an emotional fog (having just returned from a year in England to find my fiance shacked up with my best friend), I did notice that Sandra's pale skin had a rosy, polished tinge.

"It's the Rolfing," said Sandra, putting a pillow behind my back which was stiff with misery. "It's to die for."

"So I've heard."

Recognizing sarcasm as the lowest form of wit, she ignored me. "I promised myself this treat as soon as I had a little money," said Sandra, oozing her body into the deep curve of her chair. "It's wonderful. I really do think I've died and gone to heaven."

"But surely it hurts?" I said, remembering the California screamer. Sandra gave me the long look she reserves for idiots. The little worry wrinkles that usually radiate from the corners of her eyes had disappeared.

"Hurt?" she said as though she'd never heard the word before. "If it hurts, I don't notice." She sighed, and during the pause, I examined my prejudice against this "Southern California" treat. "This was my last session," she said finally, "and I never felt more grounded."

That did it. I was hooked. I wanted to be rosy and unwrinkled and grounded.

I wish I could say Rolfing was the miracle I wanted. It wasn't. So what was it?

What lasting changes did the process produce?

First, my body is more aligned. I know this because I experience fewer pulled muscles in my neck and lower back. Also, moving through space is more fun. I am a great hiker, and I noticed after the seventh session that my step was lighter, with less jarring of my frame. I have continued to enjoy this fluidity.

Second, the most dramatic change is in my breathing. The breath passage is full and clear and reaches from pubic bone to skull. At least, that's what drawing a breath feels like.

What didn't I like about the experience? With some embarrassment, I admit that I sometimes found it painful. It would be easy to dismiss this reaction as "resistance," and I tend to do so. However, such dismissal may be too self-blaming.

In the two years since my first series, I have returned on two occasions. The first was for one session a year ago to aid the healing of a sprained foot. (I walked out of Briah's office and dumped my cane in the nearest trash container.)

Last August, an unmindful driver crashed his truck into my sub-compact. Every muscle in my lower back rebelled. Five Rolfing sessions later, my back was free of strain, aligned, and deliciously relaxed. Although not without some pain, these sessions were definitely easier for me to accept than the first set.

I'm writing this Rolfing reaction during the first month of a new year in which I feel reborn. How much of this centeredness to attribute to Rolfing, to chanting, to a reformed diet, to a sustaining relationship, to better writing, and the belated acquisition of a little wisdom, I can't say since all actions are causes. Rolfing played its part, though. That's for sure.

Connie H.

I first heard about Rolfing in 1971. I was in Monterrey, California, at a communications training workshop and was overwhelmed with all the new "buzz words" I was hearing. Words like Esalen, Fritz Perls, Gestalt psychology, meditation, massage, primal scream therapy, Zen, Awareness Training, humanistic psychology, New Age, and on and on. Rolfing was one of those words. I just wanted to hurry and do it all!

I remember hearing that there were "Rolfers," just a few, who traveled the country keeping appointments with their clients who had agreed to a certain number of sessions. Rolfing was similar to massage, except that somehow it also unblocked the mind or emotions or psyche. Mostly I remember that it was supposed to be very painful!

As years passed, I heard about Rolfing occasionally, and I began meeting some people who'd been Rolfed. I had one friend who told me something about his experience. Whatever else he said I forgot, but I heard "pain" very clearly. About six or seven years ago at a gathering of "growth seekers" here in Kansas City, I heard there was a Rolfer who flew into town periodically for sessions. Evidently, I wasn't motivated enough to find out who, what, when, and where to look for them.

In January, 1986, I was in Austin, Texas, at a "Seth" workshop and met a Rolfer who was one of the participants. Out of curiosity, I decided to find out more about what Rolfing was and if it might be something I wanted to do. We talked for awhile and made arrangements for a first exploratory (my exploration!) session. I was assured that even one session would have some benefit and that if l wanted to continue, there was indeed someone in Kansas City who was a Certified Rolfer. (We learned that by looking in a little book listing Certified Rolfers all over the country.)

My first session was, hmmm, interesting. I brought with me some skepticism, lots of embarrassment when it came time for stripping down to panties and bra in front of a perfect stranger—male at that—and allowing my body to be touched from head to toe. I also brought along enough openness and trust to acknowledge those feelings and get on with it. There was no pain involved! It didn't feel invasive. It wasn't like chiropractic, and it wasn't like massage. There was breathing and concentration involved, and I liked it fine. My Rolfer assured me I'd experience definite benefits if I decided to continue.

At the time, I had some physical problems bothering me. I'd been a runner for three years but had given it up because of pain I developed in my lower back. I was also having trouble with my left hip, which occasionally felt like it slipped out of joint. I had some pain in my knees and ankles at times. I had been diagnosed medically as having a condition called costochondritis, which is inflammation of the chest tissue. The symptom was chest pain, and at first I thought I was having a heart attack! But my doctor said this wasn't the case. In addition, I had suffered with a tennis elbow for years. I had even given up playing tennis for 6 or 8 months to let it heal. When I started playing again, it was better. But while playing, I always felt my elbow. My serve was side-armed because my arm wouldn't operate in a straight down motion from the shoulder joint. Finally, I also had sinus headaches and an ache in my neck and shoulders which I attributed to stress.

About two weeks after I returned to Kansas City from Austin, I awoke one day with very severe lower back pain. It was the worst I'd ever had. It was bad enough and my schedule was light enough that I just stayed in bed for two days. I was very puzzled because I couldn't blame it on anything I had done to myself, no lifting or falling or out-of-the-ordinary exercise. Then I remembered that the Rolfer in Austin had said that sometimes symptoms in the problem areas get worse before the problem is released, rather like a final, dramatic goodbye. That's when I decided to set up an appointment.

For years I had been focusing on my own growth and self-aware-ness. It fit that Rolfing would be an enhancement to the rest of the pro-gram I'd set for myself. My only real expectations were around releasing the pain in the areas I've mentioned. Beyond that, I was just open to whatever would come. Amazingly enough, I wasn't afraid that it would be too painful, or painful at all, despite what had been planted in my head about it. I regret that I did not follow through and keep a journal throughout. After the second session, I began dreaming vividly, and I did write down some of those dreams for a while. Here is one entry after the third session:

3/14/86

Work on hips, chest, shoulders, arms and neck. Very painful . . . I had trouble syncing my breathing with the work . . . hard to empty lungs and take next deep breath.

Images appeared, very slight then pushed into my awareness . . . Egypt, Queen Nefertiti, black cat, crypt, sarcophagus . . . strong.

Pain was momentarily extreme . . . wondered why I didn't cry. Felt confused, out of it. Hard to concentrate on Briah's directions . . . also felt very relaxed at the same time.

At the end of session my upper body, arms, and legs tingled incredibly, causing visible tremor. Lasted several minutes.

Chest felt open.

It was after this third session that I noticed a marked reduction of pain in my lower back and elbow. The pain has never returned. When I look back on those weeks, I can't remember any other sessions where I had images, and very few where there was any pain other than momentary twinges. I would address those by breathing into them until they flowed through and out. I had more energy and began sleeping an hour less each night without feeling tired. My arm could move vertically from the shoulder for the first time in my memory. My tennis serve changed dramatically (for a hack anyway—it's all relative!)

I finished my initial sessions about six months ago and have just had four more sessions. I injured my other elbow playing tennis and walking while pumping hand weights that were too heavy. The pain is releasing now, and I also feel more alignment after integration time between the sessions. I intend to return at least once a year for "oil change and tune up!"

I need to add that my husband has had severe lower back problems for years. When his back goes out, he is in excruciating pain which lasts for days, even weeks. He has a disintegrated disc and has run the gamut of medical and chiropractic intervention. He always obtained some relief with chiropractic or osteopathy but was still having regular recurrences every few months. I began to notice how stiffly he was moving, always in fear that a movement or even a cough would pinch the nerve and the pain would double him over. Since his initial sessions, eleven I think, there is great improvement in his movement, and he is free from lower back pain unless he gets tired. I'm sure he'll have more sessions after a period of integration from the first set. I am also encouraging our three grown children, who all have back problems to varying degrees, to consider Rolfing for lasting improvement.

Rolfing has been as important as anything I've ever done for myself. I enthusiastically recommend it for everyone to reap whatever benefits are there. That's an individual matter. What I am sure of is that there are important benefits for each of us.

Betty B.

I first heard of Rolfing in 1984 through a close friend and, about six months later, decided to try it.

My decision was based on major upheavals in my life. Having recently moved into the area, I was experiencing anxiety about the new location. Also, different aspects of my personal life were causing problems. In short, I knew I did not want the rest of my life to mirror what I was now experiencing. I knew I had to make some very dramatic changes in my thinking and unblock areas that had been suppressed for many years. I saw Rolfing as a way to release emotional blocks so I could develop a more free, natural, centered life. I also saw it as an opportunity to create better health and posture and a total life integration.

During my initial Rolfing experience, I can't remember any sensations. In some respects, I was a little disappointed because I really did expect explosions of some sort. What I did find, however, is that my "tune-ups" are creating changes more quickly. This second tune-up is causing a lot of crying and a release of feelings of deep hurt and sadness. Wonderful!!

I feel a greater sense of ease in my body, as well as an increased awareness of movement. Because of this, I am better able to tell when my body needs another session or two. I use Rolfing to release blocks, whether old or new, and to create a better whole life integration experience.

Rolfing has been my therapy, both from a sense of the development— mental, spiritual, and physical—and from talking with my Rolfer. It's something I look forward to doing yearly and see it as my continued awakening experience.

I've noticed that the second sessions or "tune-ups" are much easier. Perhaps because I know the routine, I am better able to breathe into the movements and am more prepared for the experience. Knowing the positive things that have already occurred, I work much harder at doing my share of the Rolfing.

I would highly recommended Rolfing to those who feel the need to make physical and emotional changes in their life and are committed to a holistic approach of development.

Susan T.

I think that what goes on in Rolfing is a metaphor. It parallels so many important aspects in our lives—trusting another person to help us or working together and taking the best from it. Rolfing has a balancing effect, a way of unifying various relationships in the body. It also has the effect of bringing you even more into your own body because of the better flow, and therefore, you release things you were holding on to. The conceptual understanding comes as a result of the physical experience—the awareness and insights that come with release.

Rolfing has given me access to the best of my physical self and the ability to think and have feelings that seem right. As a counselor, it was wonderful for me to learn how much growth I could have without overtly trying to "think" it in place.

My husband recently surprised me. He wants to have my portrait painted. I had my portrait painted when I was 22 years old. If you look at that picture you notice it's pretty, but the poor subject—me—looks so very fragile. I'm excited about this portrait painting coming up, because I know my new-found vitality will come through. I can sit proudly, as if to say, "Look how far I've come. Look what I've done." And it has nothing to do with my accomplishments professionally. I was presented with an unasked-for challenge. I was given this body with these alignment and structural problems. I have done so much and learned so much about patience, persistence, open-mindedness, and pushing myself in a healthy way.

Three years ago, when I was 33, I had some structural problems that prevented me from dancing, exercising, or moving freely. My massage therapist recommended Rolfing and thought I might enjoy the experience. Movement is essential for me, whether it's jogging or dancing or whatever. I believed Rolfing might be useful to me on several different levels.

My body wasn't balanced to allow me to do any form of impact exercise without incurring swelling around the major joints. I had sore ankles, knees, arms, and hips. I used to jog daily and also took aerobic dancing. One day I woke up feeling like I had been beaten up and tossed out the window. It took several years to get to the point where I could control the pain. All of my physical activities were limited. Even walking was painful. The only thing I could do was swim and even that was stressful to my body.

I had been using anti-inflammatory medicine and learning about therapeutic breathing, but I was nowhere near where I wanted to be in terms of freedom of movement. And there were all the emotional manifestations—feeling restricted and frustrated. I always thought this shouldn't happen to someone who has the soul of a dancer.

At the clinic where I was a therapist, I learned that we store emotions in our bodies. During the Rolfing series, there were a number of sessions where, to my surprise, tears came out. Or my body would tremble. There were physical events, but there was a sense of something psychological breaking loose, too.

The emotions I had stored were being freed up along with my body. It was very liberating. Not only has the work given me a different sense of my physical boundaries, but also my emotional ones. I told my first Rolfer I used to feel like I was always about to fall on top of people, physically, as well as emotionally. The boundaries between myself and others were quite vague and that caused dependence and fusion that wasn't healthy. Rolfing really puts the boundaries in place. It puts people back in their own skin.

I find that I can stay connected to people and care for someone else without using up all the emotional energy I need for myself.

When I completed the sessions, I thought, "My God, this is how normal feels." It's as though someone brought me home and I could say, "Of course, this is where my left foot goes. That is how my hip should be." I didn't realize how adapted I had been to feeling unnatural until I began to feel natural.

Even though the Rolfing had improved my physical and emotional well-being in many ways, I still continued to have knee problems. I was in so much pain I finally went to see a specialist and was told that the only surgical procedures available were so complex, so painful, and required such heavy rehabilitation with a relatively low chance of long-term success that they had to be ruled out. The risk was not worth it. I finally found an orthopedic surgeon who discovered that my kneecaps were tracking to the outside, a congenital problem. We then proceeded with arthroscopic surgery, which was the least invasive, to release the kneecap on first one knee and then the other.

After the surgery, I called Briah, whom I had met at a Rolfing Movement workshop. I felt she was open to using Rolfing in a number of creative ways and knew I would feel comfortable with her. As soon as we began working, I felt that same sensation of, "Yes, this is where my pelvis needs to be." Or, "My feet need to be under me if my knees are ever going to have a chance to recover." Briah saw that and worked with it.

Between every Rolfing session, I exercised with a new awareness. I'd find a place that had been immobile before, but that I never knew was there. Sometimes it was a muscle, sometimes the way a bone went into a joint. I'd breathe up into it and could take it further than I'd ever been able because it was now freed up. That awareness while exercising helps integrate the Rolfing work in my body. Rolfing opens the door for me, and then I go in and see what I can do.

Had I not continued with Rolfing after the surgery, I don't think I would have gotten much better because my problem also was in the femur angle, the angle of the pelvis, and the way the femur attaches to the kneecap. My structure was so out of kilter that the amount of relief I would have gotten without Rolfing would have been limited.

I've been seeing Briah two or three times a year, for two to three sessions each time. And my mobility has increased and increased and increased.

One of the things that has been very useful in Rolfing is Briah's integrated view of things. I continue to use acupuncture along with the Rolfing and have also tried a few other techniques. However, the major movement has been achieved through Rolfing. One of the instructions Briah left with me was to learn to breathe more into my upper back, to open it up. The acupuncture has helped loosen up that area and has also been extraordinarily helpful in fortifying my blood, which is causing some of the chronic discomfort in my knees. The blood is being nourished by a better flow through the body and that has made a huge impact.

The input from Rolfing and acupuncture gave me information about myself I couldn't get from psychotherapy, because I hadn't been able to understand myself completely. Acupuncture and Rolfing make a wonderful combination. I'm learning to listen to my body and when it says, "Now it's time for more Rolfing or massage or acupuncture," then that is what I give it.

I'm continually excited with the possibility of more and more progress and of learning more about myself because I can experience all this neat body stuff at a deeper level. Plus, there are always great physical benefits.

The advanced Rolfing work was harder for me because it was more subtle, but as I became more patient with the series, I realized my rib-cage seemed to have relaxed and expanded in the right direction. I was always amazed at the Before and After photographs. I saw, as time went on, that my legs were being brought underneath my body to provide needed support. I found my gravitational line becoming apparent from my toes up to my head. The progression of photos seemed to show my body shifting or waving and eventually coming into line. Before Rolfing, my line was stuck in a certain position. In the After photos, I saw all major joints coming into alignment with one another.

I became taller, not because I was holding myself in a stretched-out position, but because I was bringing my ankles, knees, hips, and shoulders into line, so my structure changed and gave me the most freedom.

There is no question this process is an evolution. I see the world differently, and feel natural, like I belong. There must be a relationship between the world out there and what's inside the body because I'm more in harmony and feel more stable and centered. This doesn't mean I'm always calm, for the big emotions are full-bodied and not constricted.

One of the most exciting changes for me is that my knee area is not a dead zone anymore. It has taken its place in the line of things. Now the blood circulates from above and below to my knee, so it isn't numb with chronic pain. I still have to apply ice to that area after I take walks, and I can't take dance classes without worrying about it. But I recognize the process, and it seems to me that it doesn't stop but continues to evolve.

I learned another important lesson, too. I see this with other people who do body work. It's that people often go from one guru to another until they find what works. I recognize very quickly when a helper in one of these bodywork efforts knows what he or she is doing and maintains good boundaries. There's no effort to manipulate my emotional state or my body just so it fits a theory. They work in a way that complements and is respectful of who l am. I've run into plenty of people who feel they have a system that is "the answer to everything" and only they can deliver it.

Through her work, Briah simply said, "Here is some information about yourself. This is where things go in your body, and this is how they work for you." She never proceeds if she feels her client can't take that in on some level. As much as I wanted to rush ahead and have her do more, I always trusted her when she said, "That's enough for now." She never does more than is necessary and doesn't use exactly the same process on everyone, because we all have different needs.

Yesterday I attended a training session for therapists learning a particular mode of therapy. It is a very good, legitimate form of treatment and the person conducting the session is someone I know, care about and respect, but the training was very conforming, and I thought, a bit manipulative to the client. I knew very quickly that this was not for me. I knew it from my body, which was telling me about my discomfort.

I could feel myself withdrawing. My boundaries felt unsafe, as though someone was trying to invade and mold me in an inappropriate way. I felt a danger response. My body was telling me this therapy was not right for me. I am now seeing how the inner clarity I've gained is manifested in my daily life.

When people ask me about Rolfing, I tell them it has been an extremely liberating experience for me on a lot of different levels. If they strongly resist the idea of being Rolfed, my first thought is that they're probably cut off from their body. Rolfing is a re-education of the body through touch. Many people are interested, but others have the misconception that it's painful. That's a very classic reaction with acupuncture, too. The first questions is, "Does it hurt?" I tell them how I learned early on to breathe into the pressure, not to constrict or restrict myself.

In my fantasy world, I would have everyone I know and love get Rolfed, then we could have more connection between us, because it's very liberating. Because I feel so good about myself, I can respond to others in an appropriate fashion. It's what all of us spend a lot of time and energy looking for. The portrait my husband is having done for me is a symbol of the pride and joy I feel living inside this body. It's not a problem-free body, but so far it manifests the very best that I can be and am. And it feels pretty good.

Dean

This body building client saw the potential of Rolfing to help him increase strength and muscle definition. He wanted to increase strength without the use of steroids and drugs.

Before Rolfing, Dean felt tighter, heavier, and less flexible. He spent two hours a day on his workout regimen and noticed that after he started Rolfing he had more energy, more "fire." He felt that Rolfing enhanced his overall performance; he was less tired after a workout or after a day's work at the construction site.

Dean was impressed with the tremendous muscle definition he achieved through Rolfing. As his muscles became balanced and freed up, he was more flexible and less "muscle bound." He had increased length and felt as though he had more space in his body.

Dean reported that when he took a breath he had much more room to expand. He felt bigger, yet leaner.

"Strength comes from balance," explains Ida Rolf, in her book Rolfing and Physical Reality. *"Strength that comes from effort is not what you need. You need the strength that comes from ease."*

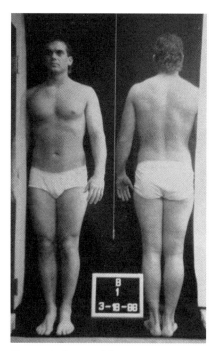
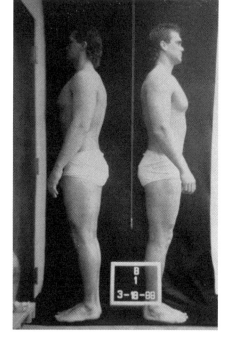

Dean, Before Rolfing

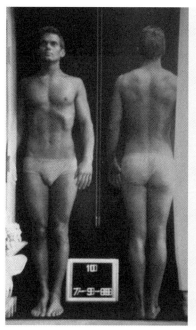
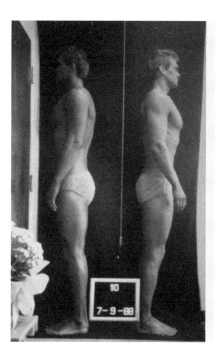

Dean, After 10 sessions.

Rolfing has to do with gravity.
Not chemistry, not medicine,
not the idea of individually fixing this
and that gone wrong. Gravity is the
one and only tool that we use. I think
my experience justifies making this
very broad assumption. Gravity is
the only tool that deals with chronic
situations in the body.

—*Ida Rolf*

Chapter 7

Rolfing and Chronic Pain

Jim A.

"At the time I started Rolfing I was in so much pain I would sit down only to drive."

Jack O., real estate developer

"With Rolfing came the realization that I no longer had to be a slave to the physical pain and could direct my energy toward dealing with the spiritual side of my life."

Suzanne A.

An artist with chronic back pain avoids surgery and gains renewed inspiration.

Germaine G.

"I am healthier now. I look younger and more approachable. Five or six years ago, I was depressed and I looked it."

Patty M.

"When I'd leave Briah's office, I would breathe and it was as if my lungs had been unlocked. I'd run out of the building singing."

Linda M.

Psychologist
"I went to a neurosurgeon whose final diagnosis regarding the numbness in my arms and neck was a combination of arthritis developing around areas where I had athletic injuries, compression of the vertebrae causing nerve pinching, and carpal tunnel syndrome."

Charlene M.

"Rolfing is really the best investment for preventative maintenance of your body."

Rocky R.

House painter
"Because my back health was always tentative, I had led a tentative life."

Ross V.

Artist and professional painter
"My body has been broken everywhere—my arm, leg, face, and skull. I felt as if I were slowly dying, but I wanted to get on with my life."

Frank W.

Engineer
"I had a myriad of problems in my back. Balance physically helps me balance mentally."

Ken R.

Rough-in carpenter, building homes
"In the past few years, I've eaten enough pain pills to fill the back end of a truck. I'd been thinking of retiring this summer, but because of Rolfing, I'll probably be good for another ten years."

Rick B.

"I feel like everything is opening up."

Jim A.

Jim came to be Rolfed because of severe back problems. "At the time I started Rolfing, I was in so much pain I would sit down only to drive," says Jim. "I had to kneel beside the table to eat dinner, and I stood all day at work."

When Jim came in, he was trying to avoid imminent back surgery for a herniated disk. A hospital administrator referred Jim to Rolfing. The administrator told Jim that many people who had back surgery faced the possibility of future surgery.

"In spite of the pain, I was a bit skeptical about being Rolfed," says Jim, "but a lot of people I knew in the hospital community had been helped by it, so I decided to give it a try."

"I've found that the process doesn't stop with the last session, the improvements go on for a long period of time. I still return for an advanced session whenever I have any back pain. Sitting in a poorly designed chair used to cause me a great deal of discomfort. But when I'm in great shape after being Rolfed, I can sit for hours in an uncomfortable chair with no pain. In other words, I can abuse my body and get away with it."

"I'll probably come back every couple of years to maintain my health. I plan to have my daughter Rolfed when she gets older. I think it's the best gift I can give her."

Jim returns yearly for some advanced work of two to four sessions and continues to show signs of improvement.

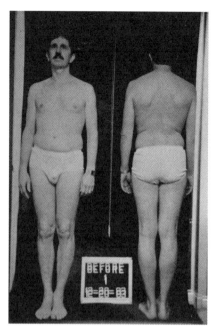
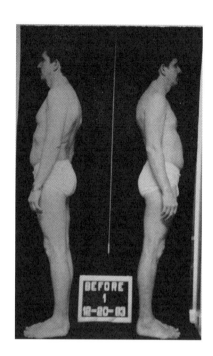

Jim, Before Rolfing

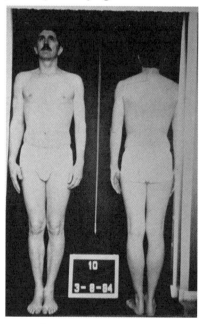
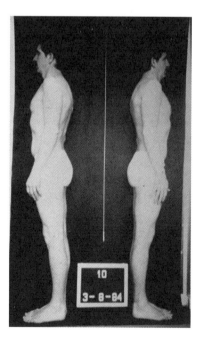

Jim, After 10 sessions

Jim A.

Notice in Jim's Before Rolfing pictures that there is no support in his lower back for his upper body, which appears to be collapsing or compressing onto the lower body. Consequently, there is no support for his neck and head to be vertical. Also, Jim's legs are not aligned directly under his torso, a common occurrence in people with chronic back pain. The legs, positioned under the pelvis and torso, give lift and support to the upper body.

After 10 sessions, notice the twist and collapse in Jim's back has been eliminated. This twist and compression of the upper body onto the lower body was responsible for his chronic lower back pain.

Notice how, in his most recent After Ten Sessions photos, taken seven years after his original Rolfing work, Jim continues to gain more vertical support and strength in his upper and lower back.

In these photos, Jim looks longer, leaner, and stronger, with the body of a younger, more virile man.

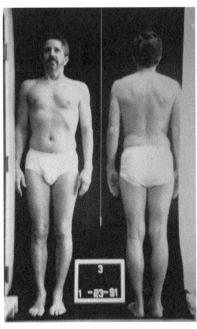
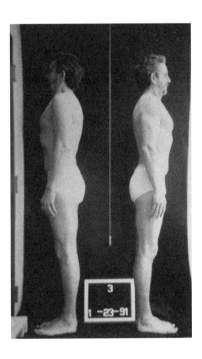

Jim, 7 years later

Jack O.

I was somewhat desperate when I made my decision to be Rolfed. I had a lot of problems with spasms in my back and neck. I'd tried all kinds of remedies over the years to alleviate the problem and the pain that I was suffering. I'm in the real estate business and that causes a lot of tension. Some people handle it better than others, and I guess I'm not real good at handling the stress. We all have spots where the tension goes. Mine goes right to my upper back and neck.

It took me some time to figure that out, but now I know what to look for and can see where it's coming from. I probably had one or two more Rolfing sessions than the norm, because the muscles were so tight in my back and neck that Briah had a more difficult time.

Throughout the entire period of the Rolfing process, I was looking more for relief from the physical pain I was suffering rather than from the emotional stress. I didn't come to the sessions looking for relief from stress. Yet Rolfing speaks to our physical and mental connection. I should have figured it out because obviously my mental stress brought on the physical pain. But as you go through Rolfing a lot of things seem to open up. It's almost like a cleansing taking place. Your mind becomes clearer; you're able to think better.

My neck pains didn't go away until we had been finished for several weeks, although my upper back pain went away much sooner. There are still times when my neck bothers me. I had this pain for about five years and had become almost accustomed to it. Now I literally have no pain, and that's an incredible change for me. Consequently, it's helped me in every other facet of my life—my relationships, my business, and my ability to cope with problems.

My wife was all for anything that would help me with my pain, but she was initially skeptical of Rolfing because I've had temporary relief from the pain before. Relief sometimes lasted for a few hours or days, but the pain would return. And when I left Rolfing I still had pain.

It was many weeks after the Rolfing process that it really started to do its thing. People look for "miracle healings," but nothing seems to work that way in reality. We tend to do things gradually over a period of time. When Briah is working on one part of my body such as my leg, I can tell it's also dealing with my back. This takes care of the overall problem, and I knew it was exactly the right way to do it.

I could sense that my body was attempting to adapt to the changes because the muscle structure had to be manipulated in such a way that it would be working together correctly. When I was about five or six years old, I was in an automobile accident. When the top of my head hit the windshield, everything in my neck was rapidly compressed. That's where a lot of my pain and migraine headaches come from. Apparently there's a nerve in the back of my neck that gets out of place, and when that happens, everything takes off.

With Rolfing came the realization that I no longer had to be a slave to the physical pain and could direct my energy toward dealing with the spiritual side of my life. I now had an opportunity to begin to feel my own presence. This was something I had always wanted. As my system was being brought back into its proper place, I experienced a sense of physical cleansing. It was like being able to breathe again. My breathing had been shallow before because of my muscle structure, but once the pain started to let go, a domino effect took hold and I could finally breathe properly.

I had a greater self-awareness and began to pay attention to my posture and gait. Rolfing doesn't just address the part of the body that aches. It takes the whole body and puts it back in place. The body is an entire entity and must interact properly to function well. If one part is out of line, then the rest of the parts start to follow. I was very patient with the whole process, and the pain gradually started to leave. I always had awareness of my pain. But today I am aware of being pain-free. When the physical part of Rolfing takes effect, it frees up the mental part. There's so much power we have as individuals. We can do great things when we're given the ability to really use that power.

One of the first things I heard about Rolfing was that it was an extremely painful process. Either I am a masochist or it wasn't as painful as it's rumored to be. There were times that it was painful, certainly, but overall I wouldn't call it a painful process. There were moments when it was like, "Ow, that hurt," and Briah would work in another area. When she came back to that spot it wouldn't hurt anymore. There were times that I came close to falling asleep during a session, but I didn't want to because I enjoyed every moment of it.

I come from a family with a lot of heart problems and have lost most of my relatives from heart attacks. As I was being Rolfed, I thought that if I had this stress in the muscles in my back and neck, then I must have tension and stress in other muscles of my body, including those connected with the heart. Whether Rolfing actually physically touches the heart or not, it has to affect it by relaxing other parts of the body. I think Rolfing helps reduce your mental stress level. I'm not a particularly patient person, but I noticed, post-Rolfing, that I would stop and think before I reacted to situations.

The ability to do that only comes from a lack of tension. I think Rolfing also works very well with other types of therapy such as counseling. It really opens a person up and enables them to express and understand their feelings clearly. If someone is in constant mental or physical pain, what do they have to look forward to? Rolfing provides a new-found hope. Hope gives you the potential for vision, and vision gives you the potential for faith. With this comes the ability to accomplish something that's meaningful for you.

Suzanne A.

I resisted being Rolfed because I thought it would be very painful. About ten years ago, I had a series of really bad falls—one from a horse and two falls down stairs. I ended up with a sinking vertebra in my lower back.

Then about two years ago, right after my child was born, I began having serious back trouble. Leaning over or trying to lift my legs while lying down would cause pain that would take my breath away. I tried Yoga, thinking it was a matter of working out something I had acquired through pregnancy. But the pain did not go away.

I went to see a very good chiropractor. He took X-rays and saw what was happening. He didn't want to touch me. He said my symptoms were very dangerous and could lead to paralysis. He suggested back exercises in hope that the muscles would help hold the vertebrae in place and said not to lift anything over twenty pounds. Since I had a child that weighed about twenty-five pounds, it was impractical to observe that rule, but I did try to be careful.

I continued to get worse. A friend of mine suggested a cranial osteopath who was able to keep me steady for almost a year. But he finally told me that I was getting progressively worse and that I needed to get Rolfed. He felt that was the only solution and that if I didn't do it soon, I was going to need back surgery.

At this point, I couldn't stand for five minutes and was in such excruciating pain that I finally listened to him and began driving from my home in Clinton, Arkansas, to Kansas City for Rolfing sessions.

After the first session I left almost bouncing and walked happily for blocks. Before, I couldn't walk but a few feet without having to sit down and rest. I doubled up on the sessions to cut down my travel time and an amazing thing happened along the way. I am an artist and my painting completely changed. I moved from doing brilliant abstracts to soft pastel landscapes and still lifes, impressionistic and soft. The difference was dramatic.

Today I had my tenth session. I still have an occasional pain when I lift something, but it's coming along; it's changing. I don't know how many sessions I'll have before I'm finished, but I don't want the Rolfing to end. Each time is an awakening. I'm learning to respect my body and listen to the messages it gives me.

I think there's something to the fact that when you get Rolfed you deal with a lot of your emotional problems. I don't think you come to get Rolfed until you are ready to deal with your emotional problems. Your inner protective forces will keep you away from healing. Rolfing lets that fear out that you've been holding onto so dearly. It's a wonderful experience.

Germaine G.

I was Rolfed in 1983. I had stomach problems and lower back problems and had been to a series of doctors and chiropractors. When I started Rolfing, it didn't provide immediate relief. My pain actually became more acute. Then, after the third session, I had no back pain at all and have had none since. As the healing process continued after the Rolfing, my back seemed to get stronger and stronger.

I also have fewer intestinal problems. I had had a lot of problems relating to tension with stomach problems and digestion. I now have less severe cramps around my menstrual period.

There were all kinds of side benefits from Rolfing that I hadn't expected. I walked more erect and my rib cage expanded about an inch and a half. After every session, my ears would clog up, my nose and eyes would run, and I'd perspire a great deal. My body seemed to be releasing all of its fluids.

My husband was different. One or two days after Rolfing, he would be open and happy and then he would be cranky and terrible for three or four days.

I am healthier now. I look younger and more approachable. Five or six years ago I was very depressed, and I looked it. I was very closed and difficult to talk to. Even though I would talk to people, I would never talk about how I felt. I think in many ways I wasn't aware of how I felt myself. I was just so lucky to find the right therapy in Rolfing.

It's funny because I don't really think about how things used to be. Living a healthy, open life is second nature to me now.

Patty M.

In 1982, I had back surgery to repair a herniated disk. After a long, unpleasant interval, I recovered. However, two years into recovery I injured my back again and was told that I might need more surgery.

At that time, Briah was Rolfing my fiance, Keith. After a lot of fast talking, he convinced me to consider Rolfing as an option to surgery. I was very skeptical about it. It sounded crazy to me, but I was frightened at the prospect of any more surgery and Keith had such faith in Briah, I decided to schedule an appointment with her.

After the first session I was angry. I didn't like having to strip down to my underwear. I didn't like what Briah was doing to me, and I was scared by the realization that I would need to be an active participant in this process. However, it did get easier with each session, and I actually began to enjoy it. Rolfing did hurt, but I think Briah must have absorbed the pain because after it was over I always felt great.

During the time I was being Rolfed, I was having some problems dealing with my Mom. She had emphysema and had been waiting to die for five years. She had simply given up on herself. I think going through Rolfing allowed me to see I was doing the same thing.

I had some strange experiences while Briah was working on my chest and neck. I would see a glowing energy force in the room, and I became very emotional. I would cry easily. I had more feeling in my chest, and for the first time in my life, I could feel my lungs and notice my breathing. Mom said that as a child I slept very little, and now I was sleeping all the time.

I went from one extreme to the other. I talked to Briah about it, and she said that once I realized that I was in control of my life and not other people, I would become a little more at ease.

I remember Briah telling me to breathe and I would, but she'd say, "Patty, you're not breathing." And I'd say, "I am, too." She would put her hands up on my chest and say "breathe," and I breathed into the top part of my lungs. She looked at me and said, "Your mother had asthma, right? You breathe like someone who is scared to death of breathing." She would have to pump my stomach with her hands to get me to push air down into my lungs. When I'd leave her office, I would breathe, and it was as if my lungs had been unlocked. There was so much emotion and feeling. I'd run out of the building singing. The process hurt like hell, but I felt much better for going through it.

When Briah began working on the back of my legs, I experienced some strange reactions to Rolfing. I dreamed that my right leg, which had suffered nerve damage, wasn't connected to my body. When I turned over in bed, I would have to take my leg and roll it over before I could complete the movement.

I also experienced disorientation after some sessions. The day after Briah worked on the back of my leg, I got lost going home. Though I finally made it home, the feeling of being lost persisted. I remember looking at a piece of paper, holding scissors and not knowing how to open them to cut. It was horrible. When I went to bed, the whole room seemed to be spinning, and I felt completely out of control.

I survived the night and called Briah the next day and went in to see her. She explained that we sometimes store emotions in a certain part of our body, and when it gets overloaded, it will shut itself off and the conscious mind loses control of it. Hearing this helped, but I still had wild thoughts about just getting in my car and driving off and becoming another person. It would scare me, but I realized that the Rolfing was bringing out emotions I had kept buried. Once I faced them, I could begin to control my life.

I began to be more assertive with people, and for the first time in my life I confronted my father and said, "This is who I am and if you don't like it, tough." I'm learning to deal with my emotions and get some direction in my life. I've started back to school. In short, I've done a major turnaround.

Linda M.

I was Rolfed the first time thirteen years ago when I was having difficulty with some old athletic injuries and spasms in my upper back. A massage therapist told me I needed to be Rolfed. There wasn't a Rolfer in town then, but a man came from Colorado once a month to work with clients. I did the series on a monthly basis the first time.

I used to play several competitive sports. I played basketball, baseball, and ran track, so I fell on my rear constantly. There's a lot of compression in my upper and lower vertebrae from falls, so I had tension and stress in those areas. I've gotten many massages over the years on a regular basis for symptom relief.

More recently, I started developing a numbness that I thought was probably a combination of emotional and physical stress. I realized that it was with me in mild form all the time. I went through a series of medical exams. My internist referred me to a neurosurgeon, Dr. Shealy. His final diagnosis was that it was probably a combination of arthritis developing around areas where I had athletic injuries and compression of the vertebrae causing nerve pinching.

Dr. Shealy is a holistic physician. Unlike most physicians I've encountered, he looks at the whole person. He is a past president of the American Holistic Medical Association and the founder and director of the Shealy Pain Clinic, now located in Springfield, Missouri. He told me he would do anything to keep me from having surgery and that he had been Rolfed several times himself. "Why don't you try a few sessions again and see what happens," he suggested. Dr. Shealy also thought I might have something called Carpel Tunnel Syndrome, and he wanted to treat that with massive doses of B Vitamins. So I started taking a lot of B Vitamins and going to see Briah.

I began an advanced series on a weekly basis. I think within the first three or four sessions the numbness was gone. If I sit in a particular position for a long time, I can feel a little of the tingling coming back, but it goes away again. I do periodic maintenance work, accepting the possibility that I may always have some difficulty with this.

I refer a lot of people to Rolfing because it promotes emotional "unsticking." Like all of us, I have unpleasant memories. When I was receiving work in the area around my face, I re-experienced the imprint of the ether mask around my face from a past surgery. During surgery, I was held down either by a nurse or a doctor because I was fighting the ether. In the Rolfing session, I could feel the imprint of the hand. It was a clear body memory.

I'm a psychologist, and I have encouraged a lot of my clients to be Rolfed and in therapy simultaneously. Many people I work with have both physical and emotional issues. I do therapy with incest survivors, and Rolfing in combination with therapy begins to release a lot of feelings, primarily sadness and anger, that have been blocked in their energy centers.

Watching things happen with clients teaches me. When I'm working with someone trying to describe an emotion, I'll ask her to put a hand on the part of the body where she feels the energy. Most women have issues around their solar plexus and in the heart and throat centers. There's often a sense of congestion there. Rolfing helps people break through barriers of denial or experiences held at the unconscious level by working with the body.

Working with incest survivors, I realize many women get body memories before they uncover content. For example, the feeling of something on them or somebody touching them or doing something to them. Or they may experience fear and the need to curl up, or anger, and they have no content to go with that. As their physical symptoms begin to come out and they gain awareness of their bodies, sometimes they'll get a massage, then they eventually can build up to Rolfing.

Once that body energy begins to be released, the content comes out. It's coded at cellular level—memory in the cells. I don't think we know much about it, but body workers are beginning to teach the rest of us more about it. I have learned from Briah. It's exciting when a Rolfer and a psychologist can work together. Briah knows a lot of things I don't know. In the exchange of ideas, we begin to think through a concept in a different way. It's exciting for me to talk to her, describe something she has come across and explore what the connection is.

I think Rolfing is such a key process because it offers you both knowledge you didn't have, and access to power that you have given away to other people, particularly medical professionals. You come to know and understand your body, and there is power in that knowledge, discovering your inner authority. Most women don't grow up testing their bodies and understanding them. Men get more opportunities for both. Rolfing offers this exploration and opportunity for insight to those seeking it.

I walk in Loose Park and notice the other walkers. I now see their tilts and protrusions that I would have never noticed before Rolfing. I see their lack of alignment and think I should give them Briah's card. They could go and get Rolfed and get straightened out in no time. I look at people's shoes, and how they run or walk in them. I never noticed how people move before I was Rolfed, and I've been exercising for years. I certainly didn't notice how my own body was off a little, one shoulder higher than the other, until I saw the first Rolfing photographs of myself.

I think that ten or fifteen years ago, if I'd had the same physical problems, I would have opted for back surgery. There wasn't a Rolfer in Kansas City then. I know people who might have avoided back surgery had Rolfing been an option.

The second time I was Rolfed with Briah differed from the first series. There was more physical pain during the first series. I screamed through nine of the ten sessions. The pain in my chest, shoulders, back, and elbows was horrible. According to Briah, the early hands-on techniques were more aggressive and invasive. I often had it planned so I could go home and crawl into bed with an electric blanket. I'd just lay there and nap, and then take a hot bath.

It was explained to me that the first series induced "productive pain." The pain I had from the muscle spasms felt so terrible I couldn't move my head. A few times they were so bad, a doctor prescribed valium as a muscle relaxant so I would be able to lower my shoulders and just get out of bed.

The day following the early Rolfing sessions, I returned to normal, but it could be pretty gruesome. There were a couple of times I thought, "Why don't you just get up and leave, Linda. It is really stupid to lay here and hurt this much." But I also knew Rolfing was helping me.

Part of the pain the first time was because of the technique. But I also think the other part had to do with a lot of body fear that I had in having somebody work on me, knowing I was already in pain and it was going to hurt. I think it was a combination of my reaction as well as his technique.

This advanced set of tools is much more gentle. I am also more comfortable having a woman work with me than a man. Thirteen years ago, only a man was available, so I didn't give it much thought. Going to a woman is more comfortable for me. There's some shorthand communication working with someone of the same sex when your body is involved.

Working with Briah, I haven't had any pain. I've had some discomfort at times in some of the areas that were really out of alignment. I'm in a different place with myself now. I wasn't looking at spiritual issues thirteen years ago, and I couldn't have if I wanted to because I hurt too much. But this time I'm comfortable with my Rolfer and myself, and there is a more spiritual quality to the work we do.

Charlene M.

I heard about Rolfing from my hairdresser, who heard about it from a friend, but it was not until my husband was Rolfed for severe migraine headaches and I saw how it helped him that I considered it for myself.

I had had a very stressful job as a vice president of corporate affairs for a large company and had just switched to an even more stressful job as property manager for one of the largest real estate firms in the country. I was storing all this stress in my body.

One fateful day, I was in bed with the flu. I rolled over to get a tissue, and my back went out. I was in too much pain to move. I called my husband, and he called Briah immediately. She worked on me for over two hours, and I felt sure that I would recover. This led to my decision to get the full ten Rolfing sessions.

I used to feel that I was developing a dumpy, frumpy, middle-aged body. It seemed like everything compacted around my waist and hips. I know that I'm carrying myself differently after being Rolfed. I'm much longer through my torso. My body is more youthful. Before Rolfing, I felt trapped in a body that I didn't like. I don't think there's any woman alive that doesn't want to look good and feel good. It's not just looking good. It's important to feel good about yourself and how you move and do things.

After two or three Rolfing sessions, I had a group of women over to my house for a Bible study. I had not lost an ounce at that time, but every single person told me that I looked like I had lost weight. It wasn't the new outfit I was wearing. It was that I had been stretched physically and felt so good.

I'm now aware of the stress in my body and can handle it better. I have a higher energy level. My husband has noticed that I get up much easier in the mornings, and there are times when I'm up before he is. He has more breakfasts because I get up and fix them.

Rolfing is really the best investment for preventative maintenance of your body. It's inexpensive and practical. But will people only turn to Rolfing when they're frustrated and desperate and feel they have no other choices? Are there some people open-minded enough to be

Rolfed when they're not in a desperate situation? I think it's too bad that most people don't know more about Rolfing. What about people who work on an assembly line? They're leaning forward all day long, five days a week, eight hours a day. If they can't release tension, they're eventually going to have problems. Many companies have cafeteria-type health plans; I don't know why Rolfing can't be included.

Rocky R.

The pain I felt had become a part of me and my everyday life, the life-altering heartbreak of back injury. I use the term heartbreak because of the restrictions—physical, emotional, and financial—my back injury created in my life.

I was the smallest player on my high school football team. In track I ran sprint races, 60-, 100-, and 220-yard and various relay team events. I was a healthy kid. Oddly enough, my back trouble started through a fairly normal daily activity.

I was employed at a local department store warehouse, working my way through college. One day I lifted a wooden coffee table from the floor and turned to place it on a higher table for inspection.

Suddenly I felt a sharp pain in my lower back, and I was unable to stand upright. I was told by the company doctor that everyone had a certain amount of back pain and I would have to learn to live with it, using muscle relaxants and wearing a back brace when it got too intense.

During that time there were certain everyday things I couldn't do. Riding in the car felt unbearable. I had to support all of my weight with both arms on the seat just to ride without intense pain. Once, just catching a frisbee, my upper back went out, and I needed multiple chiropractic treatments to remedy that situation.

Because my back health was always tentative, I had led a tentative life. I watched my every step, eliminating anything that could cause injury. I vividly remember every single day testing my back when I got up in the morning. I didn't have a lot of formal medical training, but during the years of my back trauma, I was constantly reading reports, publications, and articles about my condition. I kept searching for help—reading and talking to people—trying to discover something I hadn't tried.

I can honestly say that Rolfing opened a new chapter in my life. After just one session, I felt a release of the knots in my back muscles that I had not felt for years. I was truly amazed.

There is a cliche that says, "You don't know what you've got 'til it's gone." Over the course of my Rolfing sessions, I realized I didn't know how much I had lost through back pain, even when it was gone.

Like a receding hairline on a man who doesn't realize the progression until one day he looks in a mirror, the cumulative effects of injury became apparent. The ten plus years of back problems had robbed me slowly of activities and ease I didn't fully appreciate until Rolfing unlocked and returned these things to me. My energy level, which I never realized was so depleted, started returning.

The first three months after Rolfing, I experienced further movement in my body. Muscles felt as though they were shifting into place. It's hard to explain, but I could feel my legs, pelvis, knees, and ankles adjusting from time to time. Sometimes the shift was experienced as small quiverings, sometimes almost indiscernible, mild feelings of something being minutely relocated.

My upper body, which had also compensated to the lower back misalignment, became realigned. My spine, stomach, shoulders, and neck all harbored new positioning feelings.

Sometimes soreness would surface, not because of overwork or injury.

It seemed to be my body moving in a new alignment. This soreness would invariably decrease and leave after 2 to 3 days and be replaced with extended flexibility and a feeling of better positioning.

The second three months brought about even more subtle body changes. I had a feeling of settling in as my body became used to its new alignment. During this time I started feeling more confident in my everyday body movements. The last six months have been a continuation of the stabilizing feeling, and my energy has reached a new level. I'm returning to increased activity, and as time goes by, I find myself planning a much brighter future, with possibilities reopening in areas I had previously thought closed. There are new horizons with a course set by a more properly functioning vehicle—my body!

Ross V.

In 1974 I broke my left leg in a motorcycle accident and ended up with that leg being three-quarters of an inch shorter than my right leg. The doctor told me to wear a lift in my shoe, which I did for about ten years. I resumed my normal life, which included a fair amount of risk-taking and thrill seeking.

In the early '80s I started developing back problems, so I went to an orthopedic surgeon for X-rays and a CAT scan. Nothing showed up on the X-rays, and the doctor said the pain was probably caused by my lifestyle. There was nothing medicine could do for me. Even though there wasn't any severe damage to my back, the pain was always there: a severe, burning-type pain, as if I'd been stabbed with an iron.

I was at the end of my rope when a friend of mine told me about Rolfing. I asked my orthopedic surgeon about it first. He said he really didn't know much about it, but he had heard it was quite painful.

I had no hesitation about Rolfing whatsoever because I was looking at it as a last resort. I felt like I was slowly dying and wanted to get on with living.

After the first session, I felt so relaxed I almost fell when I got off the table. The relief from pain was immediate, and I couldn't wait for the next session. At first, relief would only last for about three days, but after the fourth session, the relief carried beyond the next session. With the pain gone, I was finally able to get the sleep I had needed so badly.

My Rolfing experience was not emotional. I let things go pretty easily, and I think my trauma was physical. My body has been broken everywhere—my arm, leg, face, and skull.

Medicine can do wonderful things for you, but a person can do much to heal himself. I believe we have a lot of healing power within ourselves, so I'm here to help bring about the change. I want to find out if there is a ceiling to what Rolfing can change. I haven't scheduled my advanced sessions yet, but I'm going to go ahead and see what my limitations are.

Frank W.

I was in a car wreck when I was just out of college in 1965. My right elbow was damaged, and I had a damaged vertebra in my lower back.

I've been Rolfed, my wife has been Rolfed, and my youngest son, Jeffrey, was Rolfed also at thirteen. Following the seventh session, Jeffrey was admitted to the hospital experiencing grand mal seizures. He went into a coma for months. The doctors were not sure of the exact cause. It could have been a head injury sustained while playing football or viral encephalitis. While in the coma he was suffering grand mal seizures every three to five minutes. The doctors predicted extensive brain damage if he survived at all.

What happened next was an absolute miracle. Briah worked with him during the hospitalization. The hospital was kind enough to look the other way as our entourage of people in various healing professions would come in to work with Jeffrey at night. As he emerged from the coma, Briah worked with him during his more lucid times. He had to relearn to eat, walk, and speak. He would allow her to work on him because it felt good.

I wonder sometimes if we hadn't done the Rolfing what would have happened to my son. There was a lot of anger removed as a result of the Rolfing. He's back in school now and is academically with his class, with the help of tutoring.

The Rolfing experience has helped to integrate me, too. With Briah's work I can now experience now my mind and body in relationship. Physical balance helps me balance mentally. I need both, but you can really speed up the process if you go in physically and balance. That will force the mental balance to come back, to accelerate. Liberating the blockage in mind and body allows energy to flow in your body. I'm an engineer and I look at balance from an engineering point of view. Rolfing ties things together in a fluid way.

I go back for advanced sessions when I feel my body is really out of whack, when I feel the energy bocks starting to come up again. I think if you can't get through these blocked areas it can be serious. I think that's why a lot of serious illness comes along.

Some emotional issues did come up for me during Rolfing. She had a terrible time getting me to me to sessions a couple of times. This anger was coming out. I was frustrated in my business. I was busy and I'd get going and I'd forget. I'd write things down but I'd forget. I was probably trying to forget, really. The Rolfing helped break through to my emotional issues, which had been a real problem to me.

I had myriad problems in my back. That was the main reason why I was Rolfed and it's been a great help. And it's helped with my posture. I'd probably be a hump backed fellow by now. It's been an incredible help. It's just a critical part of my staying alive and it's helped me stay centered.

Ken R.

In the past few years, I've eaten enough pain pills to fill the back end of a truck. At one time I was probably taking 100 to 150 aspirin a week, but it never took away the pain. I've taken everything from Bayer Aspirin to Tylenol #3 and there was nothing that ever helped.

I'd just get numb, and then I'd get sick. I'd have probably been better off drinking a quart of whiskey, which I'd tried. I haven't taken a pill since I started going to see Briah.

I'm a rough-in carpenter. I put up the sides of buildings, and it's hard, heavy work. The accumulation of 41 years of heavy labor took its toll. I hurt all over. My muscles hurt. My bones hurt. I tried doctors and chiropractors and every type of therapy, with little to no relief.

Two years ago, I became unable to do a day's work. I couldn't use my hammer or saw at all. I was on the site as an advisor, not a builder. I had been thinking about retiring, but because of Rolfing, I'll probably be good for another ten years. I still hurt, but not nearly as much as before.

When Briah first worked on my legs, it felt as if they were burning from my knee down to my shin. Later, it didn't hurt at all, and the same thing happened with my arm and left shoulder.

Before I was Rolfed, I couldn't sleep. I'd sit in a chair and doze off for a few minutes until the pain got so bad I'd have to get up and walk around. As long as I was moving, the muscles didn't hurt as bad. The only problem I have is that I go to bed before dark and don't want to get up until after daylight. I want to catch up on all the sleep I lost.

Even while Briah was working on me, I couldn't hold still for ten minutes. She'd try to get me to stay in a certain position, but my arm would hurt and I'd have to move it. It is nice now that I can move around and not hurt all the time.

One of the worst consequences of being in pain was that I couldn't ride my horse anymore. I started riding before I could walk, and it was always one of the most important things in my life. Now I can jump up and down off my horses like a two-year-old. I even do a little roping. I feel thirty years younger than I did six months ago.

There are some people who seem to want to snicker when I tell them about Rolfing, but others are really interested. They're like I was. They've tried all kinds of other things that haven't worked, and they're looking for any kind of help.

The chiropractors I tried said, "Come in and we'll loosen your joints because you have calcium deposits hurting you. We can't get them off, but we can loosen them up so you can move easier." But after a while that didn't help anymore. It felt just as bad when they finished as it did before they started. That's why I was so glad to find Rolfing.

I had forty years of cumulative injuries, falling off steel beams, having big walls fall on me. I was disabled on the job because I couldn't do the work. I was more than surprised at the amount of improvement. After the fifth or sixth session, I was as amazed as anyone could be.

Rick B.

Before Rolfing I felt curved inward, very protective of my sunken chest.

I felt pulling through my back and shoulders. It restricted my breathing greatly.

My legs felt crooked, my feet turned inward, and I walked awkwardly. I didn't have good balance and felt generally clumsy.

The tightness in my chest was terrible. I had many chiropractic sessions as well as ultrasound, ultraheat, and electronic stimulation. None of that gave me more than a few hours of relief. By the next day I always felt like my spine was back out of place.

During Rolfing I felt my breathing getting deeper; I felt like I had more lung capacity. My legs are definitely straighter; I walk taller. Rolfing gave a whole new meaning to the words "breathe deeply."

Rolfing has given me more confidence. My neck has improved immensely; I never feel like my back is out of place anymore. Now it hurts to slouch. It hurts to wrap my legs under my chair when I sit, which was a big habit. I don't feel like I have to protect my chest anymore. My back feels stronger, and I feel a lot more balanced. There is a lot less stress stored in my body

"I feel like everything is opening up."

Rick, a 24-year-old computer programmer, was so tight he hurt everywhere. Rick had a sunken chest so collapsed you could place your entire fist within his chest cavity. He lived with chronic pain. Every muscle in his body, from the bottom of his feet to the top of his head, was taut. His body was like a tightly stretched rubber band; there was no "give."

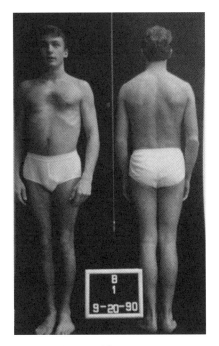

Rick, Before Rolfing

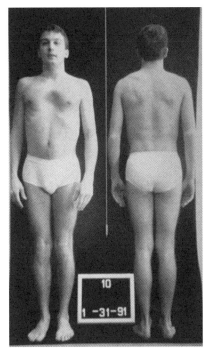
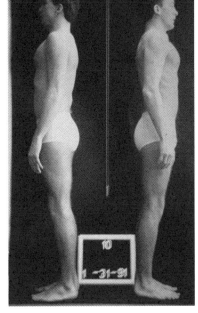

Rick, After 10 sessions

Chapter 8

Rolfing and TMJ
(Temporomandibular Joint Dysfunction)

Jack Haden, DDS

Founding member, board member, and past president of the American Academy of Craniofacial Pain (promotes advancement of knowledge in Craniofacial Pain, Temporomandibular Disorders, and Dental Sleep Medicine (AACFP)

"When patients continue to walk into my office with their heads forward and their chins pointed to the sky, the treatment path is clear—off to Rolfing."

Marilyn G.

TMJ sufferer

"I was in such bad shape that every muscle in my body hurt, but I didn't know what I could do about it."

Judy B.

Massage therapist with chronic TMJ problems

"Between myself, my parents, and my insurance company, I spent vast amounts of money on doctors and dentists."

Jack Haden, DDS

Founding member, board member, and past president of the AACFP or American Academy of Craniofacial Pain (promotes advancement of knowledge in Craniofacial Pain, Temporomandibular Disorders, and Dental Sleep Medicine

In 1982, my wife, as well as a dental colleague and I, were taking a four-day course in the Sutherland Cranio-suture manipulation technique at an osteopathic college on Long Island, New York. All three of us were inveterate joggers, but I was having a difficult time trying to run because of Achilles tendinitis in both legs.

The thirty-some participants taking the cranio course were all dentists. At lunch on the third day, I happened to sit down next to a dentist discussing Rolfing. This particular dentist from Florida was deeply involved in relating to some other people at the table how Rolfing had made an incredible impact in treating certain of his cranio-mandibular dysfunctional patients. His testimony was fascinating.

With all-out inquisitiveness, I questioned him about the concepts of Rolfing and its mechanisms. During the afternoon session, I had difficulty concentrating on the given subject because I kept on thinking of the role that fascia must have in muscular stability.

At the end of the day, I sat down and had a really "hard core" discussion with this dentist about Rolfing, Ida Rolf, fascia, etc. As it turned out, his interest in Rolfing was so great that for a period of time he had given up dentistry and had gone to the Rolf Institute to become a Certified Rolfer. As a matter of fact, he was still practicing as a Rolfer.

Wow, I thought, what an opportunity to get some aid with my Achilles tendons. Brazenly, I asked for a treatment of my tendons. He told me patiently that Rolfing was not a one-shot deal and that it was done systematically over a series of sessions. He gave me the rationale for a systematized approach. I was not to be denied. I pleaded for just one short session on one of the osteopathic tables, if for no other reason than just to see and feel the effects of being Rolfed. I prevailed, and the Rolfer/dentist, against his better judgment, did the manipulative muscle integration technique on both legs. I thanked him, hopped off the table and still felt about the same when my legs hit the floor. However, the next morning when I got out of bed, I noticed I didn't have to walk totally flat-footed for fifteen minutes to loosen up the gastrocnemius (calf muscles) as I usually had to do in the morning. It was a pleasant surprise!

When I got home I set out to see if there was a Rolfer in Kansas City and sure enough there was. I immediately called Briah Anson for an introductory appointment. We then began Rolfing's whole body approach to overcome some of the ravages that time and injuries had done to the fascia in my body. I had a terrific kyphosis that was partially inherited, partially occupational (being a dentist) and partially from the nicks and bruises of life (tennis and running).

My Rolfer took my picture before treatment, and it was a sad sight. The "building blocks" of my body were anything but lined up, and I had a big humpback. Polaroid pictures were taken throughout treatment and after the last appointment, a final Polaroid was taken. What a difference! Staring back at me was a much younger man with very little hump back, looking relatively light. I was happy and impressed.

My thoughts turned immediately to the dysfunctional patients with head and neck pain that I saw daily in my practice. For years I had a practice predominantly centered around individuals who suffered from cranio-mandibular disorders and TMJ dysfunction. Better than fifty percent of the dysfunctional patients also carried their heads forward. Some carried their heads forward with their heads slumped down on their chests.

The muscles of the upper back and neck are designed to balance and move the head. But when the head is carried forward, they are pressed into duty to support the head. These muscles are very sensitive when palpated. Some of the muscles have areas that are extremely tender, and when touched send pain to different areas of the body.

There is a shock absorber between the upper and lower jaws known as an articular disk. About seventy percent of the dysfunctional patients I see in my practice have this disk displaced in front of the joint. Some patients can relocate this disk when they open their jaws, but on closing, the disk pops back out of place. This phenomena is known as a reciprocal click, or reducible anterior dislocated disk.

Other patients with articular disk (shock absorber problems) have a disk displaced in the front of the joint, but can't get it to relocate on opening. The disk stays in front of the joint throughout the opening and closing of the jaw. This is known as an anterior displaced non-reducible disk. Almost all of these patients with disk problems have extreme forward head posture and rather than their heads slumping toward their chests, their chins are pointed up or extended. This creates a problem for the neck and upper back muscles. These muscles, which are supposed to move and balance the head, are now supporting the head and the long term consequences can prove devastating. The muscles themselves become dysfunctional and go into splinting and/or spasm.

Many of the "forward-head" patients can be helped by physical therapy and by wearing an intro-oral orthotic on their teeth. Some will be completely resistant to this treatment. Thank goodness for Rolfing. When patients continue to walk into my office with their heads forward and their·chins pointed to the sky, the treatment path is clear—off to Rolfing. I cannot remember a patient who was Rolfed and had the proper intro-oral orthotic that did not get rid of pain-inducing forward head posture.

One of the ironies of chronic head and neck dysfunctional patients is that about twenty percent of them have head and neck pain that is emanating from somewhere other than their upper quadrant. The disabling factor may be felt in the head and neck, but the source of the pain may be from the lower back, the middle back, the pelvis, a knee, both knees, the feet, a short leg, and on and on. The old song about "the dry bones" all being connected is truly appropriate. The astute diagnostician remembers that up to one fifth of the patients he sees may have a chain effect that emanates from the lower back, causing pain in the head and neck.

Although there are many therapies which deal with handling the bones in the lower extremities, unless the fascia is affected, there is no long-term effect. It is also important to note that most of the patients I see don't realize that the imbalance in their lower body could be the major factor causing their upper quadrant pain and dysfunction. Rolfing addresses whole body alignment through reorganization of fascial planes.

Awhile ago my patient, Sue, came to see me. She was suffering from severe pain with locked-out disks in both jaws. The work-up of X-rays, dental and muscular exams, and my observation of her walking and standing patterns showed me that almost everything that could be out of place was.

Sue also displayed the head forward and chin-up posturings. Weeks of intensive therapy followed. She underwent a program of physical therapy for her upper body and wore an orthotic to reposition the masticatory muscles.

However, her pain would return in a day or two after treatment, and the forward positioning of her head never changed. I then recommended that she begin Rolfing. I was amazed when I saw Sue a few weeks later. Her contorted body was almost upright and, just as important, her contorted face with its concomitant wrinkle and severeness was now bright and smiling.

Was she totally well? No, but she was much better. Sue shared some of her Rolfing experiences with me. She said that her Rolfing sessions not only helped her physically, but they had also aided a psychological catharsis for her. Sue had undergone what many people experience when Rolfed. She had emotional experiences which caused her to relive past traumas. Emotion is intimately involved with muscular tone. I believe that Sue's emotional experiences were cathartic and had as much to do with her recovery as did the changing of her muscular balance through manipulation.

Sue's pain is 90 percent relieved. Her forward-head posture is gone, and her legs are almost the same length without a shoe lift. I was not able to get her disk unlocked. Her mouth opening is slightly restricted due to her locked-out disks, but she has no more masticatory dysfunctions or pain. Her chewing, talking, and yawning are done within a parameter of opening that lets her function without discomfort.

In addition to having my patients treated for forward head posture and short limbs, I also have had patients successfully Rolfed for tight, painful cervical musculature, suprascapular musculature, thoracic outlet syndrome, carpal tunnel syndrome, lack of lordotic curve, severe kyphosis, radiculopathy, posterior nerve root impingement, etc. Rolfing is a partner in treatment against pain. This form of body therapy has not only helped me in treating my patients, but many times was the paramount factor in their recovery.

Marilyn G.

I was on vacation in Arizona, packing to go home when I heard a woman on TV describing all my symptoms—terrible headaches and low energy. I thought, "Well gosh, this sounds like me." She was describing TMJ. I had never heard of it. What is TMJ? So I said to my husband, "I think I'm going to go to the dentist she mentioned and check this out."

I was in such bad shape that the dentist had to shoot my muscles with Novocaine. The dentist said that I did have TMJ, and a bad case of it at that.

He recommended a Dr. Jack Haden, a TMJ specialist. We already knew Dr. Haden. In fact, my husband played tennis with him all the time. So when l got home I went to see him. "I wouldn't touch you," he said. "You are so bad that I can't do anything for you until you see a Rolfer." He explained a little bit about Rolfing and said, "I can't help you until you're better physically." That's how I came to work with Briah.

Briah explained that Rolfing was a series of ten treatments and that I could go to any other Rolfer in the United States and they could pick up where she left off.

The Rolfing was so painful for me that I would cry. Several times Briah said to me, "I don't think I can help you. Your muscles are like stone. You're the first person that I've ever had come to me like this."

I was in my fifties and thought, "My God, I can't go through life like this." I needed something to help me. I finished the series with Briah and had three more sessions with a Rolfer in Arizona. The Rolfing helped my headaches and my neck a great deal. I have much greater mobility and am not in constant pain anymore. I'm much more relaxed and have more energy. These changes started gradually. I didn't notice any differences for a few sessions, but slowly as things started to change in my body, my arthritis and other painful problems began to clear up. The headaches weren't as severe. I had more mobility in my movements, less pain in first one part of my body and then another. I had more energy and suddenly started feeling like a human being again.

I went back to Dr. Haden after I had finished the Rolfing and he said, "You're so much better." He made a splint for my mouth and said he could help me now.

After that, I had a few more Rolfing sessions in Arizona. I started playing tennis and basically doing whatever I wanted to do. I was back to being a normal, healthy person, exercising, swimming, walking, climbing, and never feeling like I had to force myself to do something. Looking at the pictures taken before Rolfing, I could see the strain in my face. I had been unaware of it, but you can't feel that bad and not have it show.

I used to take a lot of aspirin, easily six aspirin a day. I would use a hot pad and take jacuzzis and everything I could think of to help myself. After Rolfing I no longer needed these things.

A few years later, I had a hard fall from my bike. It resulted in a brain concussion, a bad cut on my head, and a torn rotator cuff. I went back for more Rolfing. It helped my rotator cuff a great deal and restored the mobility. I still have some pain occasionally, but nothing like it was before.

My friends ask me about Rolfing, and the only way I can describe it is to say it's like massage, but much deeper. It's a therapy that gets to the roots of a problem and works to eliminate the cause. Even though I still need a session now and then, I've never experienced the pain I had before. I had tried swimming, massage, steam rooms, saunas, and acupuncture, but only Rolfing gave me permanent relief by correcting the fundamental problem. After Rolfing, my posture has improved. My whole body is more relaxed and is beginning to heal itself.

Briah said my neck and facial muscles had been so taut that I looked like I had a mask pulled tightly over my head. If I ever have any doubts about Rolfing, all I have to do is look at my face and body and see how far I've come.

Judy B.

I wanted to be Rolfed primarily because of a chronic TMJ problem. My mandibular jaw joint would dislocate, then lock, and I would have to go in to the Emergency Room and have it relaxed. At the time I started having TMJ, there wasn't much known about it. The temporal mandible bone connects the head and jaw bone. You can feel it move when you talk. When it dislocates, it causes very painful muscle spasms in the face and neck which, if not treated, can spread to the back and arms. The key is to get it in place immediately. As I got older, I eventually learned to relax it myself.

I also had a problem with my left hip tightening up and making my left leg look shorter than the right.

I didn't know much about the process of Rolfing. I'm a massage therapist and had clients who had been Rolfed who weren't really able to explain it to me. I finally decided to see Briah. She gave me some pamphlets on Rolfing, and I got a clearer understanding of it. I already knew a lot about how parts of the body work together and that it isn't possible to fix the jaw, unless the cause of the problem, which might be in a totally different part of the body, is also fixed. I began to understand that Rolfing works toward total body alignment and not just adjusting certain points. I was driving back to work right after Briah had worked on my back and hips, and I suddenly realized that I was sitting upright. I had to reach up to readjust my rearview mirror which was too low now. I was sitting straight and tall without any effort. It was a great feeling.

It's hard to know which benefits to attribute to Rolfing because I was also going through a series of courses that worked on different chakras, or energy centers, in the body, and this was also helping me change. Between the two processes, the improvements were drastic and quick. While I was being Rolfed, I would remember different things that happened in my childhood. The memories were directly related to the specific area of work. For instance, while Briah was working on my diaphragm, I remembered an injury I had there when I was about six years old. I hadn't thought of it in years, but I could remember exactly what happened that day. I went home and confirmed it with my mother.

The greatest benefit I received from Rolfing occurred when Briah worked on the inside of my mouth. I normally had this "click" when I opened my mouth. But after that session, it was gone. I was so accustomed to having that click that it took me a while to figure out that it wasn't there anymore. From that point on, I very rarely felt any direct pain. Even now, the only time I experience any soreness is when I'm totally stressed and have been clenching my teeth all day.

My jaw hasn't locked since that session. I can yawn without dislocating my jaw, and I no longer have to cut my food into small pieces or be afraid to bite into an apple.

Once when I was in college, I dislocated my jaw. I called Mom and she told me to go to a nearby ER. I was in so much pain when I got there that I couldn't talk and the intern thought I was on drugs. By the time my mom got there, I was completely incoherent and the spasms were so bad that I had to have some kind of heavy narcotic to stop them.

I've had similar experiences like that with other doctors who didn't understand TMJ or know how to treat it. And since I couldn't talk while having the spasms, I couldn't explain.

I found one dentist who gave me exercises to help strengthen my muscles and achieved some results, but I was going to see him three times a week. He used tiny instruments to plane my teeth and readjust them so my bite would be perfect. I'd go home and two nights later I'd grind my teeth in my sleep and throw the bite off. Then I got a plate to wear in my mouth so, if I ground my teeth at night, I would be biting on it. It was gross, nasty, and very expensive, but I used it anyway.

Between myself, my parents, and my insurance company, I spent vast amounts of money on doctors and dentists.

When I became self-employed as a massage therapist, I no longer had dental insurance. I called the dentist's office and explained my problem and asked about being put on a payment plan so I could continue getting dental treatment. The receptionist agreed to the arrangement, but when I got to the office I was told I had to pay at the time of the visit and left without seeing the doctor. I had already decided to be Rolfed and had scheduled an appointment. My mother is a registered nurse, and she had watched the Rolfing video tapes with me. She was really excited about it.

So I began the Rolfing process. Now my face is filled out and my jaws are aligned. I've learned how to use my body correctly. I stand straight and balance myself while I'm working so that I'm not using one part of the body more than another. I've also learned not to drop my hip. That throws my balance off and can make one leg a teeny bit shorter than the other. My legs are a lot stronger now.

Rolfing is bone-deep tissue work, much deeper than massage. So I was afraid that I would be bruised from head to toe, but I wasn't. My legs felt more pain than the rest of my body so I did a lot of visualizations to help Briah work on them. Now I can see a change in the shape of my legs. There's more length from knee to groin. This was a plus that I really appreciated when I went swimming. I'm heavier now than ever before and my legs look a lot better.

I believe my body continued to change after I finished the sessions. Every once in a while I catch a difference, something that I hadn't noticed before.

I think Rolfing would work very well with other kinds of body therapy, such as massage or movement classes. I'm planning an open house and have invited people to come and talk to my clients about Rolfing. I see a real value to it. Some of the people I work with are hard as wood, because their bodies are so tight. They have no ability to relax.

I found that allowing Briah to work and my helping through visualization achieved quick results. I learned to participate in my Rolfing, to control my body and the things I allowed to happen to it. Briah allowed me to do that. She wasn't working on me. She was working with me, guiding me.

Chapter 9

Health Professionals and Their Personal Stories

Bill B.

Dentist

"Deep breathing and a strong posture create confidence and a better self-image."

Necia G.

Massage therapist

"Through Rolfing, my mind, my body, my heart, and my spirit were opened after years of being depressed. A technique like Rolfing allows the body to regain its integrity."

Deborah N.

Physical therapist and Certified Rolfer

"Rolfing goes beyond physical therapy and brings out the real essence of an individual, the connection of mind and body."

Bill B.

I heard about Rolfing in 1979. I had two friends who were Rolfed that year. One friend had spent a year in a body cast as a child and as a result had a sway back. After being Rolfed she had positive improvements in her posture as well as some emotional benefits. My other friend said that his breathing was improved, he felt more physically coordinated, and felt better overall after completing the initial ten Rolfing sessions.

In 1980 I was having some persistent minor back pain, which I felt was due to poor posture habits that seemed to be beyond my control. My two friends' experiences gave me hope that Rolfing might be of benefit in improving my posture and eliminating the associated pain. Something that I was unaware of at that time was that I was a shallow breather and unable to breathe with my abdominal muscles.

At the age of six weeks I had undergone a major operation to repair my pyloric valve, which is the valve between the stomach and the small intestine. In retrospect, I believe that the scar tissue and adhesions resulting from the surgery were a major cause of my posture problems and also of my inability to breathe deeply with my abdominal muscles.

I went through the ten Rolfing sessions in 1980, and each session caused a very noticeable improvement in my posture. At the end of the ten sessions, I was free of pain. Also, I was able to breathe deeper and more comfortably. As the result of Rolfing, my personal experience has been that good posture, combined with deep abdominal breathing, has had some very positive effects on my life. These effects have been a greater sense of well being, a strange feeling of inner strength, a less introverted personality, more energy, a greater ability to live in the moment, less of a tendency to worry, and a greater empathy for others. Also from a physical standpoint, activities such as running and swimming seem to be more effortless and enjoyable as a result of Rolfing.

Also, my experience has been that after the initial Rolfing the additional sessions every six to twelve months have been of benefit. Improvement seems to continue with each session and positive changes continue to occur afterward.

I believe that Rolfing would be of benefit to anyone—though some might notice more drastic changes than others, depending upon the nature of their own particular posture and breathing habits.

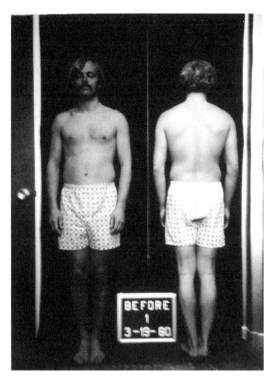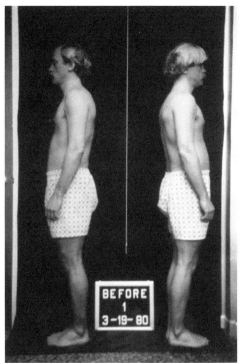

Bill, Before Rolfing

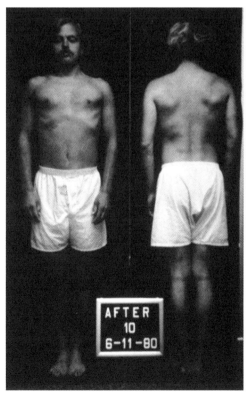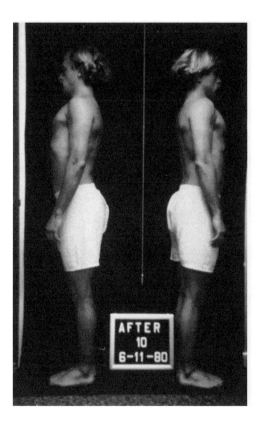

Bill, After 10 sessions

Rolfing Reflections

This series of photos shows Bill over an eleven-year span. Bill came in because of chronic back problems. He complained of low energy, shallow breathing, and problems associated with a forward head position and postural problems.

As he completed the Rolfing series, he felt that dramatic changes had taken place physically as well as emotionally. He reported a better sense of well-being, better coordination and balance, and an improved quality of life. He enjoys participating in sports more, and his skill level and endurance have increased.

"Rolfing has had a great impact on my life," says Bill. He tells me the improvements brought about through Rolfing have helped him become a more confident, stronger, and more outgoing person. "I think Rolfing helps people stay younger, and improves the physical, emotional, and spiritual aspects of life."

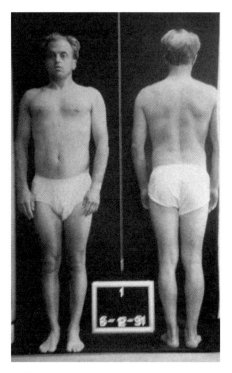

Bill, 11 years later

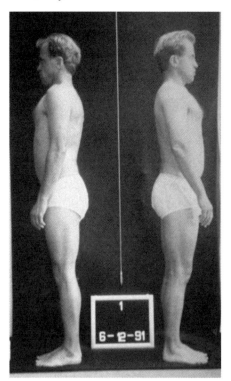

Necia G.

Ever since I can remember I always had this thing about my hands. My hands are particular. They like to be doing things. They love to touch. I am kinesthetic. That's how I relate to the world. I drew and painted. But I always came to a point of frustration because my work required that I have a tool in my hand and that wasn't what I wanted. While working at a women's health care agency as a counselor, I took part in a Gestalt training group. One of the seminars was about Rolfing—structural integration. It made total sense to me. I was taken with the truth of lda Rolf's concepts and the results I saw with my own untrained eye. After experiencing that workshop, I read every bit of information I could find about Rolfing. And I was determined that I was going to see the Rolf Institute in Boulder, Colorado. It was a sort of vision quest.

I met a woman while I was there who was studying to be a Rolfer, and I talked with her a bit. One of the things that stood out in my mind was that the majority of people who had chosen to be Rolfers had college degrees and had previously been doctors or carpenters or athletes or something kinesthetic like that. They had a predisposition towards that kind of work.

I found out how much it cost to receive training, what the process was and how to think like a Rolfer. At the end of the six-week period, you return to your home town and start a massage practice. After you had done that, you're ready for the next part of the training. Finally, you go back to learn the actual Rolfing technique and how to use your knowledge of anatomy and physiology.

I returned home and started reading about massage. I then set up a massage practice and within two weeks I had six regular clients. I continued to study both massage and Rolfing via books.

My son was Rolfed beginning at six weeks old. It was wonderful to watch him intrinsically know how to move his body when certain techniques were applied. When Jamal was born, he was almost picture perfect except for a slight depth change in the bones in his face. During his first session, Briah concentrated on his face, neck, and cranium, molding them into shape. When 1 saw his cranium shift, he peed on Briah. It was like a release, right? What made total sense to me was how his head had gotten that way in the first place. What is the head when you're born—a battering ram! What is your neck—a shock absorber! That's bound to displace bones; especially a structure that soft. It's amazing that we come out as unmutilated as we do, but the eye cannot see all the mutilations that happen with birth. Going through a birth canal is probably one of the most dramatic things that anyone will ever do. Jamal was my open door to view the truth of Rolfing firsthand—though I would not begin my Rolfing for another three years. The next level of knowing came with my own experience of the Rolfing process. I learned so much about myself and my relation to others. But it is difficult to express the depth of this experience in words on the page.

Through Rolfing, my mind, my body, my heart, and my spirit were opened after years of being depressed. When I walked home after the first session, I could feel myself moving. I was straighter, and I had a sense of freedom. During each session after that, there were times when Briah would do something that felt absolutely right. It was as if I had been waiting for someone to touch that particular spot in me because it had been hurting for so long. I felt my body welcome the Rolfer.

And my body was moving. Rolfing works with the fascia, which is the elastic sheath film that envelops the muscle and the bone. By manipulating the fascia, you can allow the body to release itself.

I have a lot of tension and congestion in my hips and legs. When Briah worked in that area, I could literally feel the fascia stretching, releasing, and getting longer. It felt so good. Sometimes there would be a tingling sensation, sometimes burning. That would be pure energy. There were times I would be breathing with the work and my teeth would chatter, my jaw would vibrate, or I would sense a pure white light in my head. It was releasing things.

Probably my favorite session of all was the fifth session. Briah was working on my back, loosening and lengthening the muscles along the sides of my spine. I started sobbing. I sensed a hole that went clean through my body, like a dark pit. I experienced images of that hole and how dark and deep it was.

Then the hole disappeared and it became light. I saw myself dancing as a beautiful Egyptian princess, moving and using my hands to twirl things. I was flying at one point, free. I continued to cry throughout the entire process.

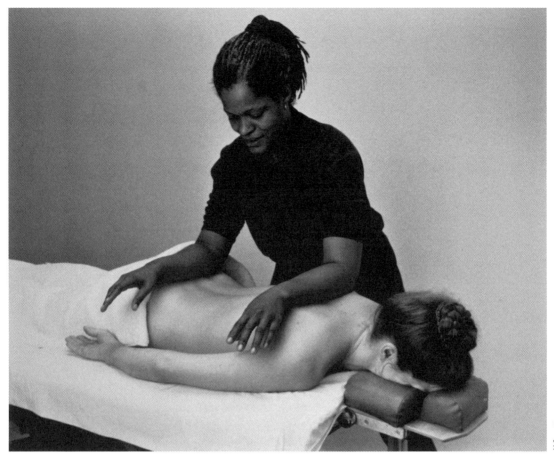

Necia performing her art of massage

That whole session was spent doing guided imagery. It wasn't guided by Briah. It was guided by my life and all that was and will be my life. There was a point where I was so ancient. And then I was a beautiful princess who was dancing Egyptian style. My whole chest and back opened up. I believe I was experiencing my birth into everything I had ever been and all I hoped to be. I gained continuity between my past, present, and future self.

When I left that session, I felt as if I were pulling my neck out of my chest for the first time. I had been hiding before, but now I could hold my head up, my arms out, and be strong. I had visualized my freedom to fly and knew I could do anything now. A technique like Rolfing allows the body to regain its integrity. There is no such thing as

Necia G., now at age 70, stands before a painting honoring her as a community leader at the Kansas City International Airport. Painting by Kwanza Humphrey

a separate body or mind process, for they are interrelated. Rolfing can help people regain their own sense of purpose, direction, and integrity at the core. That's why it's hopeful.

I learned how to work with the Rolfing technique and become a partner in my own change, as opposed to taking a passive approach. I was very much aware of how I was changing. I felt myself becoming free, moving, and thinking differently. I found myself entertaining thoughts I never had before, desiring to do things with my life and believing I could do them, such as owning my own business and practicing massage for a living. These were the changes I had wanted to make.

I completed my Rolfing over a two-year period. Each session was a time of discovery for me. I noticed how these changes affected my work as a massage therapist. I could look at a body and perceive where a person was injured or blocked. I learned how to use massage techniques to get a particular effect—how the focus of intention and concepts of integrity worked in relation to the massage technique. I was able to focus in such a way that I not only felt with my hands but with my heart, mind, and intuition. My hands felt changes in temperature, density, and texture. I sensed the emotions of the person I touched—joy, sadness, anger, whatever. I intuitively knew what techniques to use and where and when they could be applied to move the body tissue in a certain way. I instinctively knew what words to use, how a client needs to breathe with a stroke, a client's perceived boundaries that I should not cross.

My concept of breathing changed in Rolfing. With breathing you can change everything. Most people do not realize that it is possible to breathe into a body part. They don't see breathing as anything more than inflating the lungs and don't even take the diaphragm into consideration. Think how mind-opening it would be to have someone show you how to breathe into your sacrum, your arm, or your elbow. "Put your breath under my fingers" a Rolfer will tell you. It's that kind of partnership that is involved in body therapy work, whether it be Rolfing or massage. It teaches people just how wonderful the body is and how much really goes on with something as simple as breathing.

When I work with a person, I try to help them breathe and learn how to deal with discomfort. As that person's sensitivity lessens, I work deeper into the body so they can experience more, releasing toxins and things that have been stored there causing chronic problems. The shoulder girdle is a pronounced area for a lot of people. People hear little rumblings when they rotate their shoulders. That's toxins. And there is a massage technique that can help break down those toxins.

Massage is a bridge to help people on their journey to discovering themselves.

You can continue to maintain with massage. Massage is about flexibility, freeing up what already exists within a structure. Rolfing is about evolving and changing the structure of a person.

When I hear someone say they're stuck, that's when I suggest Rolfing.

Deborah N.

I'm a physical therapist and have worked both in hospitals and home care. I had heard from other physical therapists that Rolfing was really painful, but thought I would give it a try. I think horror stories about Rolfing get circulated by people who have no direct experience with it, especially physical therapists who are more concerned about doing things the "right way'" as they were taught in school.

Physical therapy only treats segments of the body. Fascia isn't considered important, and no attention is paid to the supporting network. What I'm finding out is that physical therapists can strengthen the muscles through exercise, but exercise doesn't release the tissues.

I feel that three sessions of Rolfing can accomplish what it takes 100 physical therapy treatments to do. Rolfing goes beyond physical therapy and brings out the real essence of an individual, the connection of mind and body. All of our past experiences and all of our memories are stored in the tissues of our bodies. Rolfing is a more holistic approach, while physical therapy focuses mainly on the problem.

In some hospitals in Denver and Boulder, a Rolfer and physical therapist will work together. The physical therapist teaches the patient how to walk while the Rolfer teaches them to feel how they walk. People are more aware of Rolfing in Colorado, because the Rolf Institute is located there.

After my first Rolfing session, I experienced such a freedom in my body that I knew I had to learn how to do this. So, I decided to become a Rolfer. When I told the other physical therapists about it, they thought I had been taking some kind of drug. I ignored them because Rolfing had changed my life. I hadn't realized how restricted and compressed I was until Rolfing gave me the freedom to allow myself to open up. There were some parts of the process that were painful, especially when Briah worked on my nose. But on the whole it proved a comfortable experience.

I was in therapy at this time, and I had also started chanting, so a lot of changes were going on at once. It's hard to tell where one thing stopped and another started because everything worked together.

My breathing pattern completely changed. I had much more depth and width. My vital capacity must have increased because I could get air into places I didn't even know existed. I also had huge physical changes. The whole structure of my spine and shoulders became more defined. My pelvis, hips, and legs felt less restricted and fused together, and I could feel each separate movement when I walked. The pain I had experienced from an old back injury was completely gone. Everyone could see that I was more confident and had much more energy.

While studying at the Rolf Institute in Boulder, I watched practitioners work on models and took five additional advanced sessions. I got some really big changes from those sessions, especially through my thoracic spine, my shoulders, and my neck. I felt a lot more connected and more open.

The Rolfer in Boulder was pretty amazing. His technique was very subtle. Every once in a while he would dig in pretty well and leave his initials in my back. But then he would just touch me a little here and there and the next thing I knew, my body was completely changed.

All Rolfers have their own way. Their goals are the same but their personalities are different. A lot of it has to do with what their intention is, where their hands are, and what results they are working for. The Rolfer in Boulder, Peter, had a different kind of energy than Briah because he's a different person. It was extremely powerful. I'm going to graduate from the Rolf Institute in a few months and will see what kinds of opportunities present themselves at that time. Right now I'm still doing physical therapy to pay the rent. My mom thinks I'm nuts. She can't believe I'm giving up a good job as head supervisor to go off and become a Rolfer, whatever that is.

At the Institute, I would watch children being Rolfed, and it seemed as if they changed right in front of my eyes. They were integrated right then. There was no hanging on to this for weeks. I thought it was really wonderful that a child could change so quickly, not like an older person who isn't as pliable and receptive. I think a lot of it has to do with the person wanting to change, allowing the change to happen. There were some models at the Institute who would go through all ten sessions and not know what was going on in their bodies. They'd say they supposed they felt different, but they didn't know how. I was really closed, out of touch with my feelings before Rolfing. Rolfing cut through a lot of the walls I had built. It helped me open up to the core of my being.

Chapter 10

How Can Rolfing Help People Release Problems Stemming from Physical and Sexual Abuse?

Carol C.

> "I have a certain centeredness now, a safe feeling that I'll be okay."

Nora I.

> "I was raped when I was twelve and wondered if this was going to come up in Rolfing."

Jennifer H.

> "My sexual experiences with my dad went on from the age of two until I was sixteen. Each time I left my Rolfer's office after a session, I was intensely aware that more and more 'junk' I had been carrying around for so long was slowly being worked out."

Carol C.

I was Rolfed this Spring. I had been Rolfed previously in St. Louis by a physical therapist who was also a Rolfer.

When l moved to Kansas City, I began group therapy to address my drinking. As a result of drinking, my mind got out of control. I was lonely, isolated, and miserable. The therapist suggested Rolfing.

I felt the time was right to be Rolfed again with the emotions that were coming out in therapy. I was also going to a chiropractor once or twice a week.

I always had a feeling that within the body cells, each cell has a mind of its own and has recollections of things and holds them in. I'm very intuitive and sensitive and my body has stored memories.

I was sexually abused by my father when I was very young. I think I just cut off the sexual part of my body, due to fear. I was feeling tired, overweight, numb, and generally disowning my body.

I've always favored the right side of my body, too. I felt that it was crippled. I don't know where that came from. It may be from some physical abuse and fear.

My first series of Rolfing sessions were done by a very gentle man. At first I found it definitely painful. He did a lot of work on my legs but couldn't work in the intestinal area or the rear very much. I'd had boils when I was little and I think I was spanked, too. I just couldn't handle it too much at that time. He also did a lot of work in the back and upper body area, too. I think he just saw what I needed at the time and went for it.

I found it painful, but I also needed to stand up straight and breathe better. He said, "Well, if there are any memories, just let them come up." Well, sure, I had bunches of them. I was very emotional.

I wore braces when I was a little girl. I remember he was doing some deep work around my face and I tasted and smelled metal. He smelled it, too. My body is a real storehouse for all those memories. I don't really forget.

For me, Rolfing was getting to that core place. I felt like it was the most important thing happening to me at that time. I wanted to start Rolfing again and tried to get an appointment with Briah before my group therapy sessions. It's very hard to get in to see her because she's very busy and she's real good. A friend of mine said it would be a totally different experience. I didn't find it painful. Though it burned. Even though Rolfing has had some painful aspects, nothing could do as much harm or hurt me as much as I've continued through the years to do to myself.

I felt Briah understood because she said that there was another person inside of me just dying to get out, a taller and longer person. As a young girl, I wanted to be taller and thinner and better looking. Now I am. My face has changed and people think I look very much younger.

Briah Rolfed me four or five times. And then I went to a cranial person who did some integration. In a few months when I'm ready, I'll go back to Briah again. I like myself better, and since I'm not really drinking that much, the emotional things come out hourly.

I noticed that the Rolfing has caused physical changes. People say, "My goodness, you've lost weight." The fact that I'm working on myself and feeling better about myself is really helping with my business. I have a certain centeredness now: a safe feeling that I'll be okay. That sometimes gets chipped at, but I now find myself with people that I can call on. My fear level is not totally gone. Sometimes I don't stand up for myself. Sometimes I placate people. But I find myself getting closer to my customers and letting them know me a little bit better, which is the key to selling. I'm more in tune with them because I'm more in tune with myself. It makes a big difference. And my intuitive nature is much keener.

I think I'm healthy for the first time. I'm living in a place that I love. My rooms are fine, my hair is fine, my clothes are fine, thank God my health is fine. So I'm real lucky. I feel that I'm surrounding myself, that I am in charge and I'm in control.

Nora I.

I heard about Rolfing through the center where I was studying massage. A friend of mine there had been Rolfed and talked about how intense and how important it had been. Other people told stories about getting to a certain point in their body, having flashbacks of experiences they had been holding inside, and experiencing a definite release.

I've always had severe posture problems. If I tried to stand straight, it put more stress on my body. This felt uncomfortable so I slouched. I also had stomach problems and was always in and out of hospitals for tests. Doctors would come up with a hundred different causes: stomach bugs, salmonella, spastic colon. I think a lot of it was psychosomatic: my way of looking for attention.

I always felt out of touch with my body, and one of the greatest benefits of Rolfing was the ability to feel myself in my body.

The first Rolfing session opened up my chest so that I felt as if I were breathing through my toes. The breaths were just sweeping all the way down and up, arching my feet and straightening out my knees and hips. It was terrific.

Rolfing did hurt! But feeling was part of the reason I was there. I needed to learn how to breathe through the pain to experience the intensity but have it be over and gone very quickly. Untying the knots in my back allowed me to breathe deeper and reach the point where it felt natural to stand up straight. It was worth the short-lived pain.

During these first sessions, the benefits were physical, but other people had told me how their most intense life experiences would suddenly surface while they were being Rolfed.

I was raped when I was twelve and wondered if this was going to come up in my Rolfing. In fact, the experience surfaced while Briah was working on my legs, and I felt intense pain and constriction in my chest as if my breath were being taken away. I realized what I was feeling was extreme fear and had an intense desire to run away. Instead I froze. My chest ached and I couldn't breathe.

Briah kept working and told me to breathe through this—that it was okay. I was able to physically relive that terrifying experience and finally let it go.

I had done everything intellectually and emotionally I could do.

Part of me was experiencing all of this completely, while another part of me was putting together pieces, such as, "So that's why my legs hurt and that's why this pain is in my chest." This is pretty great that I'm figuring it out.

All of a sudden I was crying. I cried and cried, and when I stopped the pain and grief were gone. It felt like I knew that I wouldn't have to deal with it ever again. I was free.

I had frozen up around the rape and that had continued as a theme throughout my whole life. My whole childhood was being shut out, I was being emotionally protective and holding everything in physically. For me, Rolfing was emotional because I had left so much hurt physically inside me.

There was much more room for me to stand up straight. I was able to control everything I did with my body. I was finally connected.

If you really have a problem, do something about it and change it. I started doing that and my attitude changed completely. I quit my job and traveled, went mountain climbing, and loved my body in a way I had never been able to before Rolfing. People have commented on the positive changes Rolfing has allowed me to make.

Jennifer H.

Without a doubt, the most painful and difficult part of my desire to grow into a healthier human being has been the process of learning to experience life inside my body. For as long as I can remember, I have disassociated my emotional self from my physical body.

Growing up in an environment that was unstable and full of fear caused me to start building my body armor at a very early age. My earliest memories of being molested by my father were when I was about two years old. It started out as molestation, and as I grew older, it included sodomy and rape. Although my self-esteem was tremendously affected by those sexual acts, it has been much harder for me to reconcile my "body esteem." I hated my body in every respect. The easiest way for me to deal with that kind of hatred was to disassociate myself from the source of it.

My sexual experiences with my dad went on from the age of two until I was sixteen. Then my parents divorced. My father had threatened me with my life if l ever told anyone about what went on between us. I was so afraid of his violent temper that I honestly believed he would kill me if I tried to get help. I can remember thinking over and over again, "If he hates me enough to be doing this to me, he probably wouldn't have second thoughts about killing me, either." At the time, it seemed easier to keep quiet and hope that someday it would stop. I remember I used to lie in bed and literally leave my body, disassociate myself from what was happening, until he was through and would leave me alone.

As I got better and better at "checking out" mentally, I began to carry that over into the other areas of my life as well. It wasn't long before I really felt like I no longer "owned" my body. It certainly wasn't something I wanted to admit owning, because then I would have had to start taking responsibility for it. I didn't know how to cope with that.

To the outside world I presented a self that was happy, easy-going, and worry free. It was my way of trying to make sure that no one would ever think there was something wrong. This caused a huge amount of inner turmoil because nothing could have been further from the truth. As I look back on those fourteen years of my life, I can see how I literally repressed everything that happened between my dad and me to an extreme. Almost as soon as he walked out of my bedroom on any given night, I had already started to "stuff" those memories. I felt so afraid and so trapped by what was going on that any attempt to deal emotionally with it was just too overwhelming for me. But my body never forgot. I have been terrified of males all my life, feeling threatened just by being in the same area with them.

I'd read something about somatic perception, and I really identified with that. Somatic perception is a person's awareness of the responses of their body to any given situation in which they find themselves. I relate to this most in the area of people in my life who love me. They say that they "love me." They do things that demonstrate love. Their body language expresses love. And I still don't feel loved!!! It's like no matter what they do or say, I still perceive that they don't love me. It has only been in the last two to three months, as I have begun to tear down my body armor, that I have started to feel the love people give me. My perception is slowly coming into alignment with reality in my world.

As I have struggled to accept and feel comfortable inside my body, there have been major areas of anxiety that have come up for me. For several years, I went through extreme bouts with anorexia because I was so obsessed with being thin. I was chubby as a child, and my sisters and friends teased me about it constantly. Add that to an already very low sense of self-esteem and it becomes easier for me to understand why I chose that self-destructive behavior.

I have avoided all physical body contact with others, even females, whenever possible because I disliked being touched so much. I still will not go to the doctor unless I am very, very sick because I don't want to have to take my clothes off or be touched by someone else. Even as I'm typing this paper, I heard my mind scream "NO!" just at the thought of going to the doctor. That's like an area of body violation for me. The same holds true for someone touching or hugging me without my permission. I am aware these areas of my life need work, since I know these attitudes are born out of the fear I grew up with.

I do want to give space to the areas in my life concerning my body where I feel I have made progress. I have recently finished a set of ten Rolfing sessions that were, without a doubt, the best present I could have given my sense of body esteem. I have to say at the onset of these sessions I was extremely apprehensive because of the very intimate hand/body contact that takes place between the Rolfer and the client. I had been told by several people that our bodies will store and remember negative and/or traumatic experiences even if our conscious minds cannot recall them. I felt if that were really true, my body had to be "overstuffed" with memories. I also knew that eventually I was going to need to confront those memories and deal with them if I were ever going to get beyond being a victim. I talked to my Rolfer before I made the decision to start the sessions. I wanted to let him know about my background and get a feel for the type of person he was before I committed myself. As it turned out, he had quite a bit of prior experience in dealing with people whose backgrounds were similar to mine, and I immediately felt very safe with him.

While it is true that as a result of the Rolfing my body posture, alignment, and muscle distribution were very positively affected, I gained the most in my "body esteem." I was amazed (and at times also frightened) at the intensity of the memories and emotions my body had stored. As I progressed through the ten sessions, many memories surfaced for me that had been buried for a long, long time. Finally, I was able to experience the emotions that went with those memories in an environment where I felt safe, secure, and nurtured.

Each time I left my Rolfer's office after a session, I was intensely aware that more and more of the "junk" I had been carrying around for so long was slowly being worked out. The sense of freedom that comes with that is incredible! After twenty four years of living outside my body and hating it, I was finally starting to come to terms with all that my body had endured. I began to embrace and nurture my hurting inner child as she began to emerge. As a direct result of the Rolfing, I feel for the first time in my life that I actually belong inside my body. I feel comfortable with my sense of self, and I am continuing to work on my issues of sensuality and sexuality in my therapy.

In the pictures taken of me at set intervals during my Rolfing sessions, you can see how my body structure has changed. The real evidence is in my face. The release that can be seen there from the beginning photos to the end speaks volumes for the freedom that my "whole self " is now experiencing.

Jennifer's Rolfer was Grant Powers of Costa Mesa, California.

Chapter 11

Rolfing and Recovery

Victor W.

Recovering alcoholic

"Rolfing gave me a jump-start into the process of the Twelve Steps."

Victor W.

To achieve sobriety, doing the 12 Steps and going to AA meetings is absolutely essential. It was necessary for me to get past a very tight knot of denial and an inability to express my own feelings. It took eight months of therapy just for me to face my alcoholic behavior. Without that, there may have been a bottom worse than I had.

Continual therapy helped me understand what my AA sponsor was talking about. The information was there in the meetings, but I didn't have the ability to integrate it; I was so closed.

I got into Rolfing on the recommendation of my sponsor and my therapist, not because I wanted psychological and emotional help. I thought I already had that. I got into Rolfing to alleviate a physical problem.

Rolfing gave me a "jump start" into the process of the 12 Steps. My hope is other people in therapy can experience that for themselves. Rolfing helped in the process of changing my life. I was fortunate enough to have a sponsor who understood this and had been Rolfed himself. It was the important combination of AA, therapy, and Rolfing that brought me to this emotional foundation where I am now able to get on with my life.

The power of Rolfing, of getting the body and its structure balanced, provides the grounding for the emotional release and depth of work, the feeling of well-being.

I started Rolfing after I had been in counseling for 18 months, and six months into sobriety in Alcoholics Anonymous. It was a time of courage. I was forced to face my fears; my sobriety was at stake. Not facing these fears meant that I would die drinking.

At the time, I was going through a lot of changes. I was on an emotional roller coaster. I had just come through a divorce, quit a job as a high-ranking corporate officer, lost a lot of money in the company stock, and moved into a new home that needed major renovation.

The reason for Rolfing was simply to do something about my sacro-iliac, a back problem I'd had over 20 years. It had gotten quite unstable, and I was becoming more reclusive. I wasn't able to participate as much in sports, such as downhill skiing, because I never knew when my back was going to give me problems. I didn't want to take risks anymore. I was always feeling insecure about my health and was going to chiropractors once or twice a week.

So many things hurt, I felt that if I were a horse, they'd shoot me. I had led an active life—boxing, Tae Kwon Do, freestyle skiing, soccer. Briah discovered during Rolfing that one leg was shorter than the other, and I was having problems with a leg that had not healed properly from a break 22 years earlier. I felt as if my body had forsaken me, and I couldn't depend on it anymore.

I talked to several people about the possibility of pain during Rolfing, but frankly that didn't bother me. I could always handle pain. I could stuff the feelings, like I had done all of my life.

The first meeting, a history-taking inventory, was a real eye-opener for me. It gave me time to develop a trusting relationship with my Rolfer. I had to tell the story of my dysfunctional relationships, talk about some of the fears I'd been having in therapy, and explain how alcoholism had affected my life. Briah asked me a lot of personal questions in order to get to know me and find out what my goals were.

The first actual physical session took place a week later. This session was like a deep muscle massage and focused mainly on breathing into the particular area she was working on. This was not an easy process for me, but I tried to be open-minded. I couldn't understand why breathing down into my legs would help, since my lungs only go to my diaphragm. But I was able to withhold my criticism. After years of Tae Kwon Do, I had seen third-degree black belts do things that didn't seem humanly possible, particularly concerning breathing, and I also knew I really didn't understand my body.

It was a pleasant experience, and I didn't have the amount of emotional feedback like I had later. Briah reminded me to drink a lot of water to wash out the toxins being released in my body. Afterwards, I felt very tired, and that night I began to recall the anxieties from my childhood.

It was after the second session I began to notice I was more emotional in an unfocused way. I began having dreams about my past. I recalled more of the old pains of my abuse, particularly around my mother. I was scared, but I felt like I was supposed to be in that place. My therapist confirmed that Rolfing was probably good for me in this stage of my therapy and helped me to deal with deeper issues.

Session three, which deals with opening up the ribcage and increasing the depth of breathing, was a whole different story. It hurt like hell and was terribly frightening. My whole body shook. I had trouble breathing, and Briah had to keep reminding me to breathe. Suddenly, I started remembering a lot of old pain I had suffered when I was 10 years old.

In AA, people talk about where they hurt and where their pain comes from. Well, mine was right in the center of my chest, where we were working. I used to have such incredible chest pain that I went to a doctor to find out if I had some kind of heart problem.

When Briah opened up my chest, I began crying, venting anger toward my father and mother, both of whom were violent alcoholics. The anger went deeper and I felt like an abandoned child. This was the emotion going through my head and body simultaneously. Suddenly, my body was reverberating with the response to these feelings. Before, they had been in my head. Now they were filling my entire body.

I had discussed it in therapy and thought I was dealing successfully with it, but my body shouted, "No! There's more!" It's not just a mental process. I realized I had gotten to this place in Rolfing because of my work in therapy and because of my belief in God.

I cried, moaned, and coughed, all at once. Then I became very quiet, withdrew into a safe place, and felt no pain. Briah stopped Rolfing and said, "What are you feeling?" I said, "Distant, spacey. But I feel less pain." She said, "Come back from that place. That's your addiction."

Briah talked me back from that old place. I had fallen into the place where I'd go when my mother would whip me, where I would anesthetize myself and not feel the pain. This was my process of denial, of withdrawing from life. When Briah said that was my "addiction," I immediately came back from that spot and allowed myself to feel again. I haven't "checked out" since that experience, but there were times when I wanted to.

I had to learn to face the fact of my own addictive personality and realize pain is part of life, but the suffering is optional. I had to stop just enduring the pain and to let it pass through me without becoming a permanent part of my being.

When I left that session, I sensed a glow above my head and rays of energy flowing from my body in all directions, through my fingers, arms, and head.

My childhood had been very repressed, abusive, and dysfunctional. I had learned denial as a survival technique to deal with my fears. My father, ex-military, had taught me never to show fear or pain. My mother used to whip us and think she hadn't gotten through to us unless we cried. I had eventually gotten to a place in my head where I really wouldn't feel pain. I just shut it off.

My father raised all of us to be soldiers. Most kids would say they wanted to be a fireman or cowboy when they grew up. I was instructed to always say I wanted to be a soldier. Our family was one of constant rules. Everything was written down. We rarely saw my father on week-days, only on weekends, and then it was like boot camp. It was very regimented with required pushups every day. There was no allowance for your own personality or things you liked to do. There was very little affirmation for me as a person. My father would say, "Well, that's not going to help you get into the service" when I wanted to do something creative, such as sing or write.

My father had decided we needed to be tough because we were Jew-ish, and he had fears of another Holocaust. He instilled that fear in us. It was embedded in my body and became part of the fabric of my life. I had no safe place in the world. There was very little touching or hold-ing, unless it was physically harmful.

My father used to make us participate in toughening exercises, such as sword fighting. We received points for how many times we cut the opponent. We got one point for a scratch, two for a welt and three if we drew blood. The first guy to get ten points won. He would pit one brother against the other and fight us himself. We wore helmets, but no shirts. By the age of 12, I thought this was great fun because, by then, I had learned to feel no pain. It was also a chance for me to strike back at him. But because he was so much bigger, I naturally lost the fights.

One thing he did teach us was to be fighters. When the going got rough, and there were some pretty rough moments in trying to become sober, I never quit. I always felt I could get through it.

I took a break after my third Rolfing session and went to California to have an eye operation. After my trip, I came back for the fourth and fifth sessions. At the same time I was going through the fourth and fifth steps of the 12 Step Program in AA. They worked together per-fectly. The fourth step in AA involves making a moral inventory of the past actions and feelings that have caused harm. It's a housecleaning, getting rid of the old stuff that inhibits recovery. This step is necessary for physical as well as emotional sobriety. If you don't face what started your drinking in the first place, it's very possible you will go back.

In the fifth step, you tell yourself, someone else, and God what your moral position is. My moral inventory started off as a novel. I took everyone else's inventory but my own.

The fifth session was especially difficult. While Briah was doing deep tissue massage on my chest and part of my legs, I had this tremendous reaction. My body started shaking, my hands cramped, and I was unable to open them. I was physically and emotionally reverberating to all that was happening to me. It was an awful experience, and when I was done, I was afraid of Rolfing. But my therapist knew I was being Rolfed; my sponsor had done it, and I had come to believe that Briah knew what she was doing. I also had my trust in God. I needed all of this support.

I talked to my therapist and my sponsor. I admitted fears. I talked to Briah. I found myself telling her about the fears I felt during AA meetings. I had never confided this to anyone except my therapist. I discovered that other people have fears that are just as crippling. I learned we are only as sick as our secrets and began to believe I could get better. I didn't have to live with these secrets.

This was a very enlightening time for me. I was able to do a lot of integrating and expunge much of the trash and garbage in my life. After my fifth session, I decided I needed a break, a hiatus, so I went to New York for several weeks. There I realized I wasn't taking my Fifth Step of the AA program honestly. I realized I had rationalized a lot of things away—it was always someone else's fault.

I got down on my knees and prayed to God to take charge of the Fifth Step. "Do it your way, not my way," I asked. "I just don't feel honest." This feeling said, "Honesty! You want honesty!" I had an avalanche of feelings. Everything broke apart. It went through me to the floor. I laid on the floor in a flood of realization.

When I met my sponsor again, I had completely re-written my moral inventory. That night, after our meeting, I had another realization of how much all this had affected my family. I felt like a spike had been driven through my chest. That pain I'd been trying to deal with in

Rolfing and therapy had centered on my sternum, and I thought I was having a heart attack.

I realized that my son and daughter were children of an alcoholic. They would have to deal with this in their lives. I also realized that my ex-wife had her own problems with my alcoholism.

I prayed, asking for relief from this incredible pain. I got this warm feeling. Some people say after their Fifth Step they have closest communication or consciousness of God. I had that feeling.

I felt enormous energy. Briah had taught me how to release accumulated energy during the Rolfing sessions when my hands would cramp up. I did the "throw the ball away" motions, stretching, and breathing through it. As I threw these balls away, they became fears and things I had done in the past. I wanted forgiveness.

I started releasing the pain, coughing, and crying. I released energy through my fingertips. I had incredible energy and was convinced that I could push through walls with my fingers, and fire bullets with my fingertips. I could feel the tension releasing.

I also did another exercise Briah had shown me, walking on my hands and knees with my head down, letting the energy go out through my body. I started breathing deeply, using every technique I had ever heard of to get rid of the pain and energy. I turned everything over to God. I asked God to take it away; it was too big for me. I surrendered.

When I was done, I felt as if I had been Rolfed on a much deeper level, as if I had been Rolfed by God. It was a very physical feeling, like a massage at a deep tissue level. I laid back and felt so calm. The pain receded and a sense of peacefulness descended upon me. The serenity was deeper than the capacity of my chest. It went all the way through me. This session marked the turning point in my recovery.

I've now worked many of these things through with my therapist, my old history and old feelings, but at a much deeper level. The five Rolfing sessions that followed were nowhere nearly as dramatic as the previous ones, although some were physically demanding. In the last five sessions, I continued to release the fear and old pain, but the Rolfing was more like a wonderful massage.

I was starting to stretch and lengthen, especially in the last three Rolfing sessions. I've probably grown an inch. I've had friends point out how great I look, how my eyes sparkle now. Before, I felt squatty and twisted. I felt older than my years. Now, I've had many people say that I look like I'm in my mid-30s, and I'm over 40 years old. I think my own feeling of suppleness, and how I respond to my world, has changed. I'm comfortable in my skin, and I feel like my body is doing what it's supposed to do. I feel vital and healthy.

It's been perhaps three months since I've finished Rolfing, and it feels like five years. I've changed dramatically as a person. It's difficult to explain how completely that integration has changed my view of life.

I'm much more aware of my body; my movements are freer. I have hardly any fear about getting a sports injury. I went down some very steep, violent ski runs with my 13-year-old son and had no trouble keeping up with him.

My friends in AA noticed a huge change. I looked like I was glowing. I've begun to have visions of what serenity can be like. I could still fall into my old patterns, but I don't have to act on them. I know that when I have anxieties, they'll pass. With this ability to be in touch with myself, I can actually have several good days in a row. The streets haven't changed, but I have.

I'm feeling great right now, and there's nothing particularly wonderful that's happening to me. In other words, I'm not dependent on other people, places, and things to make me feel okay. I'm in my twelfth month of sobriety and going through the usual anxieties that others go through as they approach their first year. My relationship with my son and daughter is excellent. I can see a huge difference in my life, and others can see it, too. I feel like I've been given a second chance, and I have the coping tools to be able to live a full life.

Many people do not believe in the benefits of counseling or Rolfing, but I also believe that God has many ways of healing the soul. The AA program works without counseling or Rolfing, but we also believe that if a person's mind is open, many benefits can be obtained from therapy and Rolfing. It can help you get past the worst parts. It can help you get to the point of being able to look at yourself.

The changes I've had in my perception of myself and the world have been incorporated into my living space. I bought two condos and opened them up into one large one. My first plan was to remodel the condo into a very glitzy bachelor's pad. I was trying to project an image of wealth, a sexy look. I was still dealing with my own male validation fears that came out of my divorce. The bathroom/bedroom was going to be some erotic, sensual manifestation of a newly-minted bachelor with the emotional stability of a 19-year-old. When you walked down the hall, which would be my art gallery, you would swing open doors to an enormous bathroom in green glass and an enormous bed. It was like turning over a blank checkbook to your teenage son and telling him he could do anything with the house he wanted to do.

In reality, I had always been looking outside of myself to feel okay. My relationships reflected that. A lot of them were very toxic during my divorce crazies. As I changed, I progressed from the "19-year-old" to an adult. I recognized that I was 42, not 19, and began to look at this residence as a place of my own, rather than a reflection of my pretensions. The whole blueprint of my condo changed as I went through my growing process.

The bathroom was diminished to a normal sized bathroom. It's not spartan, but you don't have the feeling you'll get lost in it. Rather than a huge bathroom, I put in a library. The library has a computer for my writing work and a library ladder. It's very womb-like, a place where I can feel intimate with myself.

A lot of things about the rooms reflect my inner self-concept. They are open with no hidden compartments of my soul. The place feels solid, stable, and yet there are splashes of color from the art and subtlety in the lighting. There's a feeling that someone really lives here. There is a flow from one room into another, and I feel that it reflects the new flow in my life.

I recognize my boundaries and am much more in touch with my feelings. To an alcoholic, the concept of limits or boundaries is foreign, because when we were drinking we didn't have limits. I know I can't control everything in my life, but I do have choices and can exercise those choices. During Rolfing, I had to learn to set boundaries on how much I wanted to experience at one time. One of the problems I had was that I had not taken charge of part of that experience. My body felt out of control. One of the things I am working on now is keeping a balance, learning how to say, "that's enough" to myself or someone else.

In the last five Rolfing sessions, I was less afraid of what would come next; it was much more therapeutic than I originally thought it would be. There was a better rapport between Briah and me.

During the first five sessions, I was still seeing my chiropractor, although not nearly as often. I had begun to learn how to breathe into a problem area. Now, I'll breathe into the area, slowly stretching it, fine-tuning my own body. In Rolfing and AA, you need an ability to be flexible in order to make the changes that will allow you to lead a normal life.

That explosion of emotions, the letting go of fear, was necessary for me to make the spiritual and emotional growth that I had. I was fortunate enough to have a sponsor who had been in therapy, had been Rolfed, and who had done the 12 Step Program and been sober six years. It was this important combination of all three that helped save my life—that allowed me to go on with living.

Chapter 12

Performing Artists and Other Creative People

Richard Cass

Professor of music and concert pianist
How Rolfing improved his own and his students' performances

Patricia J.

Opera singer
Patricia relates her re-birthing process and says, "I probably increased 15 to 20 percent in the upper end and fullness of voice. I could feel myself coming into being."

Camille G.

Piano student with chronic back pain also experiences spiritual renewal.

Maria F.

Dancer
"The physical changes from Rolfing have increased my confidence as a dancer which carries over into my confidence as a teacher."

David O.

Dancer, actor, singer
"My range increased a little under half an octave. Rolfing is realignment. I'd thought it was deep massage for the purpose of reliving past events, but that was a misconception on my part."

Sandy D.

Voice student studying opera

"My voice teacher was amazed and impressed. She even sent another student to be Rolfed."

Linda M.

Dancer and dance teacher

"Not only is my physical performance better, but I also have the emotional range to express myself."

Kathryn M.

Actress

"When I finished a show I would get Rolfed, just to clear the last remains of a character out of my body. I have a quality that appears very flexibly to a director."

Karin R.

Dancer

"My legs feel a lot straighter and make much nicer lines when I dance. I had blockage points that didn't allow me to express myself as fully as I could have."

Katherine W.

Professional photographer

"I grew up in a physical body which was a bundle of fear."
Can Rolfing help us work through creative blocks?

Rose S.

Professional model

"I've taken the weight of the world off my shoulders physically and mentally. You have to be completely loose, connected, spontaneous and comfortable with yourself and you have to know yourself very well. This is the artistry in my work."
Can Rolfing affect pregnancy?

Rolfing Reflections

I work with many people who use their bodies professionally—athletes, dancers, actors, musicians, martial arts instructors—people who depend on their bodies to a great extent. Rolfing helps these professionals increase performance, improve breathing and balance, and increase flexibility and freedom of movement. It is also a powerful tool for recovery from intensive efforts and injuries. Rolfing is body education.

Richard Cass, pianist
"... *technical finesse and honest musicianship*" —The New York Times
"... *an important pianist from America—a complete artist.*" —London Daily Telegraph

Richard Cass

I learned about Rolfing through a piano student of mine who was having severe physical problems. This student had been a trombone player in her undergraduate days and that in itself had created a lot of problems—the way a person has to carry the horn when they play it, and the stress and strain that is put on the right arm.

She had developed some great discomfort in her back, and as she practiced the piano and undertook more advanced literature, she began to have tendinitis and trouble with her arms and hands, including some numbness and possibly some muscle tone loss. Her back was also bothering her a great deal. She was a doctoral student between 25 and 30 years old, a person who under ordinary circumstances wouldn't be having these symptoms.

She came to me with a lot of tension and tightness in her arms and hands, and I told her that she was too tight to play with any degree of success. We had worked on this tension and had made progress up to a point. But she also had extreme attacks of stage fright that she was unable to cope with. When a piece got hard and she became emotionally involved in it, she would revert to her old ways of playing, which were a little harsh and hard. She tried various things, X-rays, chiropractic. I'm not sure how she got involved with Rolfing, but she did; and I noticed a dramatic improvement. There was a lessening of tension in her playing

One of the most gifted pianists of our time, Richard Cass continues to enrapture audiences with his flair, vitality, and dazzling technique.

Once considered "the most called-back pianist" with Columbia Artists, he has enjoyed critical acclaim for his performances throughout the United States and Europe. He was Chairman of the Piano Department at the University of North Texas and joined the faculty at the Conservatory of Music at University of Missouri, Kansas City, in 1975.

The South Carolina-born musician holds the "Distinguished Alumnus Award" from his alma mater, Furman University. Cass was a Fulbright Scholar at the Ecole Normale de Musique in Paris. He made his professional debut in Paris, followed by appearances in New York's Town Hall, Alice Tully Hall, and Carnegie Hall.

apparatus, in herself, and in her approach to the music. There was also less tension between us. The student-teacher relationship is a very intimate and very complex one. It takes a lot of work to keep the lines of communication clear. If personal things come into the picture and things become too intense, problems can be created. After the Rolfing, quite a bit of that static began to disappear.

She told me that she had experienced a tremendous release, as if the monkey that had been on her back had finally gone away. Most of her pain was gone, and we both noticed a great physical improvement.

This particular student introduced me to the concept of Rolfing. Later, I had another graduate student who was physically handicapped for playing the piano. As a child, she had severe asthma and was caved in through the front of her body. Her shoulders were pulled forward, and everything was in the wrong place. If I tried to get her wrists down where they belonged, her elbow would go out. If I brought the elbow in, her shoulder went up.

Everything was wrong.

Emotionally, she was very unstable. Because she had so many strikes against her, she was continually frustrated. When she got into Rolfing, the results were very dramatic.

I saw a total change in her body. She became a new person—straighter, more symmetrical, more filled out, and more poised. Everything improved—her posture, her appearance, her way of moving. She seemed to be, for the first time, making acquaintance with her body. I could see that in her playing. She was constantly amazed at what her limbs could do. She had never before experienced that connection between the music she was hearing in her mind and the music she was able to create through her hands. That was impressive.

Interestingly, both of these people got out of music. I tend to see that as a positive. The Rolfing may have helped them find themselves. Maybe music was not the place for them. And that might have been contributing to some of the stuff that was going on within their bodies. The end result has been that they've gone on into other fields, but that's good. People need to do what they feel they are supposed to do.

I had a third student who was also having tendinitis problems and was Rolfed at my suggestion and that of a friend. She got immediate relief from the tendinitis, plus a lot of emotional release. She had come from a rigid family and was critical of herself and, as a result, very critical of others. She imposed judgment on all of her relationships, and most piano lessons involved crying sessions at one time or another. If things went well, she cried. If things went poorly, she cried. I could see she needed some release from this situation and was delighted that Rolfing helped.

Another student came in with severe back problems. She would lie on the floor to relieve the pain and then wouldn't be able to get up because the pain was so severe. This made it very difficult, if not impossible, for her to practice. She had a very positive experience with Rolfing and went on to complete a master's degree in piano and is now working on a doctorate in voice. I think it released a lot of emotional things in her, too.

What drew me to Rolfing was the experiences of these students. It seemed to me they were having some very good results from Rolfing in psychological, psychic, and spiritual ways as well as physical. I thought I would like to experience this, and so I decided to try Rolfing for myself. I had a little bit of a problem in my right arm, which caused some numbness from time to time in my hand. Usually it went away with playing. After 10 to 15 minutes of playing, my hand would be numb, and if I practiced through that, it would go away.

But I knew I shouldn't really be experiencing this. That was the only overt physical thing that I was aware of when I got into Rolfing.

After my first session, I noticed that I had a more easily tapped reservoir of energy. That's a hard thing to describe when you're a performer. It's not just a matter of whether you're tired or not. It's not that kind of energy. It's kind of a spiritual drive towards performing. I would find, for example, that I was much more consistent in my efforts to polish a performance. Before, I would reach a point in the preparation for a public performance and say to myself, "Well, that's good enough." But my attitude changed. And I thought, "No, that's not good enough. I can do better than this, and I want to do better. Now I have the energy and force to tap into to make this better."

This new energy allowed me to break through all kinds of barriers. Then I began to realize that some of the limitations I had been applying to myself weren't real. I was fighting the performer's battle against discouragement, a discouragement caused by the absence of brilliant public acclaim. As I started accessing myself more, I realized the reason for this had nothing to do with the way the public accepted me, but the way I accepted myself. I didn't know myself that well; therefore, I didn't really know what I wanted. Rolfing increased my spirit of optimism.

When this happens to a student, I always call it a breakthrough. It was like that for me—like moving from a tiny, cramped room into a large, open one.

I slept better. I ate less, because with the increase in energy, I didn't have to keep pumping calories to feel good. I also noticed a definite increase in my desire to practice. Because of my heavy teaching schedule, I'd been lucky to average three hours a day of practice. Now I found myself wanting to practice five or six hours, and I had never done that, even as a young child. I just felt like the world's my oyster and all I have to do is crack and eat it.

The photographs taken before Rolfing showed the front view of my right side was a little torqued towards the front. Things were pulled around towards the front in my upper body, and my right shoulder was higher and pulled forward. I remember that twisted look, and I recall my head being turned to one side. My right leg seemed to want to do the opposite of my upper body and turn towards the outside. It gave my whole body a very asymmetrical look. With all that asymmetry, you can imagine all the stresses on the structure itself.

In the profile pictures, the curve in my upper back had become much more verticalized in the After Rolfing photographs.

I also found that my finger dexterity, which had been a problem in the past, had improved. My hand tends to be a little tight across the top, and I've always had to do calisthenics to keep my fingers flexible. After Rolfing, I required far less time to warm up and feel comfortable playing.

Not only did it take less time, but the fingers themselves were in better shape when they did get going. Another fine point was that I had much greater control over my fingers and could vary the speed of the finger stroke, which is very important in piano playing. It has everything to do with the loudness or the softness of the tone you make and even the quality of sound on the piano. A finger that is too fast and uncontrolled will always result in a harsh, edgy kind of sound. I noticed a big difference there. I had much greater endurance. I could play very difficult music over extended periods of time without tensing up and without tiring my fingers so much. That's important when you're playing a big concerto or pieces that require a lot of continual motion and endurance.

Rachmaninoff was a great pianist, but I had always put Rachmaninoff down. I felt that his music was cheap and too easy to listen to—gushy. I had played a little bit of Rachmaninoff's music and had always found it exceedingly difficult. It was only after I had been Rolfed that I began to play Rachmaninoff's solo pieces. I undertook to play some of his Etude Tableaux, which pianists regard as some of his most difficult music. I discovered that I loved that music. I identified with it and was successful with it. I had always felt that I didn't like the music because I was afraid I couldn't play it.

Another piece by Ravel called "Scarborough" is considered to be one of the three most difficult of all piano solos. I decided there was no reason why I couldn't play that work, even though I had always accepted the fact that these pieces were too much for me. I did learn and play that work for one entire season. I played a whole program of French piano music and ended with that piece. My creative energies and my self-confidence, my poise, were opened up to the point where I could take that challenge. That was a direct result of my Rolfing experience.

I have also found that since being Rolfed I am a much better teacher. I am more able to get into the student's work, identify with it, and lead them to something a little bit closer to what they are really capable of. Sometimes the result has been that the student gets out of music, but that's a function of good teaching, too. It's the teacher's responsibility to identify the student's situation and advise them regarding whether they should continue this particular search.

As a result of being a lot clearer about my own process, I'm able to bring this understanding to the student, rather than trying to view the student as some kind of an extension of myself. I noticed the results of their efforts were better. There was a better rapport within the class and between the students themselves. That reflects what's going on with the teacher, how the teacher is bringing the team together.

In any profession you can let yourself get down from time to time. And you can even get bored with it. I felt a revitalization coming from Rolfing. People began telling me how much younger I looked, that I was walking with a spring in my step, and my feet weren't splaying out like they used to. My posture was changing. These were unsolicited reactions. I also began to get positive reactions to my playing. People said I seemed to be entering a higher level of playing which had more emotional impact and was more expressive. Sometimes I'll hear a tape of mine on KXTR from a "Pre-Rolfing" recital from different periods, and I can hear a marked difference.

My playing is the principal thing in my life. The positive reactions to the changes in my playing really hit home. I spent the first 15 or16 years of my career touring the world playing concerts. When I first became aware that I wanted to make music my life's work, I felt very strongly about being a performer. But I also wanted to establish a relationship with a good school somewhere and teach. I had some teachers who inspired me with their dedication and ability and felt it would be nice to move people with music, move them to a deeper experience of whatever music does.

I was head of the piano department at North Texas State University, in the School of Music, for eight years and have been at the University of Missouri-Kansas City for 15 years. I average from 15 to 20 performances of one kind or another per year—recitals, concertos. A lot of my work is done in other universities where I spend three or four days playing, teaching, and lecturing on various topics involved with the piano world.

I'm 58, but since the Rolfing, I feel much younger. I realize more and more that getting to the energy and spontaneity for a peak performance is always possible. I feel much less constricted and obligated to be perfect. As a consequence, I feel that my playing is not only more meaningful for me, but for others as well.

Recently, I had several advanced Rolfing sessions and was amazed at how the whole Rolfing experience came back to me. I began to remember the whole experience. My body recognized what was happening. The immediate effect was a great improvement in the condition of my right arm. I also felt a surge of "electrical shock," as if I had been jolted back into condition. My wife told me to go back and have more sessions because she could see a big difference just in the way I used to be and the way I am today. She said I seemed more poised, more self-aware, and more relaxed.

One of the reasons I felt more relaxed was because I'm relieved of the bothersome trouble in the arm. But I also had the thought, "Uh-oh. Have I reached the end of the road here?" I've had several friends who've had to stop playing the piano entirely because they were having symptoms like this. It made me regret that I had let all that time go by and had not followed up on the original Rolfing experience with some more advanced sessions, building on what we had done then.

Rolfing is really a very surprising and amazing kind of technique. It can be approached from all different directions. If there is a student who is having particular physical problems involved in the manipulation of the instrument, Rolfing can do wonderful things to help correct these things.

The teacher also needs to provide the student with awareness of things like posture, position, and seating height.

Rolfing can also be a tremendous benefit in helping a student develop psychologically and spiritually, so they are able to open up more to their own talent. Some students are unable to recognize how gifted they are, and as a consequence, don't really know what they are after. Through Rolfing, I have been able to help my students realize their potential. This experience of opening up the paths of communication with my students carried over to my performance and allowed a great improvement in my rapport with the audience.

My playing became warmer and evoked a warmer response. Maybe I was a little less fearful about exposing my own feelings. And in my teaching, I became a little more understanding, a little more perceptive.

I've talked to a lot of people that were Rolfed and saw very dramatic changes happen to them. Several of my students changed before my eyes. My change, I think, was a little different. I think it was more of an interior change. I still find it difficult to talk to other people about Rolfing. I think it's the difficulty of communicating to another person what's going on inside you, especially something as intensely personal as your reaction to Rolfing. Ultimately, Rolfing brought about many dramatic changes in my life and has been of tremendous benefit to me.

Patricia Johnson, coloratura soprano

"I saw Rolfing as an investment in my career, a way to unlock my potential," says P.J., a lyric
coloratura soprano. She saw an immediate impact on her breathing and in her range and fullness of voice. Her range went up six half-steps. "Now I'm stretching into Fs, and even an A flat
is fairly well connected," she says. "This range is really important to me."
"Rolfing is definitely a catalyst," P.J. tells me.

Patricia J.

I had a couple of friends who had been Rolfed and said it was a very powerful experience. At the time, I was doing a lot of self-exploration and sensed a physical hindrance that I thought was tied into my emotions. I hoped that Rolfing could free me from that. I'm a lyric coloratura soprano and am just starting an opera career. I went into Rolfing as an adventure or opportunity. It was an investment in my career to unlock my potential.

After the first session, I noticed a difference immediately. It was amazing. The release in my breath and my upper ribcage was wonderful. I ran into a few friends who had been Rolfed and they could also tell the difference. For the first time, I could hit a high C easily, and after completing the Rolfing, E-flat became a guaranteed note. Now I'm stretching into Fs and have even reached a fairly well-connected A-flat. This range is important to me professionally because it's very rare. I probably increased 15 to 20 percent in the upper end and the fullness of voice, six half-steps higher.

I believe the most significant thing that happened during Rolfing was a re-birthing experience. I had heard the term before but didn't really know anything about it. There's a place in my back where I hold many emotional issues, and while Briah was working on that area, I had a strong visualization. Images of myself taking on too much in life came into my head, and I understood why I held the tension in that area. When Briah rolled me onto the other side, I felt as if I were just a few weeks old. My face became infant-like; I couldn't open my eyes, and I had this little pout.

At that time, I didn't understand. I just knew something was wrong but I couldn't express myself. Then I experienced an intense feeling of being in the womb. I had incredible energy throughout my body, even inside my mouth. My ears were ringing and everything felt energized. I cried. My skin felt irritated; it burned painfully. I was in a very hostile environment and did not like it.

At that point, Briah had me sit on the edge of the table and bend over and push back at her. It felt as if I were coming out, literally being born. I could feel myself coming into being. It was very hard for thirty or forty minutes. Getting out was so difficult. It turns out that my

Patricia singing opera

mother had toxemia very badly toward the end of her pregnancy, so my birth was traumatic. This explains so much about my personality. I'm very stand-offish. My mother used to tell stories about how I wouldn't let her hold me as a child. I'd push people away when they tried to hug me. Of course, I was still living through the irritation, the pain. Getting in touch with it and understanding it helped me to release it. I realized how much our lives are influenced by the process of our birth. It was a very enlightening experience.

My voice teacher remarked that I've opened up so much, not only my voice, but my whole self. Last year in a competition, I was second alternate and "Most Promising Young Singer." One of the judges commented on the fact I wasn't free enough onstage. This year I went and that same judge was amazed at how I was able to open up. I'm getting a lot of positive comments about how I'm able to open up.

My voice teacher thinks it's phenomenal. She says that I have 90 percent correct technique according to her standards which are very, very high. Now I'm reaching finals in competitions, breaking through levels, and getting accepted into programs. These are things I wasn't doing a year ago. The Rolfing has definitely been the catalyst to unlock all that potential and release my emotional blockages. I would not be anywhere near where I am now without it.

Rolfing even changed my attitude toward auditions. I realized that I just have to do my end of the work and the people who are listening have to make up their minds. That was a big discovery for me because I was trying to take responsibility for whether they liked me or not. To let go of that, I have even let go of my voice. My voice is beyond me. I just energize it, work for it. But never do I control it. Now that I can connect my energy to my tone, I feel grounded and solid when I perform and am no longer terrified during an audition.

My figure has also changed. My thighs are smoother and the flesh on my hips has been lengthened. The way I hold my stomach is different. My whole right side used to be shrunk in. I had a knee that was crossed over and now it's straight. In the "before" pictures I was trying to stand up straight, but my head was too far forward and my shoulders drooped. In the After pictures, my head is very straight and my shoulders seem to be resting all right. My collarbone stays parallel. Every day after the first session, I would look in the mirror and expect everything to go back the way it was, but it didn't.

Rolfing was never painful. That's what's so funny. People kept asking me, "Oh, did it hurt?" There were a couple of tense emotional places that were hard to release, but most of the time it was wonderful. I don't know how Rolfing got the reputation of being painful or negative manipulation. It helped me guide my body into a place where it wanted to be. It's not harsh at all.

If I had my picture taken again, I wouldn't be surprised if I saw more differences. I know things are still happening and even though I've finished the process, suddenly something will release again.

I remember after one session, I perspired a great deal. This was a release of some kind of toxin. Then other small things would happen. I walked differently, almost as if my feet weren't touching the ground. Everything is straight now and goes in a direct line. I also experienced times when I just wanted to sleep. At other times, I was extremely hungry or alternating depression with happiness. I recognized this as some sort of process and just allowed myself to experience it. I was releasing or reenergizing.

I had some interesting dreams. One was very powerful. It was about a friend of mine, a swimmer, who was in a competition and was being judged by a committee. It was incredibly grueling. And the committee said, "We can't accept you. You've been on drugs before." She said, "But I've taken care of that. That's totally separate." After they judged her, they walked up to her and hugged her and held her and cried. It was so powerful to really comfort somebody—something I had not done. I hadn't let anybody do it to me, so I didn't know how to do it to really, really hug. That really meant something. I was really opening up to that. I woke up and kept feeling as if I wanted to say, "I love you." But I didn't know who this feeling was for. It was so powerful and so genuine and real. I talked to Briah and she said, "It's probably for you." Wow! Knowing I can love myself the same way I love someone else is wonderful! I had denied myself that feeling before, but I seem to be in touch with myself and reality now and can deal with difficult situations in a truthful way.

Rolfing in itself doesn't cause all these changes. The person who is being Rolfed has to participate and make it work. It's a way of teaching yourself. You can take it as far as you want, or you can be totally unmoved by it. It's all up to the individual. I'm still looking for more opportunities to grow and know I'll come back for more Rolfing in the future.

Camille G.

Rolfing was recommended to me by my piano teacher, Mr. Cass. My back had been hurting so badly that one day I went to his studio and said, "I don't think I can take this lesson. I'm not sure I can even get back downstairs."

I had had severe back problems all through high school and college. The lower right side of my back would get stiff and eventually go into muscle spasms. When this happened, I would have to go to bed. I didn't have any other choice.

I literally could not move for a day or two. Even with pain killers and muscle relaxers, I would be flat on my back for a week and unable to walk for several more weeks.

Finally, Mr. Cass said, "If you don't get Rolfed, I won't continue to take you as a student. I will pay for your first session if you'll just go. It worked wonders with me."

I didn't have any other options, so that's how I ended up being Rolfed. I was desperate.

I think I went for a total of thirteen sessions. For a year, I had no pain and could do anything I wanted to do. I knew I was on the right track. Family members would ask about Rolfing and say, "What is this?" I'd try to explain to them by saying, "Well, she massages me with her knuckles, kind of like kneading dough." My family is very conservative and traditional, so Rolfing was a very difficult thing for them to understand. They still don't understand, but they don't bother me about it now. Many of the other members of my family suffer from back problems but, because of their rigid religious beliefs, refused to consider Rolfing.

The biggest thing Rolfing did was to teach me a lot of lessons about myself. I grew up in a fundamentalist religious background. It was very rules-oriented. We had a lot of back problems in our family. My brother, father, mother, aunts, and uncles also all had back problems.

When Mr. Cass told me about Rolfing and what it would do, I explained it to my mother who really didn't understand. My family saw Rolfing as some kind of Eastern philosophy, which, in our religion, must be shunned. Fundamentalists are supposed to stay within their own confines, be separate. This strictness in my religion was a problem for me. When I started Rolfing, I explained what it was and my family kind of turned up their noses. I'm surprised when I look back on it that I even started the Rolfing. It was the first time I had ever broken away from or questioned what I had been taught. Even though there was nothing wrong with Rolfing, it went against my family. It was something that came along when I needed it, and caused so many other things to happen. I think I was meant to be Rolfed at this time.

Briah talked with me while she worked on my body and helped me realize that the pressure I was under was causing my physical problems. The degeneration of the disc was due to rigidity. I was pounding it to death trying to live up to everyone else's expectations, always doing well in everything I tried. I never seemed to get upset, but I knew that inside I wasn't really happy, so I felt like a hypocrite.

I worked a lot on self-image in those sessions. I had to learn that it was okay to be myself. I am definitely a perfectionist. This is one of my biggest problems, and I have to work on it constantly.

I put a great deal of pressure on myself in graduate school to be the best because I wanted to be the one that went on to the "Big Career." It was difficult to learn that I could still be a fine person and not have to be the best in graduate school.

Fundamentalists have to work hard to keep their natures under control. Some things in my nature just don't fit into fundamentalism. And yet, I can't feel bad about that. I am a deeply religious person and have since become a member of a liberal congregation which believes in God but also that we are in control of our lives and, with God's help, can live them well. I think a person has to be completely open to what is happening in order to get all the benefits of Rolfing. Briah said, "Some people are Rolfable, and some are not because they don't want to work with me." I had to learn to let go, to relax and to feel my body. I believe successful Rolfing depends on how open a person is. I remember being particularly withdrawn during some of the sessions. On those days, I wouldn't get as much benefit from what Briah was doing.

Each time Briah worked on my lower back, I experienced a lot of pain. But as I learned to relax and release the tension I had been carrying around, I was able to bend over and move. I hadn't realized I was creating that tension myself because I was not in touch with my body at all. When the doctor discovered the degenerating disc and bone spurs, he told me to do anything I could to increase flexibility and that he hoped the disc would regenerate, and the pain lessen. I believe Rolfing will help.

It has taught me how the problem started and what I can do to prevent it from coming back. Twice since Rolfing, the pain has returned, but I realized both times that I was working too much and putting too much pressure on my body. Now, because of the Rolfing, I've learned how to work with my body every day to keep myself functioning.

One of my goals in Rolfing was to improve the technicality of my playing. In order to play the piano well, it is necessary to be totally relaxed, both physically and mentally. I did an hour's worth of warm-ups each day of technical exercises to increase the speed at which I could do the scales. I use a metronome and have worked for years to be able to move it up one notch at a time, but the day after a Rolfing session, I would be able to move the metronome up three markings. It was incredible.

My piano teacher noticed an overall improvement in my playing as well as my ability to relax.

Maria F. and Linda M., Susan Warden Dancers

Maria F.

I'm in the Susan Warden Dance Company. Everyone else in the company had been Rolfed and used to tease me and ask when I was going to get Rolfed. I was looking forward to it because of the changes I saw in the other dancers' bodies. Linda's chest really opened up and seemed to grow. She was better able to hold her shoulders back and they, too, became larger. At the same time, her arms got stronger.

The dancer is always struggling with the chest, fighting to lift the sternum and pull the shoulders back. It always seemed so difficult—something you had to hold in or push out or manipulate to get that lifted stance. Suddenly Linda was standing taller without manipulating her torso.

I felt the enhanced posture would make it easier to dance because I would no longer have to concentrate on it. I would already be lifted and spread throughout the shoulders and more relaxed.

I noticed that when Karen was Rolfed her legs became longer, less bowed, and she was more sure-footed. Her chest broadened and her back was more relaxed and bigger.

With David, there was a new refinement and suppleness in his dancing as well as more subtlety. He always had very high arches which caused his feet to pound the floor audibly when he ran. He had beautiful feet and Rolfing softened his arches. He could run, jump, and land noiselessly because his arches were more balanced.

The first session instantly gave me what I was most interested in, a lifted chest. Everything seemed to lighten up without my having to use my muscles to lift my chest. All the work in the center of my rib cage allowed my chest to expand, and I worked on breathing deeper, taller, and wider.

I used to sleep curled up; because if I slept flat, I would wake up in the morning with an aching back. Now I can wake up flat on my back or my stomach and my lower back doesn't ache. Dancing is my daily life. I teach or rehearse or perform. The physical changes from Rolfing have increased my confidence as a dancer which carries over into my confidence as a teacher. I'm able to trust myself to teach correctly because I can see it in my body. Dancers train their eyes to see dance and movement, and what I see reinforces what I'm feeling. My students can see it, too.

One of my students has also been Rolfed. She's a masseuse and dances for physical exercise. I'm able to help her integrate her Rolfing even though she did it several years ago, because I'm able to show her the placement of her upper body, her shoulder girdle, and her arms when she's dancing. We discovered one day in jazz class that she had been pressing her shoulders down in front of her rib cage and that it was giving her cramps in her arms.

I've been with The Susan Warden Dance Company for the past four years. Susan always does work on the floor that uses the arms, such as pratfalls—where you fall and catch yourself with your arms—and handstands. This year my arms look stronger because of the Rolfing. I feel like they are getting bigger and releasing more energy when I work.

In the profile photographs taken before Rolfing, my shoulder girdle and upper arms seem to drop forward. The After pictures show my head up, shoulders square and the arms dropping directly down rather than to the front.

My legs appear longer and lifted. My knees and ankles are in a straight line. My entire back and neck are longer. My right hip, which looked higher than the left before, is now down and more grounded while my left shoulder is opened back and on the same plane as the right shoulder.

My eyes look out of my head differently. Before, I looked up to look out. Now I'm looking straight out. My whole body is centered, and I look as if I'm really stretched through space even though I'm just standing.

Being a dancer, I watch my body very closely and have noticed many changes due to Rolfing. My dimensions from side to side, top to bottom, and front to back are more in line. Because I'm more relaxed, that alignment has been much easier to achieve. This has made a big difference, especially in ballet class which used to be such a struggle for me.

During Rolfing, my body always called out for the next session. Something would start to hurt and Briah would say, "That's what we"ll be working on next week." I think my body was eagerly awaiting those adjustments and dancing became more challenging and rewarding.

The Rolfing also helped me adjust to some emotional changes—to resolve the residual feelings of fear I still had in my body. I don't feel like I'm vulnerable to those anymore. During the seventh and eighth sessions I pulled something in my inner thigh and shoulder, and it seemed like everything hurt. I'd been dancing a lot. We had a big performance coming up, and I didn't want to feel like this. I couldn't even turn my head to the left. After the eighth and ninth session, I felt so much better. The eighth session was on my hips and legs, and it released the pressure on my back and gave me vitality. The ninth session released the pull in my back and lifted me up. The discomfort was gone!

Rolfing is maintenance for dancers because they use their bodies so much. I think pain is experienced before an injury and that being Rolfed right at that time can realign and release all those places that are tense and pulling so that injuries don't get worse.

As a teacher, l can observe a student's body structure and be able to predict where they're likely to have injuries. I can see the places where they are limiting their dance and movement and can help them become aware of these "holding" places and the interrelationship that takes place when the rest of the body has to compensate for the symptoms of weaker areas.

I discovered this interrelationship through Rolfing and am now beginning to work on the cause of a weak area rather than the symptom.

I now have a better ability to talk about alignment and the proper placement of the hips or direction of energy that the body should take to support it. This heightened awareness of my own alignment has been helpful in working with my students.

The members of the dance company are still integrating the changes from Rolfing. Each individual opened up and changed. And as we've all released and broadened, we've come to a better understanding of each other. After the Rolfing, we can go back and dance and work better as a group.

This is especially important in contact improvisation, which depends on knowing the people you're working with and being able to trust them. Being extremely sensitive to the quality of the contact and support builds a network or mesh. The more the group works together, the more woven and secure the mesh becomes. This security allows each individual to take more risks, which causes the performance to be more exciting and spontaneous. Incredible things can happen within this mesh.

Karin and I were talking the other day about how, as you work with other people, you are always reweaving that fabric, reweaving, reinforcing, reconnecting. When we're away over the summer or when the group forms again, we have to reconnect, reattach, refamiliarize ourselves with each other and open up to the new things we each have to offer. We're continually reweaving that fabric and making it stronger.

David O.

I began Rolfing on the recommendation of one of the dancers in the company I perform with. Eventually, the whole dance company is going to be Rolfed. I was interested in improving my dancing but was delighted to find that Rolfing also helped with my singing and acting.

I was taking weekly voice lessons as I was getting Rolfed and immediately saw a dramatic change in my voice. My range increased a little under half an octave. I made better friends with my "break," and I got up into my higher register. I was really pleased with that. I also developed a larger lung capacity and more energy.

I was hoping to get in touch with some emotions that might come in handy in playing roles. I did break down a couple of times and cry in the sessions, but I didn't flash on anything in the past, which I thought would happen.

I can see many of the benefits of Rolfing in my dancing. I've always had very high arches, which I thought was an asset. People were always complimenting me on how well I could point my foot. It wasn't until Briah was working with me that I realized that a high arch was a handicap in some ways.

My arches are more relaxed now. Before the Rolfing, I would make noises. When I ran, you'd hear bump, bump, bump over the floor. Now I can run quietly.

Briah did a lot of work in my shoulders which has really helped. I had a very inflexible shoulder socket and was not able to lift my arms as high as most dancers. Because dance is so leg oriented, it wasn't until I had been dancing for maybe eight or nine years that I realized I needed to stretch my arms, too.

I was also hoping for more flexibility in my arms. It hasn't improved as much as I'd like, but Briah assures me that if I keep working, it will come. I've been very lucky as a dancer because I haven't had any leg injuries. I've broken fingers and an arm. I've had pains in my shoulders and couldn't move my arm in a certain way without having it pop. I've had a lot of stiff necks, but I could always keep dancing.

I still have several goals to achieve with Rolfing. For example, my shoulders are still askew in the After pictures. I'm going to be

Susan Warden Dancers in action

in Dallas/Ft. Worth next year and Briah has recommended some Rolfers there I can work with.

When I first heard of Rolfing, it sounded more like a release of old tensions. But I didn't understand the primary goal of Rolfing is realignment. I'd thought it was deep massage for the purpose of reliving past events, but that was a misconception on my part. A friend of mine had a bad experience with Rolfing. Her first response was that it was very painful. That's not the first thing I would say about it. I've talked to her extensively and finally convinced her that she was Rolfed by somebody who didn't know what they were doing, and that my experiences were very different than hers. During my weekly sessions with Briah, I did as much work as she did. I would move part of my body while she was working against it. It was always on the breath, and it seemed a very natural thing, sort of going where the body was supposed to reach, as opposed to working against the body's natural occurrence.

A lot of people have never heard of Rolfing. I was lucky to have heard of it when I was studying acting. I'm sometimes surprised at how

Susan Warden Dance Company
Maria, Linda, Karin, David, Susan

many theater people don't know about Rolfing. It seems like a therapy tailor-made for theater people. Then there are people I can't imagine knowing about it who say, "Oh, yeah, I got Rolfed."

Rolfing has been a great thing for me, and I'm looking forward to the post-Rolfing work, too.

Sandy D.

I think the first time I heard about Rolfing was in the movie "The Longest Yard." There was a scene where a lady was doing something with her elbow to a guy screaming in pain. I thought they must be really blowing this out of proportion.

I got a massage for a Christmas present years ago, and the masseuse talked to me about Rolfing. I said I had heard it was painful. She told me that she had been Rolfed and sometimes it hurt and sometimes it didn't. A friend of mine took a body mechanics class and would give me a massage using some Rolfing techniques. I really wanted to invest in Rolfing, but the raises didn't come through. I actually went out and got another job and finally did have enough money. I was really excited and ready for Rolfing. I'm studying to be an opera singer, and it takes tremendous preparation.

The Rolfing has really helped. I was so locked up and tight before Rolfing, and now I have the posture, control, and the nice line of gravity that I had been working so hard to achieve. It's as if I've skipped half a year's worth of lessons.

My voice teacher was amazed and impressed. She even sent another student to be Rolfed and is considering it herself.

I approached Rolfing more from the physical standpoint than the emotional, although I had heard that it could be a very emotional experience. That turned out to be more true than I expected. While Rolfing helped a lot with my body, it also addressed the emotional baggage I had carried with me.

During the first session, the Rolfer worked on my legs and I remember them stiffening, almost like being paralyzed. It was energy releasing. I got off the table and my whole center of gravity had shifted. I actually did feel much more centered. I wasn't leaning back. I was straighter.

The most significant thing that happened to me was when the Rolfer was working on my left leg, which had been broken right above the ankle. It's always been terribly painful when touched. I didn't realize it, but it was really twisted, and my whole left side was lower than my right side because I was protecting my left leg. When she worked on this area, it was intense. I felt frightened. Briah would ask, "How old do you feel?" I was afraid to let go, but she helped me get through it. She never asked me leading questions, but helped me to express all of my negative feelings. I was able to scream, cry, and let all of my anger out.

I've always had a thing about not getting angry in front of other people. My dad used to get mad, and it was a negative experience for me. Expressing anger publicly made me feel very vulnerable. And here I was, flat on the table, naked, just about as vulnerable as you can be, getting really angry. I screamed and cried and Briah kept saying, "Keep going, keep going." I didn't want to let this stuff out, but I kept going. I felt so much better afterwards. It was like some part of me that had always been upset was suddenly at peace. Afterwards, the side that she worked on didn't hurt nearly as badly. I've always known that the body and the emotions are really connected, but somehow this experience made it concrete.

This was a real turning point after which I was able to release a lot of emotions. At this time, Briah suggested that I get into therapy. I took her suggestion and it has been really good for me.

Between Rolfing, chanting, therapy, and a Feldenkrais workshop, I left no healing stone unturned.

The next big session, which I think was about the seventh, dealt with my shoulders. I had a cold or the flu and throughout the Rolfing so much energy was coming out that my limbs were started feeling paralyzed. Energy was just coursing through my fingertips. It didn't scare me. I had learned not to be afraid of this, but it was amazing how strong the feeling was. The room was warm, Briah's hands were warm, everything around me was warm, but I was shivering and so cold I could barely maintain consciousness. We decided to delay that session, since I was sick. I came back the next week to finish it and once again began to feel paralyzed. Briah asked, "How are you feeling? How old do you feel?"

I felt very young and wanted to yell, "I want my mommy!" I think I was reliving birth, in the birth canal. It was dark and warm, and I was constricted, frightened, and possibly hyperventilating. My mother had complications during her labor. She thinks they gave her the wrong kind of drug by mistake which left her unable to push, so the doctor had to use some old-fashioned metal forceps to pull me out. I was reliving this experience. I was very angry. I was mad at the doctor and mad because the lights were too bright. It seemed so impersonal and I wanted my mother. I realized how important it was for my mother to be there, but she was asleep so there was no nurturing quality about my birth. It was just a clinical event.

I saw this entire theme of unnurturing throughout my life. I was not nurturing myself and wouldn't let others nurture me. All these things clicked into place. At that point Briah said, "You can give yourself a nurturing birth now." She was working on my shoulders and I felt, literally, as if my head were out of the birth canal, but the rest of me wasn't out yet. So we went further. Briah put her hands on my head and told me to push against her hands. I was pushing and felt as if I were giving birth and being reborn, at the same time. Suddenly I was letting myself nurture myself, and it was like cleansing away that old experience. I felt as if I could start life fresh. It was a solid, deep experience. Afterwards, I felt contented, peaceful and centered in a way I had never felt before. It was one of the most nurturing things I had ever done for myself.

I called my mother that week and had a really long talk with her. She didn't say much, just listened to me, and I felt close to her in a way that I hadn't felt before. I understood a lot of things she had done for the first time.

She's getting divorced from my dad, and we talked about their relationship, things that as a child I had never seen, and how she felt. I see my mom as a person now. I've always felt love and sympathy and affection and understanding, but not empathy. That was something that changed.

I noticed a lot of physical changes, too. In the photographs taken before Rolfing I was knock-kneed, my right side curved out, and I was much broader in the right shoulder than the left. I was standing as straight as I could and yet my shoulders were very rounded. After Rolfing, my chest is expanded, my shoulders are squared, and there's a big difference in the left/right relationship of my body. I imagine a picture of me now would show even more differences. I think more changes occurred after I had completed Rolfing than when I was going through it.

I feel a great difference in my breathing now. Before Rolfing, I would struggle when singing as if I were bent over and locked shut. My chest was constricted which made singing very difficult. A lot of this constriction and tension was caused by emotional issues. Coming to grips with certain things and beginning to make peace with them made a big difference. My teacher noticed a great deal of improvement and was impressed.

I also had to go out and buy new shoes because my old ones didn't feel right. I can't wear hard shoes anymore. When I first began Rolfing my husband would say, "Six hundred dollars! What if this thing is dangerous?" He's supportive of the Rolfing now. The more changes he sees in me, the more curious he becomes and the more he likes the idea of Rolfing. He has noticed how much calmer I am now. He respects Rolfing and would like to try it. I hope he will, because he has asthma and his lungs are hyperextended.

Rolfing unlocked so much for me. Positive things are happening as a result of it. Even though I've finished the sessions, I am still growing and expanding. It's still making a huge difference. I attribute my progress and successes of this year entirely to Rolfing. Before, I was struggling, and now I'm zooming along at the speed of light.

Linda M.

I was the first person in the dance company to get involved with Rolfing. The physical changes that resulted were so dramatic people noticed them immediately. The Rolfing process was one of completely letting go and allowing myself to be myself. Being a dancer, I learn by doing, and it's difficult for me to make changes in my life without making changes in my body as well.

Before Rolfing, I read a book entitled *Body Mind*. It described my own physical condition perfectly and I thought, "How can this author know me so well?" I knew that I needed to integrate my body and mind and that Rolfing could help me do it.

I went in for my initial interview with Briah. We spent a long time talking about my injuries and surgeries. I was the classic accident-prone child, followed by years of dance-related injuries and compensations. As it happened, the next client canceled, so I was free to have my first session immediately after the interview.

It was really interesting. I had always seen myself as being pear shaped because my hips were out of proportion to my chest, rib cage, and shoulders. After that first session, my shoulders had widened so dramatically that everybody commented on it and asked if it had been painful.

The only pain I had found during Rolfing was in my right arm which would become uncomfortably numb from shoulder to fingers. It became very obvious a lot of the holding was going on in my arm.

Rolfing brought up emotions that I thought were buried. My mother, who is a very bright, intelligent woman, has put herself aside for our family. This became an issue for me.

Why? Because suddenly, I was beginning to resemble my mother physically. After the session on my hips, I went home and I hated myself. I wanted to pound myself. I told Briah I looked like my mother. She had wide hips from bearing six children, and the Rolfing had freed up my hips so now they looked like hers.

The epitome of a ballet dancer is, of course, no hips at all, so I was very upset.

However, there was a benefit because the internal rotation in my legs increased.

Linda's performance shows her incredible balance and flexibility.

Suddenly I was letting go of my negative body image and the tendency to disassociate my emotions and my brain from my physical self. I had a high level of self-hatred, and at one point in my life was anorexic. I was five feet eight inches tall and weighed ninety-eight pounds.

I wasn't able to integrate with myself. I could have discussed it on an intellectual level for a long time and not gotten anywhere because I integrate by doing, and working through the Rolfing process brought about the integration.

I thought the changes would stop with the end of my sessions, but what I find is that each month my level of strength, acceptance, and security in my physical abilities improves. I finished Rolfing three months ago and just recently noticed an increased capacity in my lungs. So I know that the changes from Rolfing spiral and continue because I've seen it.

Other dancers in the group have had significant changes as well. Karin has had remarkable integration through her pelvic area. I had always felt that she had been dancing in pieces. Karin has a body structure which allows for very little external rotation in the hips. Her legs were a separate piece from her pelvis and with that came a shortening through the torso. Every time she would try to rotate, she would pull into herself. Now, with release, she connects between her hip and leg and uses all the rotation she does have.

Susan is a pretty integrated dancer, strong dancer, even with all the compensations that she has. She's come back after her pregnancy, and I'm amazed at how fast she's been able to regain her extension ability and create a more integrated flexibility/strength ratio. She's always been very strong, but now she also can use all the flexibility she has.

Before Rolfing, most people saw me as a technical dancer, very efficient, and a quick study, but not emotional. Now I am finding that "play" between the two types of dancing. I'm so thankful that I found Rolfing at a time when I can use that balance in my performance. Not only is my physical performance better, but I also have more emotional range to express myself.

I haven't put on any weight, but I've softened dramatically. I've opened up in my shoulders and rib cage and grown an inch. I look stronger and broader. I talk about Rolfing to everybody, and if anyone says it costs too much I just say, "It's worth it, because it really helps."

Kathryn M.

KATHRYN G. MAJOR

When I was a undergraduate in California, I had a friend named Mary who had gone to the University of Milwaukee, where Rolfing is close to being a requirement for theater students. Mary and I were doing a show together, and one night she walked into the dressing room looking as if she had lost about ten pounds overnight. I mentioned that to her and she said, "I just had a Rolfing session." I was amazed that it made such an obvious difference.

When I came to Kansas City, the movement teacher in the graduate program talked about Rolfing, and we read a few books about it.

I had very bad shin splints from ballet work which caused a problem with my movement class. My movement teacher suggested Rolfing to address my condition. She said that maybe I could get some spot work done on my legs. I made an appointment with Briah. She explained that she didn't do spot work, but I could certainly do the first session, and if I didn't like it, I didn't have to continue with it. There was no pressure to continue. I didn't have to do all ten sessions, and the more I thought about it, the more excited I became to begin.

My first session was wonderful. We concentrated on releasing the upper body and breathing deeply. I came out of the session feeling as if I were walking on air. The increase in my breathing capacity proved a real help with acting. After the second session, I got very sick. I had cramps, diarrhea, and felt awful. I called up Briah and asked what was going on. She said to relax—these unremarkable symptoms usually happen when we work on the spot where we're holding our main tensions. Release floods your system with toxins that were in those cells and your body has a reaction to it. "Drink a lot of water, take vitamin C and you'll feel better in a couple of days," she advised. And sure enough, in about three days, all the symptoms went away.

I found Rolfing to be a great experience and would have kept going

Kathryn playing the Wardrobe in Beauty and the Beast. *Heavy costume piece!
This role definitely led to a Rolfing tune-up session.*

after the 11 sessions, but Briah said it was best to wait 6 months to a year after the first series to give your body a chance to settle and adapt.

So I took some time to let my body adjust to the changes. Over that period, I got a lot of positive comments from faculty members and fellow students who were very interested in what I was doing. They noticed, too, that I was a lot more friendly and outgoing and that I expressed myself better.

Part of that was because I was getting to know them, but there was also a part of me that didn't care about being a perfect person anymore. I decided to act the way I wanted and say the things that needed to be said.

When I perform a role, I incorporate the physical mannerisms of the character into my own body so that after a show, I am holding tension in different parts of my body for different characters. For instance, when I was understudying Laura in "The Glass Menagerie," she has to limp. I realized that my muscles could get used to that pattern, and it would be hard for them to go back to a normal position again.

So when I finished a show, I would get Rolfed to clear the remains of a character out of my system. That helped me move on to a new character. If I can keep myself in prime condition all the time without having to wait for things to accumulate, it's going to be a lot more beneficial to me in the long run.

I have a quality that appears very flexible to a director. I can take an idea they have for a character and know how to put it in my body, producing something that meets their requirements. I believe this ability stems from an awareness of my body and its holding patterns. Rolfing has given me this awareness and it helps get me jobs.

I've talked to a lot of actors who say they've heard Rolfing was painful. I tell them that it didn't hurt me, but that they have to decide for themselves about it. If they're really excited about Rolfing and eager to do it, they will relax at the right times and it will be an easy thing for them.

I intend to continue Rolfing, using it as a finishing process. I want to maintain the positive changes I see in myself.

Karin R.

I've always been interested in Rolfing, and when Linda came into dance rehearsal one day and said she was going to get Rolfed, I thought, "Wow, that's wonderful." Then she mentioned that Briah was interested in Rolfing the entire dance company, and I thought that would be great.

When I went in to Rolfing, I was hoping it would make me feel taller and more alive. I also wanted to get my legs straightened out because they were bowed which made me look funny when I was dancing. I was sure Rolfing would help.

When I was little, I was pigeon-toed and wore corrective shoes until I was four or five. Now when I stand, the weight is distributed evenly on my feet rather than falling to the outside. It's interesting trying to get used to the feeling that everything is centered. I'll be doing something like brushing my teeth and can't believe that I'm completely balanced on my feet.

I've also noticed that when I put on a pair of shoes I haven't had on for a while, they feel uncomfortable because of the way they've been worn on the heel. Now I feel as if I need to get new heels on all my shoes.

My legs feel a lot straighter and make much nicer lines when I dance. I'm much happier about the way they look. There is also much more open space in my shoulders and arms and more range of motion than I ever noticed before. I used to feel as if I had blockage points that didn't allow me to express myself as much as I could have. Now I feel these points releasing and am hoping my legs will become more unblocked in time. It's just going to take a while because of all the "warping." There was always a kind of space between my legs that bothered me because I thought there was nothing I could do about it.

Then I discovered Rolfing and my legs did change. I would never have thought it was possible. Even if I lost ten pounds, it would not have made my legs look any different. But Rolfing did.

I think everyone should be Rolfed. I wish my whole family, especially my dad, could be Rolfed. As a matter of fact, I think everyone should try it. Linda, who is the ballet instructor of the dance company, has mentioned how much she thinks my legs have improved and that my torso is so much more open and in line with my body. I feel I have so much more space to breathe with now and that's an eye opener.

Karin is able to express beautiful movements without pain

I don't think I ever really thought of this before, but I remember times when my brothers and sisters would make me so angry I would hold my breath until I turned blue. It's funny to make that connection now, but I'm sure that must have a lot to do with my breathing.

I have also noticed that I have more stamina for dancing. Doing three or four pieces used to take a lot of energy. The difference after Rolfing is really apparent to me in terms of the increase in both my mental and physical energy level.

There have been so many changes in the way my body reacts. I remember after the first session I went to the movies and that the movie seat was not hitting my back right. I was really uncomfortable. I also used to walk around with my head down, but that's not comfortable for me anymore either. So I've been changing that and feeling more open to the world. I'm having fun going out and reexperiencing walking—just the simple act of walking down the street and what it feels like.

Katherine W.

I was afraid of Rolfing for three reasons. First, I would have to take off all my clothes. Second, I was sure I would be invaded, and I had fears about that. Third, the possibility of tapping and releasing memories I had buried terrified me.

I had been thinking about Rolfing for six months and wanted to know the specifics. Was it painful? What happens? I was doing my own research to build up courage.

I had been in therapy for a number of years and had reached the point where I needed to connect with my process on a physical level. I felt that Rolfing could be the vehicle that would allow me to burst through some of the psychological barriers I had erected. I needed to look back on my childhood to understand why I was having so many physical problems as an adult. I had had several surgeries for endometriosis, which is very painful. My back and neck bothered me constantly, and my body was very constricted, especially my shoulders. Part of that may be due to the fact that I'm a professional photographer and have to lug around heavy equipment.

Rolfing made me aware of how I had locked myself up physically. It was my inner child's way of surviving, of protecting myself. I've spent most of my life in that condition, but with therapy and Rolfing I've been able to pull my mind and body back together. The hardest thing for me is allowing physical contact. I never realized it before, but I didn't let people touch me. I was totally detached from physical sensations.

My mother abandoned me when I was about eight years old.

Actually, she abandoned me in the womb. I was an unwanted child. I had no adult support, no mother-daughter or father-daughter contact, no holding, touching, or hugging. There was no verbal communication or positive reinforcement. No one said, "I love you," or, "You're a good person." They just didn't have it to give.

So I grew up in a physical body that was a bundle of fear. My muscles retracted. I withdrew from my environment and lived in my head.

I walked out of the first Rolfing session with more physical awareness than I had ever had before. I could feel my feet, my legs. I was no longer broken into sections and disconnected.

Each session brought me closer in touch with my body. Midway through the Rolfing, I developed a lot of anger and experienced it in therapy as well. I started letting go of old ways and released a lot. Anger was probably the biggest emotion I had to deal with, and I'm still dealing with it.

The session I feared the most was the seventh session, the head session. I was able to discover the amount of tension that I had in my face, especially around my mouth. It wasn't painful like I feared it would be. I could breathe more clearly because my sinuses had opened up. I started looking at myself in the mirror after that session, and I liked what I saw.

For the first time I was seeing myself in a new way, and wasn't seeing this ugly broken little girl. My facial structure had changed. I was seeing an adult, a woman.

My body is still going through changes. Sometimes I will notice when I've been asleep that my leg turns out. When it starts to go back into its old pattern, I worry, "Oh, no, I'm sliding back into that old space." I believe the body does have a memory and that Rolfing doesn't completely change it. You still fall back a little bit into who you were before you were Rolfed. But it's easier to integrate now.

I didn't stand up straight before. I was contracted and looked heavy, tired, and probably older. Now I feel lighter. I'm standing taller. Sometimes I feel I'm walking straight, and sometimes awkwardly. Briah explained my body is still integrating these changes; that there is an unwinding process. And there are points in the process where I feel oiled and together and other places where I feel clumsy. At one time I had scar tissue from my endometriosis surgery that went from my ovary to my lower intestine and caused a lot of pain. These areas were contracted within my body. I think the Rolfing released that tension. My periods are very short lived, light, and painless. Sometimes I'll get a sharp pain, but it's not like the old pain. Things are still working down there, still releasing and letting go.

I pay attention to my neck and shoulders and am very aware if I let my shoulders stoop. I was so ashamed of my body I used to slump to hide my breasts. Now I find myself wearing clothes that define my body. I'm getting more comfortable with showing my body, which is ironic since, even though I had done a lot of nude modeling, I hated the way my body looked. When I look at myself in the mirror now, I'm not attacking myself like I used to.

I haven't lost any weight, yet my clothes fit differently. They fit better around the waist. My jackets and blouses are a bit tighter through the chest because I'm standing straighter, more uplifted. My shoulders used to be rounded; my chest was caved in and collapsed.

I'm also changing professionally. I had been blocked creatively. Before Rolfing, I was living separately in my mind, body, and spirit, so everything I photographed was somewhat isolated and detached.

One of the goals of my Rolfing was to help me tap into my creativity again, maybe through photography, writing, or sculpting. I know Rolfing helped with that because I'm seeing things differently and am more in touch with my feelings.

Now I'm doing more portrait work, which requires a lot of interpersonal communication and a tremendous amount of trust and touching. I am able to get beyond my own personal space.

I used to have a shell around me, but I've been able to chisel away at it so it isn't as thick, and I can be more sensitive to others. I feel more comfortable artistically. I haven't painted for ten years because I thought my ideas were blocked. I used to paint or photograph something, and I always felt as if it had to be a masterpiece. I was doing it to please the world, not me. I'm not so hard on myself now. I'm doing it for pleasure—getting all kinds of ideas and not putting all these judgments on them.

I'm moving, which is a big transition in my life, and I'm going to be involved in direct sales for the company. I'm going to be dealing with museums and libraries and connecting with people in the arts. It's going to be a whole new field—a whole new kind of energy. And it feels very right. It feels like it's time.

Scott Allan Barker, The Prodigal Son, *Kansas City, 1989*

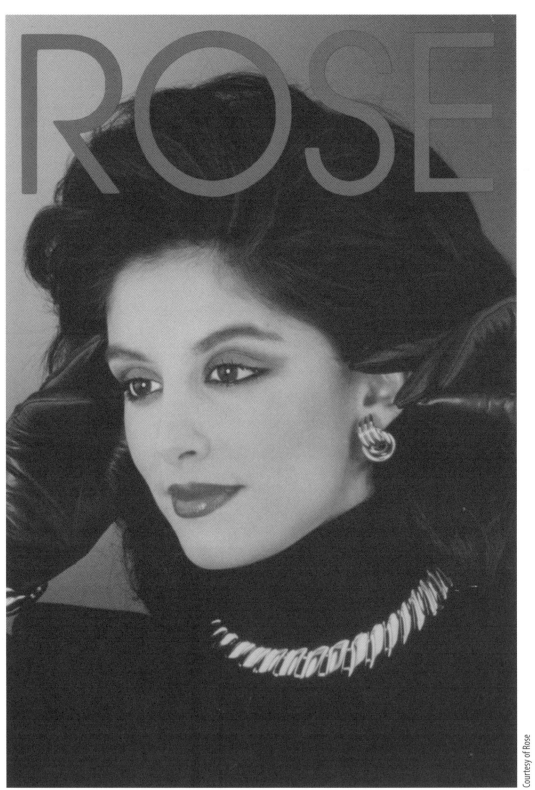

Rose, professional model

Rose S.

Maria, a friend and fellow model, first told me about Rolfing. She had scoliosis and said Rolfing had straightened her spine out. "Now, I feel wonderful," she said. I had also been diagnosed with scoliosis and had lost close to an inch in height. Even though Maria's experience was so positive, it still took me a whole year to get aggravated enough with my own body to seek out Rolfing.

During that year, I had been going to a chiropractor because my shoulder was constantly bothering me. I thought it was the model's bag pulling me down. The chiropractor would help for a while, but it would take two days for me to feel good. That feeling would last for about a week and then I'd be back where I started from. The same pain would return—the same out-of-joint feeling. I got to the point where I decided I had to do something permanent and decided to find out more about Rolfing.

Before the Rolfing, I remember being beside myself with tension and anger. My dad had been ill; my grandmother was dying of cancer; I didn't like my marriage or my in-laws; and I had just had a baby. It was such a change for me. I came from a modeling background where I was able to get up and go and be anywhere, anytime. Suddenly, I felt like my shoes were nailed to the floor. I had a lot of internal problems.

Now, nothing matters to that degree anymore because the tension and anger no longer stick inside of me. People don't aggravate me as much, not because they've changed but because I've become more accepting. I think that constant pain aggravated me to the point where I didn't have tolerance for anything. Now, I'm more comfortable with myself, and I can be more comfortable with everyone else. I'm not in pain, so nobody else has to be a pain to me.

I used to have severe colon problems. If I ate nuts or popcorn, I would pay for it hours later with cramps. That's gone now. A lot of things have healed themselves. Many of these problems were stress-induced, and I've kept most of that stress at bay.

Modeling is a very physical type of profession. You work with your mind and body. When you're working, you think about where your body is, how to make it more attractive, what the purpose is in showing clothes or demonstrating how a shoe looks or how a garment fits. You have to think ahead because the photographer shoots frame after frame. You have to keep thinking and moving. They'll ask you to do an instant replay, and you have to remember where your body was five seconds ago—was your hand on your hip? It is very taxing mentally and it isn't natural.

Photographers always say, "If it's a really uncomfortable position, then you know it's right." The positions are not natural. You have to twist your torso and hold it steady for long periods of time.

A model will go on the set, and the crew will be setting lighting, doing a slow exposure, and they'll say, "You're going to have to hold that." And you're stuck for hours in one position, sitting in a chair where the clothing is perfectly draped and you can't move. You can't just pop up and say, "I'm not comfortable. I have to switch." You may be stuck on one hip until your leg goes numb underneath, and some of the work can be very detailed. It's exhausting and probably not very good for your body, but it's what I do for a living.

Rolfing has helped me balance it out more easily. I don't come away devastated after a shoot. I just breathe it all back again—take a nice, cleansing breath—clean out all the cobwebs and stand up straight. It always comes back—the way I'm supposed to line up. Before, I would get off a set and my leg would hurt for the rest of the week. I bruised my elbow one time because I had to sit with my head on it for an hour. I don't have that problem anymore. I have integrated it so I can breathe out that tension and get rid of it. My body doesn't retain a character position like before. I can go back to what it's supposed to be.

Without the Rolfing, if I bent over for a long time, the act of pulling up and standing up would be so much more painful. It would stay with me for the rest of the day, like rigor mortis. With the Rolfing I have much more flexibility. My body is stronger now. I also have a lot more inner strength and stamina that I can rely on. I used to get out of breath, and now I can jump into anything, and it doesn't show the effects it did before.

I once went into a fitting for a show, and the client mentioned my right shoulder was lower than my left shoulder. I didn't even know it, that's how out of tune I was. Even being more in tune with my body than most people, I had never looked at my structure. It's one thing to look at the shape, but I had never looked at the framework. There was a good half-inch difference in the shoulders.

When I looked at the Before and After Rolfing pictures, Briah showed me the *linea nigra*, the natural line that runs up the center of your body. Mine was more pronounced because I had just gone through a pregnancy, so it hadn't faded yet. I could see the curvature better and asked, "Well, what do you think that is?" Briah said, "That's where your body is out of kilter. That's the way your body is going. It's not straight."

I also felt pulled, more from the right than the left. My shoulders were completely turned in, depressed, and concave. And my upper back was curved. Perhaps a person in their 60s would have that type of profile, but I was a youthful 31. And I took good care of myself. I exercised and tried to eat well.

I'm one of the top five models in this city, and in this business you learn to take care of your body—the skin, the hair, keeping your eyes clear, your teeth nice. You become very conscious of taking care of yourself. I haven't gone out in the sun in ten years. I don't eat chocolate or junk food, and I don't go snow skiing because I might break a leg. I'm very in tune with the demands of my profession. Yet this physical condition is something that came with the territory. It's not something I did and am now trying to correct. It's something that probably developed at birth or when I was very young, and I grew up with it. It was a natural part of me that I had overlooked.

Once I put the clothes on, especially those with big shoulder pads, it's camouflaged. Other than the nagging pain I would have in my right shoulder, neck, and mid-back and between the shoulder blades, I didn't even connect with the problem. I can't imagine I went through life that much out of alignment and never noticed it.

If I hadn't gone through the Rolfing, I would still be seeing chiropractors every two weeks. No matter how much I'd try to jam those bones into alignment, the muscles were just going to pop right back out. I just thought I had moving bones, never thinking that there was muscle connecting these bones, that there's fascia connecting the muscle to the bone. I never took the time to explore why I felt like this until I ran into Maria one day and the light went on. I realized, "I'm out of alignment. There's something bad going on here. I'm a whole inch shorter, and I can't just attribute it to the energy that's gone out of me."

And I did get my inch in height back. I see so many people that need Rolfing, and I don't know why they don't try it. I think it's the time

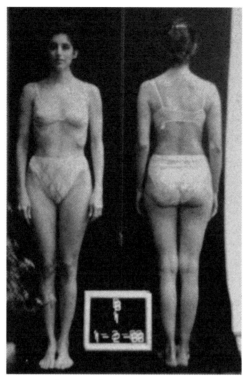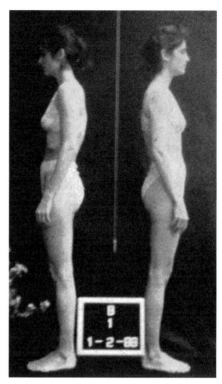

Rose, Before Rolfing

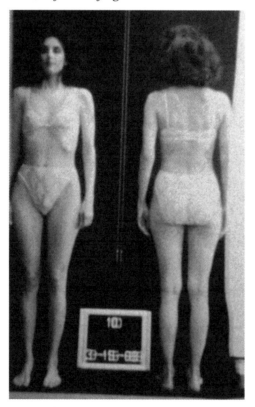

Rose, After 10 sessions

and investment or they don't have the right information. They want an instant cure, a cortisone shot, which to me is painful. It can't be the cost-effectiveness. I spent far more with a chiropractor than I ever spent with Rolfing, and I'd still be paying for a chiropractor. It would be the same if I were going to an orthopedic doctor and getting cortisone shots. I would have spent the money 20 times over and still have the pain. So I don't think it's the expense. I think people want to get rid of their pain instantly.

When I was Rolfed, I thought it would take a long time for the pain to go away, but it's a fast release. The muscles get stretched out; you move things around, and the pain is gone. You work on a part, and it feels better immediately. Rolfing is definitely the most direct and least painful of everything I've tried. It also seems the least radical. I went to a chiropractor, and believe me, when they start popping your bones and cracking your back, you think, "This is too much. It can't be good for my body."

Rolfing Reflections

"I had been diagnosed as having scoliosis and had lost close to an inch in height," says this professional model. "The constant pain was aggravating me to the point where I didn't have tolerance for anything," says Rose.

In the Before Rolfing pictures, Rose has a "tired" posture, and it seems to take a lot of energy for her just to hold herself up. She has rounded shoulders, a forward head posture, and curved back.

In the After photos, Rose's shoulders and back are straight and strong. Her neck and head are more supported, and she looks a lot more confident and self-possessed. Rose regained her inch in height and was better able to handle the tension in her life. She had more energy and felt less pressure on her back.

"My life runs at an even flow." she now says.

I don't know what images people have of Rolfing—maybe that the Rolfer comes in with a bat and beats on their muscles—but it's a very controlled, very slow process. It's not snap, snap, snap.

I've noticed I'm not as tense as I used to be. My energy has a better flow, nothing gets kinked up, nothing gets held up any place. I should be under a lot of stress with two babies under 20 months old and with my demanding professional life. I might get a call at 5 p.m. and have to be at work at 9:00 the next morning, maybe in St. Louis or another city, and I'm trying to make connecting flights and arrange transportation at the last minute, as well as finding someone to take care of my babies. So it's very stressful.

I used to "stroke out" trying to get everything done. Now I just go at my own pace and everything falls into place. The Rolfing has changed that part of me. It's also changed a part of me that was angry. I'm not angry anymore, and I've adopted a whole new theory. I used to be a very sympathetic, empathetic type of person, wanting more for the person than they wanted for themselves sometimes. A lot of that stuff has been released. I've taken the weight of the world off my shoulders physically and mentally.

I don't have the pressure on my back anymore. I think anyone who's bent over like a little old lady is going to be bound up and crabby. Nothing can be pleasant when you're like that.

Rolfing did an awful lot for my mental state. Everything is connected, and my life runs at an even flow. Not every day is wonderful. There are certain problems with every day. But they certainly don't affect me like they used to. I still get the same amount of things done, if not more. I probably get more done now with less stress.

At the end of the Rolfing series, I found out I was again pregnant. Briah worked on opening my rib cage and giving me some length, more expansion along the back and the ribs. I never got that I-can't-wait-to-have-this-baby feeling; there was plenty of room for him. After the pregnancy with Philip, I stayed thinner. I didn't gain as much weight, and I had a lot more energy. People couldn't believe how great I looked, and I felt terrific. Even though the second pregnancy was a C-section, the next Cesarean was actually less taxing than the first one. I think I would have done a lot worse with a C-section delivery if I hadn't been Rolfed first. During the surgery I was so tense. I tried to relax. I started deep breathing and was able to let go just as I had done in Rolfing. The pregnancy was wonderful, but Philip kept turning on his cord, and the distressed fetus syndrome caused the need for the C-section.

Three months after having the baby, I came back for two more Rolfing sessions. It was actually more about body awareness than the first series of Rolfing. I felt things open up. This time, I could instantly tell where my body was aligning. I could even sense the sensation of the tissue opening up. It felt rather strange. I could feel one side of my rib cage all bunched up, and the other side where we were working was where it was supposed to be. I was surprised after what I had been through with the C-section and nursing that everything could come together that fast. I would bring the meditation techniques with me when we worked—taking a nice big breath, filling my chest cavity, and becoming more in-tune with my body.

There are many models who are substantially taller than I am. But when I photograph, I dwarf them; I become "extra bigger." That's called "carrying a photo." If there are three models on a set, there's always one that carries the energy of the photo. I can do this. I go with the adrenaline and feel the blood flowing. I'm thinking sharply; I'm thinking ahead, and I'm carrying the whole photo. This is something totally visible. It's looking at the photo and asking, "Who looks confident? Who is selling it? Who has the bright eyes?" It's the difference between just looking like you're there and really being there.

I am a lot more creative now after the Rolfing work. I'm more in sync with what the photographer's doing. The connections feel stronger. My attention is all there. I'm not drifting off someplace else. I get a rhythm going with the photographer. A lot of times on the set, the models will run through the same poses and motions they've always done. I'm a little freer, not intimidated with trying something new.

The biggest thing we fight in the profession is feeling inhibited and shy, afraid to do things with our expression. This feeling makes every move stiff. It's much easier to shoot if you're a little more fluid and if the photographer is more relaxed. Now I can get that concentrated, focused effort, move easily. I just get up there and flow, and I connect with whoever is at the end of the camera.

Right after I was Rolfed, I was probably in the best condition I had ever been in since Michael, the first baby, was born—size wise, looking good in clothes, the balance between the upper and lower body, the whole bit. Everything was more connected for me. And right out of the blue, I mean out of far left field, came a phenomenal client, and they were sold on me. They wanted me for their whole campaign, for the entire year. And the campaign turned out to be wonderful. It was an editorial image. Not just selling a blouse. It was a good shoot and a good opportunity, and I was much more relaxed. It was more about personality and energy. That's what they were looking for. They wanted someone who was so relaxed that the photo would look like a pretty woman in beautiful clothes was caught out in the forest or a girl in shorts with a sweater tied around her neck was riding on the handlebars of someone's bike. That's much more spontaneous than anything I'd done since I was 15 or 16 years old.

You have to be completely loose, connected, spontaneous, and comfortable with yourself. And you have to know yourself very, very well. This is the real artistry of my work. The other type of work is very mechanical and technical. But now, I've been able to add flow to the technical parts as well. I look forward to going to work. It has become more enjoyable, more fun.

When you're in pain, you're totally affected by it. Every part of you is consumed with that pain. Everyone thinks you have to make such a drastic move to be Rolfed. I wish I had done it long ago. I found that it was far more helpful for me in much more than just the physical aspect. It's worked for me on many different levels.

When the tone of the soft tissue is balanced,
there is a sensation of lightness in the body.

—*Ida Rolf*

Athletic Performers

Brian Orser, professional figure skater

Athletic Performers

P. Tractman

Nanette L., black-belt Aikido instructor

Professional athletes and performers often have high pain levels. "No pain, no gain" is their motto. One world-class runner remarked that athletes probably have forty different words for pain, just as Eskimos have fifteen different words for snow. Athletes often train themselves not to feel the pain because they feel they won't be able to excel. They're masters at concentration, blocking out everything but the performance. I often find that professional athletes are afraid to restructure the body, or fix the pain, because they are afraid it will affect their performance.

By restoring their bodies to proper order, Rolfing offers them greater potential, freedom from chronic pain caused by their body being out of balance and at war with gravity.

Athletic Performers

Craig Swan, pitcher for the New York Mets

Chapter 13

Can Rolfing Enhance Athletic Performance?

Mark W. Pflughoeft

Men's gymnastics coach, University of Wisconsin-Madison
Note from a coach on Rolfing

Bret Saberhagen

Pitcher for the Kansas City Royals and two-time winner of the
Cy Young Award (1985 and 1989)
"I think if somebody got Rolfing done, just an average person,
they're going to feel a lot better about themselves, and they're
probably going to have a lot more energy. I experienced that
myself."

Sara C.

Swimmer
"No matter how hard I tried to breathe on both sides, I always
gagged and choked. I just couldn't get the air right. After just a
few sessions, I could breathe on both sides comfortably; having
increased range of motion, more flexibility and no pain was a
dramatic change."

Alexi Grewal

Cyclist, Olympic gold medalist, member of the Coors Cycling Team
"Rolfing helped make my body more pain free."

Nanette L.

Black-belt Aikido instructor

"I didn't expect much, because I thought I knew all about my body from Aikido, but lo and behold, my eyes were opened."

Craig Swan

Former pitcher for the New York Mets and currently a Certified Rolfer

"I truly believe if I had been Rolfed earlier in my career, I'd still be pitching today. It's ironic that now I'm a Rolfer working on the same thing that ended my career."

Brian Orser

Figure skater, Olympic silver medalist (1984 and 1988), World Champion (1987)

"I know my body better than ever, and I think the Rolfing helped me become more aware of my body. It made me feel compact, like a cat ready to spring. It became a part of my system."

Mark W. Pflughoeft
Note from a coach on Rolfing

East Indian sage, Krishnamurti, defined human intelligence as "sensitivity." Krishnamurti thought that one must be able to feel or read one's physical, mental, or emotional sensors from an extreme sensitivity base in order to react with extreme intelligence.

The process of Rolfing is a sensitizing experience that helps bring one in tune with one's body. It is a study of and a practical application on "What one's body was made to do." Its emphasis is basic body alignment through correct positioning and use of one's muscles.

In athletics, one develops an appreciation for sensitively re fined, basic body movement. The benefit of spending hours and hours on "basics" is that athletes will eventually develop a wide base of correct movement that will allow the development of more advanced skills with relative ease. Metaphorically speaking, the athlete will widen the base of the pyramid of knowledge so that a new height of learning will be reached by the pyramid peak. Rolfing then will aid those who strive to naturalize or idealize their movements, and with Rolfing a sensitivity to very basic physiology will develop. Rolfing makes conscious those physical problems that have arisen unconsciously. It then goes on to remedy those old physical habits and, in doing so, it opens previously undiscovered sources of energy that then create changes, not only on the physical level, but often on emotional and mental levels as well.

—*Mark W. Pflughoeft*
University of Wisconsin-Madison
Men's Gymnastic Coach

Bret Saberhagen, Pitcher, Kansas City Royals
1985 and 1989 American League Cy Young Award Winner

Bret Saberhagen

Bret started the Rolfing series in 1986. He was suffering from arm and shoulder problems, muscle strain, and tendonitis. Bret didn't really have good alignment before he was Rolfed. He had a curve in his back, a tipped pelvic position, and his shoulders didn't really have anything to sit on. This misalignment was causing him to be off center. After he finished the ten session series, he returned a year later for an additional three sessions. In July 1990, Bret had a series of five sessions as a general tune-up and to facilitate surgery and recovery on his right elbow.

I had heard about Rolfing from my agent. I was having some problems with my knees at that time; they were constantly getting sore. My agent told me about a guy he went to out in California. I was leery at first. I didn't know what to expect. I thought I would lay on my back and get a massage type of thing. I only had one session with the man in California. After a few days I was feeling better, and I didn't go through all ten sessions at that time.

In August of '86, I was having arm and shoulder problems, including tendonitis and some muscle strain. At that point, I was all messed up. You come into Rolfing because you have wear and tear on one part of your body or another, and after a while you have to readjust that particular muscle. It might not necessarily be where you're hurting. It could be somewhere else that's affecting you. The spot where you feel pain isn't necessarily where the pain is coming from. Like right now, I feel it in the top of my shoulder, but I think the pain is coming from lower down.

Rolfing gives you more of an idea of how your body works. After each session, you feel more comfortable about yourself. The way you walk, the way your body is programmed, you realize the way each muscle is in tune with all the other muscles. After the tenth session, it took me a while to recuperate. It takes some time after you're done with the Rolfing work to relax and let it integrate, to work your way slowly back up to par. It takes some time to build up the strength you had.

It's amazing the way you feel. The soreness you have when you get Rolfed is a good soreness. Everything's getting unjammed, things just seem to get tight and tense, and after the session's over, you feel better.

It takes a day or two for the soreness or stiffness to get out of there, but it works its way out.

Regarding pitching: one thing that started feeling better first was the arch in my foot. Once that started feeling better, my knees, hips and shoulders also started feeling better. It was a progression up my body. I think my arch being sore might have caused my knee to be sore. And my knee being sore might have caused my hip and shoulder to get sore. So it's a kind of "trickle up" theory.

Once I started getting my body back in tune and feeling better, I could definitely tell the difference in my pitching. Mechanics were a lot smoother, a lot more at ease. Once your body starts feeling better you're more at ease, more focused, and things just seem to happen easier.

For instance, the one thing I try to work on is my tempo, having the same flow all the way through, not being too quick or too slow. Once my tempo starts becoming consistent, my arm's going to find the same spot pretty much all the time. My release point is going to be the same. When something starts aggravating me, it starts throwing off my tempo because I'm trying to make up for wherever it's affecting me, compensating for that loss of rhythm.

The other big thing for me is not throwing across my body. If my hips are jammed up, it's going to be tough to get them open. You don't want to throw across your body, but you also don't want to fly open, that is, open up too much. It's a fine situation. There isn't much margin for error. You can get away with doing these things, but in the long run your arm's going to be hurting. It's going to hamper your mechanics. For the most part, you're going to make some mistakes with a few pitches and end up getting hurt by them.

When things start hurting, you try to compensate, and that's usually when you come up with some problems. The day-in day-out general aches are something you have to put up with. Most pitchers realize the different kinds of soreness in their shoulders. You realize whether it's a general ache or a surgery-type injury. When you go out there, your arm is not going to feel great every time. I can generally tell when I'm going to have the velocity I need on a certain pitch once I get to the bullpen. I can tell how my body feels and how my legs are feeling.

Consequently, I work a lot on my legs, doing as much running as I can. But it seems as if my shins hurt and my knees hurt when I'm running, so I also try to get on the Lifestep to get my legs strong. I lift light weights, a lot of repetitions, three to four sets, for my arms. And I do some Theravan for my shoulder.

After a game there isn't much we can do. Right after I get done pitching, I throw some ice on to take off the swelling or any inflammation that's built up from all the use. The following day I get on the Lifestep again, do a little bit of extra running with the team, come back and do my arm weights—a lot of things to get the blood flowing and get the arm back into throwing shape for the next time out. A lot of my conditioning is working on the whole body, like working on the legs which power the rest of the throw through the arm.

I throw around 100 pitches a day. When I get up to 125 or so, I get tired. I usually don't get more than 100 to 130 pitches on the mound. Warmup is about 60 pitches; you start off slow and work up to how you'll be throwing in a game. In between innings, I usually throw nine pitches. Depending on how many innings you go, you could throw 200 plus pitches in a ball game. After throwing that many pitches, I feel pretty exhausted. I really feel drained.

It usually takes me about four days afterwards to feel like I'm ready to go again. The day after, I'm very stiff and that's why I try to get a lot of blood flowing back, starting with my legs and working back up into my arms. When I'm doing my running, I'll be pumping my arms to get some blood flowing there. I do a bit of throwing, probably some long tosses, to try to get out the stiffness and get the arm back in throwing motion. My entire body is tired. But I feel the brunt of it in my shoulder and arm.

At certain periods of time, your body starts feeling like it needs something. Rolfing is a good thing that has come across in my life and that I feel helps me out from time to time, such as when I'm feeling soreness in one area where a trainer can't really help me out. The soreness might be in a shoulder, but a lot of times that's not where the problem is occurring. I don't think a trainer does the job that a Rolfer does. The advanced Rolfing sessions I had were basically a tune-up. There was a lot of wear and tear throughout the year on my shoulder, on my right knee, from pulling and twisting on it. It's basically like preparing for seasons. You've got to get your body prepared. After the initial ten sessions in 1986, I came back a year later for three sessions.

Bret Saberhagen

Colin Braley, courtesy of Bret Saberhagen

The thing is, as much as we travel, it's tough to have somebody there all the time. Our schedules don't really allow it unless the person travels with us. As far as when to be Rolfed, I think there's no time like the present. It doesn't matter what walk of life you come from, I think it's going to help you out in whatever you do, because different people use different muscles. When I watch TV, I will see an announcer holding a microphone or carrying a camera. They're using some muscles to do that. After a while, they can become stiff and sore.

In July of '90, I had surgery on my right elbow. The surgery was basically to break up a lot of tissue build-up. I had some tendinitis in my elbow, and I was feeling some aches and pains that I needed to get rid of. At that point, I knew I had a lot of time to rest and relax because I knew I wasn't going to be doing any throwing. In surgery, they removed a bone fragment about the size of a grain of rice. It wasn't as large as some bone fragments can get. Usually when you find one, you find a few more, but all I had was one. It wasn't really in a spot that was affecting me, but it could have in the future. It could have gotten to a spot where it could have rubbed up against a ligament and done some damage.

I recovered from the surgery faster than the doctors thought I would. But I always expect to come back from injuries as fast as I can, and I'm sure the Rolfing helped me out. I did two Rolfing sessions before surgery and three afterwards.

I talk about Rolfing a little bit to my teammates and colleagues. Everybody has their own theories or feeling about things. I know of a few ball players that stand heavily by Rolfing. Tim Leary and I have talked about it quite a bit. Tim actually told me of a few different Rolfers around the league I could contact if I ever had problems. My wife, Janeane, was having some headaches. Her neck was getting stiff and tense. It was caused by everyday tension, from having two kids running around, trying to keep up with them. After her first session, she felt a big difference. She had three or four sessions. After she had it done, she understood anybody could go in and get a few sessions, and it can make a big difference.

Anyone can quickly feel the differences, the changes that come about from Rolfing. As soon as you get off the table, you notice your walk has changed. Rolfing puts you back in a good frame of mind, and you're going to look at some Rolfing photos and say, "It's hard to believe that's what I looked like before and what I look like after."

Rolfing isn't like massage, where you sit down and it relaxes you, and it's going to feel good for that day. With a Rolfing session, you're going to feel more intense work on your muscles. You might be sore for the rest of that day, but it's going to help you out for a longer period of time.

Rolfing is good for anybody in any walk of life, because it's going to put you in focus with your body, to realize what kind of beating your body takes from an average day, and not just necessarily an athlete's day. If an average person got this done, someone with a nine-to-five-type of job, they're going to feel a lot better about themselves and they're probably going to have a lot more energy. I experienced that myself.

Sara C.

At the time I was being Rolfed, I was training for competitive swimming. As a child, I was very asthmatic, and from ages 26 to 28 I had to carry around a compressor mixed with medicine. I was dealing with a lot of asthmatic and postural problems and had the characteristic rounding of my shoulders, even though I'm very athletic and have broad shoulders. A Yoga instructor (the director of the Iyengar Institute in San Francisco) once said, "You look like you're afraid of something. Your body posture looks like you're afraid." I felt I must have some fears if I was expressing them physically.

During a Yoga session, I got a cramp in the middle of my back and the instructor asked Briah, a Rolfer, to get the cramp out of me. I found out that Briah was a Certified Advanced Rolfer. I had considered Rolfing 15 years ago, and all of a sudden, here it was, back in my life.

Having met Briah, I decided that perhaps Rolfing would help ease some of the physiological reflexes that cause asthmatic problems. I started Rolfing while I was competing in swimming. I was active in competitions and swam about 2,000 to 3,000 meters a day, 5 days a week, and later after a number of Rolfing sessions increased to 5,000 meters a day. I was active in the master's swimming organization which holds local, regional, and national competitions, as well as international competitions.

After the fourth session of the ten session Rolfing series, I went to the pool to work out. We were doing some distance drills and suddenly I realized that I could alternate breathe now. I had been breathing on one side all the time during my freestyle stroke and had developed problems with the side of my neck and trapezius muscles. I'd had terrible stiffness and soreness in my neck and shoulders. No matter how hard I tried to breathe on both sides, I always gagged and choked. I just couldn't get the air right.

That day, I was breathing on both sides comfortably. That was one of the most dramatic changes. I stood up in the middle of the pool—I didn't even finish the length—and shouted, "I can breathe on both sides" to my coach. It sounds minor, but it was a big deal to me because I was swimming so much. What this meant for me was the ability to do bilateral breathing. It was a real achievement, and I was able to get more out of swimming because I had an increased lung capacity.

When you're swimming 200 laps per workout this averages out to be about 1,000 to 1,200 times you are rotating your head to breathe. Having increased range of motion, more flexibility, and no pain was a dramatic change.

Thirty-three years later at age 68, Sara swims between 2000–3500 yards, 3–4 times a week, 80–140 lengths, which is equivalent to 40–70 laps.

I had been doing 100- and 200-meter events and started competing in the 400-meter individual medley. I was able to do longer distance events, and the Rolfing work brought my time down in the 500-yard drastically. Everything felt better. I went to Wisconsin to the Nationals, and I swam the 500-yard free and dropped my time down to 5:40. I got second place. The first place person is a world record holder, so I didn't feel too bad about getting second place. Then I went to Toronto in 1985 and got fourth in the 200-meter individual medley at the World Masters' Games.

My breathing capacity greatly improved. I was able to expand the whole ribcage, and I could feel the upper thoracic cavity move and expand. I was teaching Yoga at the time and tried to teach my students about that expansion. I would be able to breathe in and feel the whole rib cage open up from the back. Being able to breathe feels good!

In 1986, as I was preparing to go to the Nationals, I was in a car wreck. I had already finished my Rolfing sessions, and it was ten days until the national meet. Someone ran a stop sign and hit my car on the driver's side. It was a pretty severe accident. Because it had been raining, the road was slick, and the car spun around so that I had a lateral whiplash to my neck. I had trained for over a year and a half for this meet! From the scene of the accident, I called Briah, and she came over to the house to help me. She worked on me twice before the swim meet. I wore a soft collar that I had gotten when I was in the emergency room of the hospital and wore it the entire time until I got on the plane to go to the Nationals.

I was really scared to dive off those blocks at the meet. I had to dive head first, and I knew it would be a blow to my neck. But I did dive and managed to place in everything, though I didn't do as well as I would have liked. My distance wasn't as good because I had to lay off practice for ten days before the meet.

Even to this day, I have repercussions from that accident, and it's been almost four years. I come back every year to get a Rolfing tune-up. As I went through the Rolfing, I noticed a lot of changes. As my swimming improved, my confidence improved. I never had any emotional outpourings from the sessions, though Briah warned I might. I had slow, steady growth and was doing nothing but improving. I was also going through many other changes, and looking at other alternative methods of healing. It was a time of great alteration.

The chiropractor who had been taking care of me since 1979 said that I was working within 20 percent of my capacity. I was really working at a very high level of intensity in my training. To me, the Rolfing was one of those things that allowed me to work up to my limit, my potential, without injuring myself.

I wanted to heal the different layers of myself. As we release the body, we also release the spirit. It's like the healing comes naturally when everything is in its right place, like peeling onion layers. You start with a physical structure and work down into the glandular, and then you work down into the spiritual and psychological layers.

I was adopted when I was one month old and became interested in finding my biological parents. I hadn't thought about it much in 35 years, but suddenly I wanted to do this. Two weeks after I wrote the County Juvenile Court requesting information about my background, I got a description of my biological parents. I found out their health history and that my mother's interests were similar to mine. She liked to swim, and I've been a swimmer since I was three, which incidentally was when my asthma started. She was German, and I love the German language and culture. I had been to Germany after I graduated from college. She was musically oriented, and so am I.

I felt as if I had learned something about inclinations, desires, and predilections and finally had some roots. It was good to learn about my parents and to know that they cared about me, the "unborn" me, and felt responsible to find the best outcome for me. I had always been an oddball in my family. None of them had the same interests or traits that I had. They accepted them, but they didn't know where they came from. So it was nice to know why I am the way I am. So, perhaps, that was some of the emotional trauma and burden that caused the asthma. They've found that with asthma, there's a grief component. It had never occurred to me to think that I might be carrying along an emotional disposition from birth.

When you see me now, you would think that I'm the picture of health. But you'd have no concept of how sickly I really was. I was sick every two or three months, and on bronchodilators, antibiotics, antihistamines, and allergy shots. It went on and on in a cycle. I was afraid to leave the house without them. During my pregnancies, I was terribly afraid I'd have to take these drugs because I'd get an asthma attack.

Now, people would never guess I was so ill all the time because I look so athletic. I don't look stoop-shouldered anymore.

I look better, and I face the world better. When your shoulders aren't rounded and you don't have that fearful look, you project a positive, healthy attitude. People see that, and you get feedback on that positive attitude. Everybody wants to approach you if you're healthy and alive and open, but they'll be tentative with someone stooped and looking fearful and withdrawn. I was never aware of looking fearful, but when I look back at pictures of myself, I see that.

Briah also Rolfed my two children, both of whom were in the car accident with me. They both went through the entire series. Teddy has had severe asthma since he was two and had eczema and other allergic skin reactions. I took him to the doctor a lot, and he sometimes had to be rushed to the hospital for adrenalin shots. I was determined that I was going to find a way to help him, without giving him a lot of drugs. It's bad enough when you're sick, but when you see your child heaving on the floor because he can't breathe, it drives you nuts. I felt that if I were helping myself out through Rolfing, I could at least help my child.

Teddy also had curvature of the spine, and his chest was caved in. He had the posture of an old man, with a rounded curvature at the top of his thoracic spine and a sway back towards the lumbar region. His neck was torqued off to one side.

I knew that there were physiological traits that contribute to asthma attacks. We tried a multi-pronged attack on healing Teddy without a lot of drugs. I took him to an osteopath, and we made nutritional changes and alternative methods for healing him.

We took Before and After pictures as Teddy went through the ten Rolfing sessions. His posture is much better now, and his asthma did get much better. He's eight now, and it's been five years since his first Rolfing series. His posture is still much better. I've brought him back twice for some advanced work. At his age, children grow up so fast, and three advanced sessions a year help them continue to grow into the length that their bones are accumulating. Rolfing lets their soft tissue out. Teddy is not at all crunched over, curved, or crooked.

My daughter Emily was Rolfed when she was five. She didn't really have any problems, but I thought since she is athletic and interested in ballet, it would benefit her. She had just a little bit of scoliosis, but it wasn't visible to the inexperienced eye. She has well-developed muscles and an athletic build, but I thought since the Rolfing helped me and Teddy, I wouldn't deny her that opportunity.

When I was in high school, I received some information from the Rolf Institute in Colorado. I remember thinking that I would like to be a Rolfer until I read that I would have to take a lot of science courses and weigh at least 140 pounds. That's not true now, but at the time I just threw the whole idea out the window.

Rolfing came back into my life at a good time—when I was ready to make changes in my life. I was ready to deal with a lot of unfinished business, and determined to get over my asthma and health problems.

Alexi Grewal

Olympic gold medalist in cycling, 1984

Alexi Grewal, an Olympic medal winning cyclist, is currently in competition with the Coors cycling team. Alexi currently works with Advanced Rolfer Ray McCall.

In 1983, I had ten sessions of Rolfing in Boulder, Colorado. I noticed at the time that I had a lot of physical changes. My structure was more integrated, and I had a degree of more efficiency. I am a cyclist, and even though the Rolfing really didn't change the way I rode a bike, it helped make my body more pain free.

I have a high pain tolerance, and during the first ten sessions, Dia, my Rolfer, took it to the limits. It wasn't easy. The restructuring of the body created a lot of discomfort. These first sessions were trying at times. I also went into a heavy training program shortly afterwards and knew a lot of pain and restructuring would result from that.

Starting in 1988, I began working with Ray. I have four or five sessions before the cycling season begins and two or three sessions during the season.

I also train on the bike, and I have a specific exercise program which trains the antagonistic muscles isotonically to the cycling position. This is specifically to strengthen my genetically weak muscles.

When I first saw Ray, I had been pretty severely injured. A non-functional psoas had turned my whole left side into a knot. It was caused by racing without enough base training.

When you push your body to the max without training, it tends to accentuate the imbalance already present and creates problems. I did that in '85, '86 and '87 and felt like my left leg wasn't attached to my body by the psoas and was going to get injured.

My first big ride is in December. I start doing four or five hour rides then and continue through the year. With Rolfing, I don't have to take much more than a day off.

During the first ten sessions, I underwent a deep nervous reorganization of my muscle tissues. Since my nerve synapses were not developed yet and the neural pathways weren't tromped on, they just didn't work. I'm now undergoing a continual neural re-education in my body with the Rolfing and physical therapy.

I believe I gained better balance being Rolfed, but it wasn't something I really concentrated on. I didn't, bingo, have better balance. I think it's a by-product. But Rolfing opens up the possibilities for different neuropathways to be used, and this develops a better balance. This doesn't happen immediately because the neuroreceptors have to be better developed. When the receptors are open and used, they start to fire. Eventually a better body and improved balance results.

As stress patterns are removed or unblocked in Rolfing sessions, I feel lighter and can move with less resistance. There's no doubt, especially in the first ten sessions, that I appeared to lengthen and have more mass.

When I reach full form in the summer, I notice I am more efficient, and my muscles appear to be more supple than the year before.

I think Rolfing is a very individual thing. If a cyclist is basically pain-free and doing well without Rolfing, I don't usually suggest it because a cyclist's body tends to revert to the old patterns or positions.

When I'm working with my team, I will usually recommend a comprehensive physical training program first to keep the body balanced and conform the antagonistic muscles to the correct position. Rolfing will open up the neuropathways and strengthen the body. But without training, the old body patterns will set back in, especially in the case of a cyclist, who always has to hold the head up and look forward, causing an imbalance in the neck muscles.

Relying solely on Rolfing will bring some success, but, after a six-month period, the body may move back to where it started. So I also work with the Pilates system and Mercury machines on basic, specific muscle exercises.

Nanette L.

When I was 18, I started practicing Aikido. I'm 25 now and teaching at two schools in Kansas City. Aikido is very different from any other martial art because the main focus is not to break and maim, merely to get out of someone's way and redirect an opponent's energy. I call it the karma-free martial art because no one gets hurt. Some people say the best defense is a good offense. Well, that's just total nonsense to us. If you're trying to hurt other people, something is wrong. Aikido is a very gentle, free-flowing martial art. Some of the other martial arts can cause back or knee problems, but Aikido is very healthy.

Aikido appeals to people of all ages because it isn't necessary to be big and strong to throw somebody. If you can do this, you know how to use your rhythm and chi, or life force.

When I was teaching Aikido in Columbia, Missouri, one of my students, a professional psychologist, told me about Rolfing and how wonderful it was. I thought, "Oh, great. I don't need a massage, and I'm not going to pay 50 to 75 bucks for one." He spent several months trying to get me to go, and finally, because of chronic back pain, I decided to try it once. If I didn't like it, I wouldn't go back. I scheduled an appointment with a man named Mark, who was fresh out of Rolfing school. I didn't expect much because I thought I already knew all about my body from Aikido, but lo and behold, my eyes were opened.

The first session was incredible. I felt wired afterwards. I had so much energy. He worked on my chest and rib area and all this air came rushing into my lungs. My ribs were expanded and I felt like I could really breathe for the first time in years.

Some of the Rolfing was uncomfortable, but I knew I was releasing a lot of tension and it was great. I loved it. When I walked out of there, I could take in three times the amount of air. I was energized for weeks after that.

The next sessions were less intense, and the experience was more subtle, but I noticed many changes. My posture was improved. I've always had this kind of pouch in my belly, even when I was underweight. That started to straighten out because my posture was getting better. I could stand straight without any effort or tension. My clothes

Nanette L., black-belt Aikido instructor

fit and even though I gained a few pounds, my pants seemed looser. I
believe my shape was molding itself correctly to my body structure.

When Mark worked on my feet, I felt a lot better. I've been injured
there, and it's a sensitive area. Sometimes I would laugh hysterically. It
was very uncomfortable, but I could feel the energy being released and
see the changes in my performance when I practiced Aikido. I noticed
as I'd turn, move, and hop that my feet were making better contact with
the mat, especially when I landed after jumping. My weight would find
a comfortable place very quickly. My balance was so much better. My
neck relaxed, and I held my head up naturally.

The Rolfing process with Mark took a year, and the changes in my
body were incredible. About two years later, between a difficult relationship and a stressful employment situation, I felt that I was falling back
into my old postures and habits. I had a list of little aches and pains,
things that were starting to go wrong from my toes to my head, and many
stressful things were coming together. Being Rolfed seemed to be the best
thing I could do for myself at that time. So I came to Briah.

She did a lot of work with my legs and knees, and I could feel an incredible difference in how they were tracking, moving smoothly without the joints rubbing together.

I also feel more comfortable about my abdomen, hips, and certain other parts of my body. As a child, I had gotten some negative messages about my body. Rolfing helped me develop a positive self-image.

My reactions to Briah's Rolfing have not been as intense as those with Mark. Her technique is more gentle, but also I am older now and have already worked through and released some of my most intense emotions.

In the first ten sessions with Mark, I had more turbulent reactions emotionally. I went from feeling ecstatic in some sessions to really disturbed in others. I felt fear when Mark Rolfed my feet. I've always been injured there, and it's a scary area in my body for other people to touch. Sometimes I would laugh hysterically when he would Rolf my legs and abdomen. I could not stop laughing, it was such an intense feeling. Again, I was remembering things from when I was little. I was putting different aspects of my life together. Images would come to me. When I was Rolfed in my solar plexus area, I had a dream that night about this Indian dying in a field. He had an arrow stuck right there going through him and he was hunched over, dying. I had been hit in that area several years ago, and it was all I could do to hold myself in that position. Until the pain went away, I was doubled over.

Three years later, the emotions are more subtle. I've had three sessions with Briah, and when I look in the mirror now, I can see that my muscles have stretched and my knees and legs are straighter. I don't have the vocabulary to talk about what Rolfing is, what it does and how to describe the changes. But basically I look longer, stretched from my knees to my collar bone. I went for a walk after my third session and felt that my hips were more fluid, not stuck and rigid. I really enjoyed the walk. I would recommend Rolfing to anyone who feels stuck and is ready for a change.

I knew I had some physical problems when I was younger. I didn't know what to do about it. Rolfing gave me a kind of mirror to see myself in. I saw other people balancing their bodies, and even though I practiced and practiced Aikido, I still felt as if I were being held back. After the first session, I firmly believed that Rolfing could help break that rigidity and let me go forward. It was an incredible revelation for me. I wish I had found it when I was twelve.

The main event (of Rolfing) lies with the individual's use of energy, both his own and the environment's. Human energy is evanescent and invisible; it is difficult to define or measure.

—*Ida Rolf*

Craig Swan

*Craig Swan, former pitcher for the New York Mets,
now a Certified Rolfer*

One thing I always worked hard on as a pitcher in the major leagues was
the mechanics. I knew the mechanics and the habits I picked up when
I was younger were stressful to my elbow. But I was young, and my cells
regenerated faster. I thought I could put up with the pain in the major
leagues because a starting pitcher only plays once every five days.

In 1974, my very first year in the majors, I broke my elbow and got
my first taste of what an overabundance of stress can do to structure. I
had a fracture of the olecranon process.

As the injury progressed, the stress shifted from my elbow to my
shoulder and eventually caused a tear in my rotator cuff. I was throwing mostly fast balls in the velocity of the mid '90s when I threw with
my shoulder and upper body. After I tore my rotator cuff, I couldn't
pitch that fast again until I was Rolfed. That was my first experience
with Rolfing. I was in a pretty unique situation because the Mets doctor
didn't want to perform surgery. I had a grade two tear, and we were
going to treat it with rest and a lot of physical therapy.

I had heard about Rolfing from a beach bum friend in St. Petersburg.
He had been in a motorcycle accident and had a pin in his ankle. He
limped for five or six years with that injury and then found a Rolfer
who cured him. I was a little skeptical about Rolfing because I didn't
know anything about it. But I've always thought it's important to try
everything. It doesn't matter what works.

When I went through the Rolfing with Ron Thompson, I had been
in the big leagues for six years. Ron was not only Rolfing me but giving
me movement tips as well. At first I thought, "Wait a minute here. I've
been pitching in the big leagues and this Rolfer is telling me about basic
movement!" He taught me how to take my arm out of the glove, how
to feel my muscles, what kind of texture or feeling I should be having
through my musculature.

He was trying to give me enough length in my joints to create
leverage in a pitch. When you can keep the space in your joint, keep
the musculature fairly relaxed but still use it, you can then get your

Craig Swan exhibiting great pitching form

shoulder girdle and arm away from your body. This creates velocity on the fast balls, or any kind of throw, because it develops leverage. It's not so much a muscular move as it is a mechanical move throw. Since I've become a Rolfer, I try to teach this to most of my clients. It's a most important thing to learn, but it's tricky. Some people can do it easily, and others can't at all.

I truly believe if I had been Rolfed in the early part of my career, I would still be pitching. I started focusing on pitching when I was a 13-year-old kid in Southern California. I went to Arizona State and led the league with the most wins by a college pitcher for about six years and made two All-America teams my junior and senior years in college. I was drafted by the Mets in the third round in 1972 and was doing well in the majors, throwing very hard. The thing that stopped me from playing baseball was a tear in the fascia on my triceps. The fascia grouped itself over a nerve leading down into my arm and eventually tore in 1983 during spring training. It was a strange injury because there was very little pain. I just started losing 7 to 8 mph on the fast ball after about 45 pitches.

A surgeon went into my tricep and found that I hadn't torn muscle cells, I had torn fascia cells. It is ironic that I'm now a Rolfer, working on the same thing that ended my career.

I had a lot of Rolfing after I tore the tricep and recovered faster from my injury than anyone expected. Because of this, I was named "Come Back Player of the Year" in 1982. For the first twenty Rolfing sessions, I went about twice a week. Ron would come up and work on me at Shea Stadium. We usually ended up in the laundry room because Ron had done one session on me in the training room and that was all the trainers could take. They couldn't watch. They thought it was some far-out thing I was trying, and they really didn't want to see people like me getting Rolfed. They felt threatened, as if there were some kind of competition between Rolfing and them. They thought their way was the only right way.

Team owners lose millions of dollars each year to player injuries, and Rolfing is a powerful preventative tool. One of my first goals as a Rolfer was to get the team doctor Rolfed. I would call him every week over the winter, and he just kept putting me off, saying he wanted to try it but would never commit to any sessions. My goal now is to go down to the Mets and present it to the front office or maybe Rolf a trainer.

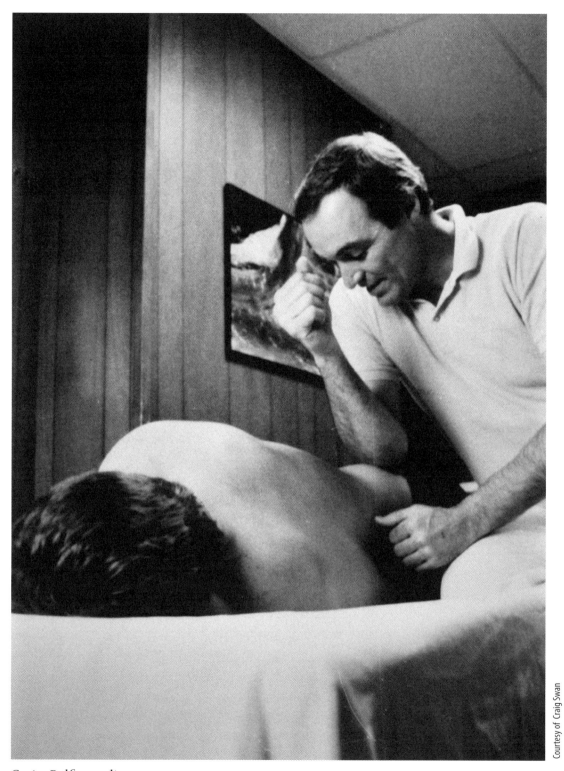

Craig, Rolfing a client

I recently Rolfed a catcher who had been in the major leagues for 15 years. You can imagine squatting for all those years. I got into his hips in the first and third sessions, and he appreciated it, but he went through a lot of pain in those sessions. His hips were very locked up, and he also had knee problems. After the third session, his knee started hurting so badly he had to stop and was put on the DL (disabled list). In the first three sessions of Rolfing, he became much more aware of his body.

He stopped blocking the pain and had his knee checked out by the doctor who found fine bone chips floating in there. He hadn't been owning up to that. He was blocking the pain and doing a good job of it. The Rolfing made him so aware of his body, he realized that he had a severe problem. He had surgery and four weeks later, we started on sessions four through seven. After the seventh session the season began, and he couldn't come anymore. He later signed with another team and decided to finish the series with an Advanced Rolfer in West Palm Beach, Florida. He must be feeling fairly well now.

At the time I was working with him, he was getting his hips through the ball and was grounded into his feet. He had never done that before. He had never really bent his knees and used his legs. Being a very massive person from the waist up, he had always used his upper body for hitting. After he was Rolfed, he doubled his batting average. He was hitting 110 for the first half of the year and 260 the last half. His numbers really jumped. It was hard to try to change the way he had been hitting because he had been successful. He had been on the all-star team for eight years, but he made the changes because he knew his old way didn't work. He was willing to try anything.

Another ball player I Rolfed had a bad back and came in for a few sessions. I tried to do the whole series on him, but as soon as he started feeling better, he quit. His thinking was, "If I'm not hurting, I don't need work."

I think there are a lot of professional athletes who don't understand their bodies well enough to tell where they're putting stress and how to make appropriate adjustments.

That's what Rolfing gives people, an awareness of their body and the ability through movement to make minor adjustments that release stress in their problem areas and prevent further injury. Before Rolfing,

I could read my body the day after pitching and know, "Oh God, did I overuse that!" I felt it all the way from my feet to the end of my fingers.

After I was Rolfed, I noticed an improvement in all forms of movement, especially in running. Pitchers do a lot of running—race and long distance. That became easier for me for the first time in my life. My energy level wasn't being drained, and I noticed that my feet and legs were tracking much, much better. I remember feeling as if I were riding a bicycle when I was doing sprints, I felt so well-oiled, and it was fun to run.

I used to have stomach spasms, possibly duodenitis. Part of that was caused by stress, emotional factors, but after the fifth Rolfing session, the problems went away.

Ron gave me a visualization and I used it quite often when I pitched. I would try to make my muscles feel like rubber, not soft rubber or extremely hard rubber. That helped me to keep my intrinsics in balance with my extrinsics, but I didn't know that as a "Rolfee." I remember tracking my movement, letting my elbow float away and go long rather than contracting or muscling up the ball. There's a point when you take the ball out of your glove and your arm starts to come up and gets ready for the throw. That's the time I'd let my elbow and arm go long.

Practice days for pitchers are usually filled with pain. You throw to loosen your arm up, to find the right mechanism, the right feel to throw the ball. Every time I went out to the mound, it was a new experience. All starting pitchers usually struggle through the first few innings of the game trying to find the correct mechanism, the right feel of a pitch. As soon as we grasp that in the kinetic sense, we can mimic it for the rest of the game.

As a Rolfer, I now try to get my clients to feel the movement by having them produce the movement in my office and have them feel what is correct so they can mimic it outside the office. It's a certain sense of timing, and when that's there, everything is easy. When it's not there, you're all over the place.

It was apparent with the baseball players I have Rolfed that they were trapped in the thought that velocity came from strength. They were still wrapped up in the old ways of thinking and believed they needed to make their muscles stronger rather than use them in a balanced way. They were from the "bulk up to be stronger" school. These guys are plenty big and strong, yet they wanted to be bigger. It made no sense.

Craig Swan leaping a foot and a half off the ground as he delivers a pitch

Here I was, a fairly big person, but my arms were like noodles, and I could throw 95 miles per hour. Most players think if something is sore or weak, they need to strengthen it. As we know, that is not the case. These guys all had injuries, bad backs, bad knees. When you are constantly overusing particular sets of muscles, these joints and tissues get very tight. Rolfing opens them up and gives you the resilience. Rolfing enabled me to know when I was getting too tight and needed more work.

I certainly could have used a Rolfer on hand. Rolfing lengthens the connective tissues and opens up the circulation. Trainers use hot packs, ultrasound, and stimulators to increase circulation, but lengthening the collagen fibers is a better way.

I'm pursuing a video production with a famous pitcher, Tom Seever. Our goal in the video is to explain the Rolfing process. Tom hasn't gone through it yet, and I want him to work with a Rolfer and maybe a Rolfing Movement teacher so he can understand the pitching mechanics. The video is going to be instructional and will show proper mechanics of a throw that reduces stress on the structure and, at the same time, increases velocity. It's also important to work with a proper mindset, so negative and positive factors don't influence performance. If you're a little on the wild side, you don't want to forget the source or the basic movements. You can get a little too tricky sometimes on the mound, especially if you've had some success.

When I went to the Rolf Institute, I was very skeptical about Rolfing. I knew what it had done for me, but I wasn't convinced that it worked. I thought, "Maybe this was an unusual Rolfer, maybe it was a fluke." I always question everything, and I think that's a healthy attitude. It was a good learning experience for me.

I feel grateful to do what I do. I get so much from my work and from my clients. I learn more about people, and it's been a great way to make the transition from being a baseball player back into the real world. I'm with people in a real way. At the Rolf Institute, other Rolfers would say how they would get so much back from their clients. I'm able to understand that now. When I see people wake up with new hope about their lives, it's very exciting to be a part of that.

Brian Orser demonstrating his athletic and artistic talents

Brian Orser

Brian Orser, O.C. (Order of Canada), is one of the greatest competitors in the history of figure skating. Since 1984, he has ranked as the number one freestyle skater in the world.

Orser took skating by storm in 1978 when he became the first man to land the daunting Triple Axel (3½ rotations in the air) correctly in competition. For the next four years, he was the only competitor to land it consistently. It became his signature move. But it was not long before the world realized that there was much more to Brian Orser than a breathtaking jump.

Orser's ability to combine the artistry of his countryman Toller Cranston with the physical prowess of Scott Hamilton has carried him to the very forefront of his sport. The "completeness" of his skating has not only helped Orser raise the sport to a new level, it has also captured the imagination and won the respect of fans and critics all over the world. At the 1987 World Championships in Budapest, Orser won the long program and gave the most stunning performance of his career; he scored three 6.0s for artistic impression. The 1987 World Championship was his last amateur competition. He moved to professional figure skating as the reigning World Freestyle Skating Champion.

When I first got into Rolfing, I thought I would have a couple of sessions just to experience it. I noticed a visible difference the first day. We took some photographs, and I noticed my stance—my ankles and feet were somewhat turned in, and my pelvis was turned back a little bit. I was having a lot of trouble with my lower back at this time also. My neck, shoulders, hips, knees—it just snowballed from one problem to another.

When I was younger, I had some ankle problems. I broke my ankle three times when I was around 15, twice landing and once toeing in for a jump. Other than that, I haven't had any major skating injuries.

I completed the Rolfing series three or four years ago and haven't had any problems since then. Helen James, my Rolfer, is a physiotherapist and a Professor Emerita of Physical Therapy at California State University-Fresno. "Jimmer" was a long-time acquaintance of my aunt, and when she came to Canada, she introduced me to Rolfing.

The Rolfing series was administered at many different locations, depending on where I was performing, training, or competing. I would be skating and would fly Jimmer in to work with me. We would have a session or two, and then we'd go our separate ways and try to meet up again. Often, I would get a session in the morning and perform in the evening. Jimmer was afraid, at first, that the Rolfing work might affect my balance, but I never had any problems.

One thing I did notice was a pair of skates that had fit like a glove suddenly were causing blisters on my feet. I thought that was really strange. My feet had changed a little bit during the Rolfing sessions. My center of gravity was changing. I knew that something was happening, but I trusted Jimmer and knew that everything was happening for the better. It didn't turn me against Rolfing.

A wonderful benefit, particularly on the ice, was a sense of lightness right after the first session. It was great to experience total effortlessness and lightness. But at the same time, I felt very compact and totally in control. I had increased energy, and it took a lot less effort. I found I had extra agility. Compulsory figures are a real test of balance, and I found a difference there, too. My balance was better when I was doing particular turns on the ice.

Compulsory figures count for thirty percent of competition and are very technical. A lot of the time that was my downfall until I started making progress in 1985. After the Rolfing, I felt better doing them. My turns were cleaner; my balance was better; my tracings were better; my foot was steadier. The balance point of a skate blade is like the point of a pencil when you are tracing a pattern. You have to know exactly where the point of the pencil is when you're drawing, and I knew when I stepped on my foot to trace a figure exactly at what point I was standing on.

I'd gotten myself into a rut with the judges. I didn't have an understanding of compulsory figures. I worked three, four, five hours a day on them, but I would just never seem to click. However, my figures did get a lot better, better than the actual placings did because the judges were already used to seeing me at a certain performance level. There was one time when I won a compulsory figure at a world championship, which shocked the world because no one ever thought I could do it. That was in 1987 at the World Championships. [Ed.note: This was after the initial Rolfing series.]

When I worked with Jimmer, we would communicate through my muscles and her fingers. I would suddenly relax when she wanted me to relax. It felt mentally draining because I didn't just sit there and let her work on my body. I worked in sync with her. There were times when she would finish an area and we'd both have to take a breather because it was so demanding. We worked together and the trust had to be there. We felt we accomplished so much. I knew I was making so much progress, even though it hurt sometimes. I mean, nothing comes easy.

I tried to read up on the technical aspects of Rolfing, but to me it was a sensation. That's what I was after. I am more into sensation than what is happening in technical terms. As I got more sessions, it became easier. Sometimes Jimmer and Kathy Robertson would work together on me, and we made a lot of progress then. When we worked for an hour it seemed like two, because there were two people working. They worked well together, and the three of us worked well in harmony. I could feel everything letting go.

I know my body better than ever, and I think the Rolfing helped me become more aware of my body. I always thought I knew every muscle, but I didn't until I did this, until I discovered new things through Rolfing. Now I feel I'm totally in sync with my body. I think I'll always continue to get Rolfed.

When I would come back to Jimmer for the "post-ten" sessions (we called it a "tune-up" because we weren't making any major changes), she would find an area in my body that needed a change and continue to go forward with it. You can always continue to get better and more detailed.

Right after the ten sessions, we were getting into the competitive season, heading towards the World Championships. At that point she stopped making changes. We had some post-ten sessions, but it wasn't the time to risk changing anything in a major way. Everything was going well. I was skating well. I felt really good with everything. It was a time to smooth out the body, get a little bit more lift and length.

During the sessions we did during competitions, Jimmer would work my mind a little bit as well. She reinforced me. Getting some Rolfing an hour or two before competition helped me become more centered. I usually felt a little bit of anxiety, like my mind was racing

*Brian Orser, Olympic Silver Medalist, 1984 and 1988, Men's Figure Skating,
1987 World Champion*

Brian Orser leaping with great ease and lightness

ahead of my body. I needed the centering. There were absolutely no distractions. Physical input is better than verbal input because I'm more of a physical person. I use my body to talk.

Jimmer joined the Canadian Figure Skating Team in 1987. She came with me to the World Championships, to the 1988 Olympics, and to the Canadian National Championships in 1988. We would work together for an hour and a half before leaving for the rink. I've learned to incorporate the Rolfing into that training and preparation for performance. The Rolfing is also a way of warming up for me, helping me to be exact with all this extra energy. I had always felt in the past that I had a hard time getting warmed up, and I would be tight. The Rolfing made me feel compact, like a cat ready to spring. That stayed with me the whole time I was on the ice. It became a part of my system.

I'd do the Rolfing, go for a walk on my own, and then I'd come back and get my costume together. I'd walk through my program. And then I'd get on the bus and go to the rink in a very quiet mood. All of these steps were part of the focusing. It was nice to have that hour and a half of Rolfing because I had no distractions. The room was always very quiet, and I was with someone I really trusted. It was a nice safe place to be, and I was filled with positive energy.

I know some other skaters who have been Rolfed, but they haven't given it a chance, partly because they're always on the run. Getting a session here and there every two months, they're not able to make the connections. Several skaters have been Rolfed by Jimmer, but she is in California, while they're in Montreal or Toronto.

I've actually had more luck educating non-skaters about Rolfing. The skaters seem to be more uncertain and afraid of change. They resist doing something different, which is unfortunate because a lot of them could afford to do it. Ice skating can change a person's body for the worse, particularly the pelvis, ankles, and knees. In my "After Ten" photos of Rolfing, I noticed a big change in my stance and the sway of my back. The pictures were taken using a plumb line which gives you a perfect vertical line. I noticed that I wasn't standing like a gorilla. After the Rolfing work, my feet were closer together and my ankles were more in line with my knees and hips. The line of transmission went through my pelvis rather than around it. I gained 5/8 of an inch in height through the Rolfing. I have changed in clothing size. I used to buy T-shirts in a men's small size, now I definitely have to buy a medium since my chest is larger.

The nice thing about Rolfing is that it promotes expansion. Artistic and creative growth comes from within, and after Rolfing you follow through with an idea. Limitations are fewer because you have so much more freedom and range of motion. Uschi Keszler, my choreographer, works mainly with motion, and Rolfing was right up her alley. Motion and freedom of movement are all part of modern dance. That's why Rolfing and modem dance go hand in hand with the skating, any kind of activity that requires movement. It didn't make me any more creative, but it helped me follow through with my ideas.

I definitely had more range of motion, flexibility, and extension, with side to side and front to back movements. Choreography is not necessarily the actual steps or positions. It's the way you can translate the music through motion and the ability to get this feeling and go with it, with nothing holding you back. It's improving and putting patterns together and seeing what will evolve. I'm one of the few skaters who will improvise. Each night my performance is a little bit different from the night before. Some of the basic steps are the same, of course, and the preparations to jump are the same, but it's a very spontaneous kind of thing.

For example, tonight there were some children in the auditorium with a sign, and as I went by, I'd connect with them. Some of my large, more dramatic jumps happened right where that energy was. It's my way of interacting with the audience. I get energy back from them. It's nice to be able to change a program like that, to innovate and be spontaneous.

When I first started skating, and until I was about 16 or 17, I didn't know I was creative. I started working with Uschi Keszler when I was 19 years old. She found a way of getting all this energy and creativity out of me. She helped me find a way I could be creative on ice. Our stage is so big, and we have the element of speed and flow and balance. All these things are enhanced by Rolfing. You can fill things out, use full range of motion and find total freedom, lightness, and effortlessness. If you can sense it, it will come out.

When I strain or pull a muscle, I bounce back very fast. For what I do and for what I am trying to achieve, I have to be in great shape. I work out a lot, skating, putting myself through my programs, running, doing aerobics classes, and weight lifting. Flexibility is very, very important. I feel great as a result of the Rolfing, but when I step on the ice, if I'm not in great shape, I can tell. Nothing can camouflage that. I feel I can get in shape faster now. The difference between being out of shape and in shape may be a three-week time span, but it's an incredible difference in how my body feels and how I feel about myself and about skating. In Olympic experiences and World Championships, the tension and stress is unbelievable. I had to get up at about 5:30 a.m., and I was on the ice for seven hours a day. It was an intense 12 years of my life. Now that I've turned professional, I don't have to train as hard, my body is different than it was then. In retrospect, I don't know how I did that, how I was so focused. After a competition, I would be laid out for a couple of days. I didn't realize how much pressure I had until the competition was over. Jimmer would detect these problems in my shoulders and neck. She knew where I carried everything and she would try to work out the kinks. I didn't realize how much pressure I was carrying around with me until it was gone.

I love the performing. I see myself doing this for another five or six more years, as long as I'm healthy and in good shape. If you really want to and your body allows you to, you can skate as long as you want. The problem is that the body deteriorates first. There are so many professional skaters that really want to be as good as they were, but their bodies won't allow them to be. Toller Cranston is a great Canadian skater and he still performs. He is 41 and still in good shape. But I have seen skaters lose it physically. They have injuries and can't do what they used to.

Had I not been Rolfed, I would be in big trouble. I am totally in touch with every part of my body, and to perform I know where I have to be. If I start to slip a bit, I work to get back to the place where I can perform well. I think if I didn't have the Rolfing, I would never have gained this sensitivity to my body. I'm really aware when I start to slip, when I'm tight, when the elasticity is gone. And I do something about it, whether it's flexibility exercises, concentrating on my posture, or having a few tune up sessions of Rolfing with Jimmer.

I tend to get tight in my lower back and everything seems to tighten up towards there. I do a lot of loosening up in that area. Every once in a while you find yourself slumping, trying to get air in the body areas. If

I'm wondering why I'm not feeling great, why I don't have that feeling I like, I stand back and look at myself and notice that I'm letting things slip a little bit. You have to work at it constantly.

You have to get the structural change, and then use your awareness to educate your body and maximize your potential. The one thing that turned me on to Rolfing was the freedom I had, the lightness. I felt so much lighter from my fingertips to my toes, all through my joints and my hips. Everywhere I felt light and airy, as if bubbles floated between every cell. And yet, I have a really hard time talking to people about Rolfing.

Some skaters have a repetition of doing certain things over and over. They put themselves deeper and deeper in trouble, structurally. But the Rolfing totally frees you up.

Rolfing also heightened my confidence. When you see someone standing erect, you can feel the confidence they project. It's there. Suddenly, you are confident. You're not trying to be confident, but you just are. People see that in you, and that's important in skating and any judged sport. The judges will see it; people will see it; and suddenly you're a leader.

Before, I was a little bit inhibited and intimidated by others. My skating was an escape for me. But suddenly I could go and meet with certain officials and business people and feel more comfortable with myself. I felt good and looked very confident.

I see myself skating longer because I haven't had the injuries, which I know is a result of the Rolfing. And I know I will be skating longer. I love to skate. I love the sensations. I love to throw myself in the air with control and feel the suspension and sort of caress the ice as I land. Rolfing has helped me maintain that sensation and even improve it.

Helen James, Advanced Certified Rolfer from Clovis, California, is Brian's Rolfer..

Chapter 14

Can Rolfing Help Rehabilitate Injured Animals?

Fred K.

Horse trainer and equestrian
Fred tells of his own Rolfing and the Rolfing of two of his horses.

Rolfing birds of prey

Rolfing a mountain lion

Fred K., horse trainer and equestrian

Fred K.

I was Rolfed several years ago in Seattle, then again in Colorado. I met Briah in Kansas City five or six years ago and was interested to see how her technique compared to the other Rolfers. My first, a male Rolfer, was very powerful and made some powerful changes in me. The second Rolfer was much more subtle and into fine tuning. She was more of a detail Rolfer, and my life was also becoming more detailed and more organized. Briah approaches Rolfing from a spiritual viewpoint and makes me feel and think about the bigger picture. She hits a level of consciousness that makes me think of more important things than my next appointment at work.

How did I get into Rolfing originally? As a horse trainer, I encountered many physical problems. Case in point: It is important when you are on a horse to have a straight line from shoulders to hip joint to ankle. I always seemed to have my feet out in front which caused me to roll onto my tailbone behind the horse's motion and be unable to pull my leg back. I thought, "Wow, I need some real help in changing the way I sit." I looked into lots of things. One was Feldenkrais work which was wonderful, but slow. It works well with Rolfing, but it wasn't enough. It was subtle, but I wasn't getting results. As I was looking into other things, I kept running into Rolfing but was afraid of it because I had heard it was painful.

Finally I decided to look in the phone book and found a Rolfer. I scheduled an appointment and after the first session, knew Rolfing was for me. It did a lot more than get my leg right under the horse. It changed my position and sense of timing. I was more relaxed and could move with the horse. It changed my teaching also because I was able to recognize different movement blocks other people had. I couldn't Rolf them, but I could understand their limits and help them find a way around a particular block.

My own range of motion became so much bigger and freer. I used to have such a closed upper body and shallow breath. Wow, my chest opened up; my lungs opened up. I could smell things again.

I took ten sessions, one a week, and I tell people those were the best ten weeks of my life. Not just looking back but during those sessions, I knew the changes were wonderful, and wondered why I had waited so long.

I had always had a very low pain tolerance. My first ten sessions were powerful, and there was pain involved with each one. I never enjoyed it, but I began to understand that pain isn't so bad and was no longer afraid of it. That was a wonderful and powerful realization. I remember at first that I would close my eyes and go into an altered state. I didn't like that. It wasn't comfortable. I don't even think that is what Rolfing is all about. I believe it is about being here, now and aware. If I kept my eyes open, I could see how patterns and my vision changed.

During my sessions in Colorado, we would focus on a particular group of muscles and go right at them. I would learn different options of movement with each muscle. I would move one knee clockwise or counter-clockwise while keeping the other knee still. I could feel the difference. We also worked on the whole body. If you tell a Rolfer you have a problem with your knee, they will start working on your ear because it's all connected.

I will probably continue to get Rolfed when I have problems or when I am trying to get to a different point in my riding. I use it as a tool to help me with the horses and am sure it helps in other parts of my life, too. I am relaxed after a session and ready to get organized. The Rolfer helps organize my body, but I in turn try to organize my finances, my social activities, and achieve a balance in my life.

Every time I get Rolfed I see, smell, and hear better. I can come in with an allergy and have the sniffles and go out without the feeling of fluid in my face. Everything opens up. Also, I can tolerate the hay, straw, and mold from the dust better after being Rolfed.

After I got Rolfed—the first ten sessions—it was wild how I saw a tree in my own yard I never knew was there. I noticed the fields are plowed in rectangles. I don't think I ever looked at the sky before I was Rolfed. Maybe I saw a star or two, but I never noticed the different patterns in the sky or was aware of the different brightness of the sun throughout the day. I am much more aware of my environment now.

Fred K: Discussion about horses

I've been working with horses since the age of ten. I breed, train, buy, and sell them and am also a professional riding instructor. Rolfing was such a positive experience for me that I wanted to see if it would unlock some structural problems in Petey, a four-year-old mare that I raised. Petey was stiff and tense. She was nervous around strangers, new things, and generally fearful of the world. Sometimes when she was ridden she went under the saddle, causing a splint or formation of calcium on the cannon bones in her front legs. She jarred her legs too hard.

I asked Briah to work on Petey. At first Petey was suspicious of what we were doing, but as Briah worked on her head, Petey's eyelids got heavier and she appeared to be tranquilized. Their rapport began immediately after that. It was a bonding experience for both of them.

As Briah worked on Petey's pole, the top part of a horse's neck, and down the lower part of their neck, I had my hands on the mare and could feel the Rolfing going through her body. We took a picture of her then, and her head, which had been startled and so high in the air, was down below my kneecaps. She had relaxed so much that her head went way down to the ground. This is the way a horse shows trust.

When Briah started working at the top of Petey's shoulder, she needed more leverage, so Briah got on top of Petey and worked downwards on the muscles.

As Briah worked on the side of Petey's neck, the veins became more prominent. I could actually see the blood circulating and her breathing becoming deeper. The barn animals all came over to watch when Briah started Rolfing. She worked for two hours on Petey, climbing all over her and at one point using a ladder to get leverage. It was intense work, and Briah would have to rest for hours afterwards. After five sessions, Petey's coat became lighter and healthier. It remained lighter for the rest of the time that I owned her. In the After pictures that we took of her, she has a longer neck, and her muscles are more pronounced. She's standing more upright on her legs instead of her legs being sort of sprawled out like a baby horse would stand. She had big, thick muscles on the under part of her neck from tensing up so often, and they are beginning to go away. Her neck isn't underslung. She has some pretty muscles coming out on top of her neck now. She's more alert after five sessions in terms of using her ears and eyes, her collar, the way she's standing up. Before Rolfing, Petey looked like a barnyard horse. Now she's bright and alert like a showhorse. She stands base wide, centered perfectly over the tops of her feet. Her legs come straight down rather than spreading out. In the Before pictures, she is standing on the

Petey, Before Rolfing

Petey, After 5 sessions

outside of her feet, like some people walk, and in the After pictures, you can tell that she's standing right over the center, on the tops of her feet. Her weight is shifted back to her hocks, making her look more capable of bearing more weight and producing more athletic movements. Her rhythm at trotting is synchronized now, and, because her shoulders are freed up, she uses them more effectively. Less restriction in her hind quarters has significantly improved her jumping.

Petey really seemed to love the Rolfing and afterwards would be relaxed and appear to vibrate positive energy. As she opened up in the chest, I could tell that a lot of intense energy was being released. It was very powerful.

Now when I ride Petey she puts her head down for the bridle and stands quietly while I tighten the girth on the saddle. Her overall attitude is more amiable. She is more likable and likes everything a lot more.

House

Briah also worked on another horse, named House, because he is so wonderfully big. He's really come a long way. She worked on House twice for several hours each time, and he loves people and was very trusting. House had a terribly short neck that was inhibiting his jumping style and movement. He did learn to stretch out and stretch down into the bit. Before, he was so far behind the bit that it threw his balance off. The Rolfing facilitated the training. Now he seems so huge. I have to stretch my elbows out now, he's so long.

The potential for Rolfing is great. There's a lot of room to do Rolfing with horses. There are a lot of body adjustments and chiropractics with horses at the racetrack. There has always been potential with the riders, because riding is so hard on the body. In terms of Rolfing, though, it hasn't yet soaked in. I don't know many Rolfers that work with horses, but the potential for it is great. The horse has less risk of injury because its body is aligned and more relaxed, but if an injury should occur, the recuperation is quicker. Rolfing also improves the horse's performance, and I know from my own experience that it also improves that of the rider.

I would really like to see Rolfing workshops set up with local equestrian teams. Whether the horse gets Rolfed or the rider gets Rolfed, it seems to help the riding experience. It builds

House looking beautifully Rolfed

self-confidence and creates a sense of well-being that is essential for a good performance. I'm interested in the self-confidence that Rolfing provides, especially with horses. Because when the horses feel a sense of well-being, I think they perform at higher levels. I saw that in the two horses that Briah Rolfed.

Dennis A.

Rolfing birds of prey

In my very first session of Rolfing, the first thing I noticed that surprised and impressed me was the fact that my lung capacity increased between 15 and 20 percent. I was amazed because I was in good shape. I had been doing triathlons and was having tightness in my legs which would occur about 15 to 20 miles into a bike ride. There were a number of things besides my legs that were affected, but that was the most obvious thing. I started seeing changes in my legs after the third or fourth session.

I broke my back six or seven years ago. The break caused a 65 percent compression factor. The vertebrae could not sit on a horizontal plane. They became twisted, so I had a very deep curvature of the spine. I couldn't sit straight. I would slouch after only a few minutes of trying to sit up. Since the Rolfing, there is a substantial difference. I feel stronger. In the past when I ran, my feet slapped the pavement. It was very hard for me to land softly on my feet no matter how hard I would try. It was uncomfortable. Now, about a year after the Rolfing, it's very easy to run. My feet land where they are supposed to.

I've not only found Rolfing to be very beneficial to me and my body, but also I have seen the same type of therapy benefit birds of prey. Any body with muscle tissue can benefit from Rolfing.

Early in the summer, I began working with birds of prey at a petting zoo. One was a male golden eagle that had been shot. The shot was apparently from beneath the bird while it was roosting, affecting a little bit of wing, the main joint on the wrist, and the right side of the skull. With the golden eagle, I was curious to see how depth perception was affected with just one eye. I found there was very little change when the bird flew from the air to the fist. It seemed to land as well with one eye as with two. This nine-year-old bird had never been handled with human hands. Basically a wild bird, it had been kept in a cage but no one had ever handled it.

I started working with the bird, putting some jesses on it. Jesses are the leather bracelets around the wrists of the bird, so you can keep the bird close to you. The bird can be taken outside without worrying about it flying off. It's on a leash just like a dog would be.

Dennis and Desiré, one of his falcons

I worked with the bird about an hour every day. My objective was to get the bird outside so that people could see it fly. Some days I would get the bird to fly to the fist fairly easily. It would go three or four days before it was ready to fly to the fist again. I was using food as the key to training, but eagles can eat a lot of food at one time and then they won't get hungry for four or five days after feeding.

My long-term goal was to get the bird to fly to the glove consistently enough so that I could release him to hunt normal prey, such as rabbits, snakes, mice, and so forth. My hopes and aspirations were to release the bird back to the wild. I had been working with the bird about five months when I mentioned the experience to Briah during my regular Rolfing session.

Cinnabar

Briah had Rolfed a couple of thoroughbred jumping horses, as well as a couple of quarter horses. I thought it would be interesting to see what kind of results would occur with a bird. When I initially proposed it, Briah was a little bit hesitant. Cinnabar was a very wild bird. When I would stroke the bird's neck, he would always attempt to bite me.

I didn't know what would happen or how Cinnabar would respond to being touched. I decided to construct a makeshift hood because I didn't have one large enough to fit him.

There's usually no reason to hood an eagle. Hooding basically calms the bird because he cannot see. I wanted a hood that would work so when Briah started Rolfing the bird, it wouldn't get too excited, biting her or clawing her. The hood didn't work very well, so we decided to try Rolfing him without it to see what would happen.

When I work with a bird, I have a very large, multi-layered leather gauntlet that I made for my left hand. The bird sits on that. The arm is covered about halfway up, five or six inches above the elbow. On my other hand, the hand I would use to feed the bird, I would wear a large welder's glove which is very thick.

For safety, and to try to ensure the best opportunity to actually Rolf the bird, I placed my gloved hand and arm on Cinnabar's perch and then had him stand on my glove. Next, I took his jesses and pulled them tight under my hand so he couldn't "foot" Briah. The feet are the most dangerous part of a bird of prey. The power of the talons going

Note how Cinnabar extends his feathers in a beautiful cape

through the spinal column is strong enough to kill a dog. I'm nervous around even smaller birds, such as redtails, which weigh maybe a pound and a half. The redtail can go through several layers of glove and a quarter inch into the skin. Cinnabar weighs more than 9½ pounds and is about 18 inches tall with a wingspan of six to 6½ feet.

When Briah started Rolfing Cinnabar, she approached the bird from the back. I think she wanted to be as far away from his head as possible. She went behind the bird and underneath the wings into the body of the bird. I was immediately surprised. Cinnabar is very nervous and usually turns immediately to face the person. He didn't do that. He didn't even turn his head around!

When she first made contact, Cinnabar extended both wings and made a loud sound. Briah kept her hands on the bird to maintain control and immediately started Rolfing. It was about 15 minutes before Cinnabar even looked at her. Anytime I would stroke his feet, whether he's on my fist or on a perch, he would immediately look down to see what I was doing. He's a very sensitive bird. He didn't do that while Briah

Cinnabar being Rolfed, obviously at ease with what's going on

was Rolfing him with her hands underneath both his wings. He finally looked around very calmly and acknowledged that Briah was there. He looked back around as if it were just as natural as could be. He continued to calm down, making this frequent "chirping" sound, which he does sometimes when I am around him with food or after he has just eaten. He doesn't do it frequently. However, during the entire two-hour session, he continued to make this sound. It was a very calming sound. I don't know if there is a term for it. His beak was partially open and his tongue was hanging out a bit. It's like a very relaxed talking.

As the bird relaxed, he started to recline towards Briah, even though he was still fully supporting his weight and had his feet in a very powerful grip. This state of relaxation lasted for the first 30 minutes. His legs were nearly on a horizontal plane but still totally supporting his weight. At that point, I realized I didn't have to worry about his "footing" Briah or being aggressive.

Cinnabar was very much in an altered state, relaxing and going with the Rolfing. Sometimes Briah would get into a painful part on the wing or body where he had been injured. The bird would almost "wake up," even though his eye was open. He'd make a high-pitched shrill noise indicating his pain and irritation. It was as if Briah hit a sore spot while working on a patient. He let her know where he was very tender. Cinnabar even flapped his wings a bit. But within a minute or two he was back in the same position, laying back but still gripping and holding himself in a horizontal position.

Briah was struck by the massive and multi-layered musculature of this 9½ pound bird. She said that at times it almost felt like she was Rolfing a horse. During the session, one could almost see how the bird began to relax. His eye was not focused. It was a distant stare, very calm, very relaxed. Several times we would have to reposition him because it was difficult for Briah to bend over for long periods of time. The perch was about two or 2½ feet tall. The bird was about 18 inches above that. So about 45 minutes into the session, I picked Cinnabar up on my arm, and Briah Rolfed him at her shoulder level. Within a few minutes, he was very relaxed and started lying down against me. I had to support him with my chest, because he was leaning against me as if he wanted to lie down. Again, these birds never lie down. The only time they do is in a nesting environment. They sleep upright; they stand upright, all day long and all night long. They never lie down. So when he did, I was a little surprised.

At one point, he laid down on the glove next to my body and his right wing was totally relaxed, lying fully extended, hanging from the glove down past my knees. It was like a cape of feathers. Briah took the wing and started lifting it to work on it, extending it and so forth. The bird behaved as if he were sedated, something more akin to what one would expect from a pet chicken rather than a powerful bird of prey. If I had moved my hand in front of him, he would not have acknowledged it. And remember, this was a wild bird, very alert, very keen. I was amazed. It was beautiful.

Every 15 or 20 minutes, Cinnabar would appear to wake himself up, analyze the situation, and within a minute or two get back into the altered state again. When Briah was working under his wings she remarked how his wings were almost like a shade. She extended his wing over the top of her so she could see underneath.

We progressed down Cinnabar's body. Briah started working on the legs. Cinnabar would have had easy access to Briah's hand if he wanted it. As she worked, he didn't even look down. When she worked on the back of his neck, right up at the top, he put his head down as if he were guiding her. He was very much in tune with the whole process. Briah said that Cinnabar seemed much more appreciative than some of the other animals she has worked with, even though the others had been domestic.

After the session, I fed the bird. I remembered that every time I got out of a Rolfing session, one of the very first things I would have to do is eat. Even if I had eaten an hour before I went in, I was famished. Thinking that it might be the same with the bird, I fed him.

Briah then suggested we have the bird fly to the glove a few times. I told her I would try. However, since he had just eaten, it might be two or three days before he would eat again. I might not be able to get him to fly. He flew three or four times to the glove, which surprised me. I noticed that he landed much softer than he had before. In the past, he would land at the same speed at which he was flying. Other birds I had worked with would use their wings in a braking method, their tails fully fanned. This was the first time he had done it right in the six months I had worked with him. This was about 30 minutes after the Rolfing.

In analyzing the pictures, I noticed Cinnabar was more balanced. The left side looked more like the right side. The bird used to look as if he had bowed legs. One leg went further up into the body and that side of the body seemed turned and twisted a bit. The neck and head were rather short, shrunken into the shoulders. After Rolfing, the rest of his body looked fuller, more rounded and filled out. It was as if he had grown two or three sizes. His weight hadn't changed, but he looked as though he'd gained a few pounds from the way his body had expanded.

Cinnabar's neck was larger, fuller, taller. This bird is very powerful. When he flies, his wings should be fully extended. Prior to the Rolfing, I realized that his wings were never fully extended. The photographs are quite dramatic. They show the improved power of flight after the Rolfing session.

About a month later, Briah had a second Rolfing session with Cinnabar. During that month, he hadn't seemed quite as frightened. He had more confidence. Before, Cinnabar seemed rather timid and weak, not only in his physical body, but also in his overall posture. It was noticeable in the way he carried himself and the way he stood on his perch.

He learned—probably relearned—how to slow down in flight for a stop. Previously he would land on my fist at full speed, knocking me back a step or two. His mass of 9½ pounds, combined with his momentum, forced me to hold my gloved fist overhead to avoid having his wings hit me in the face and head. Cinnabar has a lot more control over his body now. He is more coordinated, more like a bird from the wild would be. They can land softly on anything. There was a gracefulness that he regained. Before the Rolfing, he would come in for a crash landing. The first time or two that he flew to the glove at a distance of six to eight feet, I had to step back to regain my balance because there's so much force and energy coming toward me. During the months after he was Rolfed, Cinnabar would come in and slow down, landing right on that spot. I wouldn't have to take a step backwards.

When we did the second session, it was videotaped by a local TV station. It was a very windy day. With the lifting strength of these birds, it was difficult to hold onto Cinnabar's leash. He would hover right above the glove about two or three inches. It was like flying a kite. The wind constantly threw him off balance. So we moved to work with him around the side of the barn.

Briah seemed more relaxed, having worked with him before. It seemed to take only a few minutes for Cinnabar to get into that altered state again. He recognized Briah, just like he recognized me. He was very calm and very relaxed. I didn't have him on the perch. He laid down several times during that session which lasted an hour or two. We reworked those areas where the injury had occurred. Briah was able to do some very specific work inbetween the joint in the right wing and through the entire wing.

The structure of the wing is similar to a person's arm. Imagine bringing your wrist up next to your shoulder. Your wrist and shoulder represent the thick mass you see on bird's wing when it's folded. The other part of the elbow is actually back below the softer tissue that makes a slight "U" shape from the shoulder to the elbow. When you extend that, the tissue extends as well, stretching and actually covering the elbow that's now extended.

The first time Briah worked with him, she didn't do much with that area. It was very tense and tight. She spent a lot of time freeing up that entire wing structure during the second session. Cinnabar was able to relax and allow her to work in those very sensitive areas. Once when she was working on him, a muscle in his wing twitched and quivered. He was again in an altered state. Briah was able to get deeper. A friend of ours put her hands on Briah's hands. She could feel some of the tissue releasing. I was holding the bird upright to keep him from falling off. By this time, he was lying down, which is very unnatural for these birds.

We had problems getting him to stand back up a couple of times. He was so into the altered state that he didn't want to finish the session. We had to stand him back up so Briah could work on his chest and legs some more. She even kissed the back of his head because she was so comfortable with him.

Before this session, I noticed that Cinnabar's eye was looking really dry. During the session, it started to look shinier, a little more oily. The eye was able to rotate in the socket better. After Briah Rolfed Cinnabar, we decided to try Rolfing an owl.

Rufus, the Great Horned Owl

Rufus is a male owl about 12 inches tall. An owl's normal tendency is to bite. This owl had been injured when it flew in front of a car five or six years ago. Its jaw was broken, and it wasn't able to survive in the wild. It couldn't pull meat apart because the lower mandible was about a half-inch left of the upper mandible. We maintained him on a diet of ground entrails, meat, and bones, which is very similar to an owl's natural diet. These meals aren't as good as live or freshly killed prey, but Rufus was not capable of pulling anything apart. He could not grab prey with his beak because it overlapped so much. Two surgeries had been performed on his beak, which was very thin, almost like a fingernail. Rufus had the best surgical care an owl could receive. When the veterinary school realized he couldn't survive in the wild, they gave him to the zoo for display and educational purposes.

The problem with this owl was his natural instinct to bite. He's ornery. Briah would approach him from the back side and he would nip her. We finally got her a fairly thin pair of leather gloves after she had worked on him as much as possible without them. He bit on a piece of the leather glove like a pacifier, watching what was going on. As long as he had something in his mouth, Rufus seemed to be somewhat content to let Briah work with him. He wasn't as cooperative as Cinnabar

Rufus, Before his Rolfing session. Note the tremendous overlapped misalignment of the beak.

After one session of Rolfing. Notice the realignment of the beak.

had been. Briah wasn't able to work with him as in-depth. She worked with his wings a little and with his body a little. However, Rufus didn't require as much work as Cinnabar because there wasn't as much mass to work with.

Owls have two sets of eyelids. They have eyelids from the side that actually go toward the beak at a right angle. The other set closes from top to bottom. Sometimes Rufus would close one eyelid. Sometimes he would close both. At other times he would close both eyelids on both eyes. He made little sounds. With the piece of leather in his mouth, he thought he was in full control.

After a while, Briah wanted to work with his jaw. This presented a problem since he had a piece of leather in his jaw as a pacifier. Briah used a glove to protect her hands and worked inside Rufus' mouth, try-ing to get the cranium to better fit the mandible. The changes we saw were amazing. It appeared that the alignment of the beak had changed substantially. It had moved three-eighths of an inch. At that point, the right side of his lower mandible would touch the upper right side of his upper mandible. Before, the two mandibles looked like a pair of scis-sors which were wide open.

I had not realized, before the session, the length of his lower mandi-ble. It was actually too long to fit below the upper mandible properly. It occurred to me that, after the session, we were going to have to clip the lower mandible because it's supposed to fit under the upper mandible.

When Briah worked with Rufus' mouth, he made chirping noises. Occasionally, I saw him swallow. At times, it looked as if he were chirping bloody murder. His eyes were saying, "Don't stop." It was very entertaining, very funny. There was no struggling at all. There was no one holding the bird.

His instinct to bite is not as pronounced as it was before. He now seems calmer and less agitated. When a friend of mine works with him, Rufus doesn't seem to want to bite as often. He doesn't seem to want to protect himself as much as before.

Rufus can now take small rodents in his talons, then tear and pull them apart with his beak. There was no way he could do this prior to Rolfing because his beak was so far off. It's a lot better for him to eat more of his normal prey. When an owl holds prey with their feet and pulls it apart, it strengthens the back muscles. It's good exercise, and it helps keep the beak from being overgrown. Feeding Rufus something that's ground up doesn't allow him to stretch those back muscles or keep his beak in proper shape. Filing, or coping, a bird's beak is required when they're maintained on an improper diet.

Working with the face or beak requires two strong people to hold the bird completely stationary. If those powerful feet get loose for an instant, they can grab an arm or something and they don't let go. The talons are thrust deep into the flesh, and they are needle sharp. At the same time, the bird is trying to bite. It's a huge ordeal. So the Rolfing work was relaxed compared to the ordeal of filing a beak down.

The reason for Rolfing Rufus was to see if we could get the mandible to move.

And it did—dramatically!

There are other animals and other situations in which Briah and I would like to try Rolfing, just to see what happens. We are going to document this. Of all the animals in the animal kingdom, birds probably have the least amount of muscle tissue. I want to try a more massive animal in order to see what happens with an animal that's healthy. The next animal we're going to try Rolfing is a mountain lion. He is about two years old and perfectly healthy.

We want to see if his movement, his walk, changes and becomes more powerful. We'll get a videotape of before and after Rolfing and document every bit of it. If you can find a Rolfer who's willing to work on an animal that's injured, I suggest you do it. It's definitely worthwhile.

I suggested Rolfing these animals after seeing and feeling the changes I experienced.

I've referred some twenty friends and relatives to Rolfing. Their stories are all different. Perhaps some stories are not as dramatic as mine, but still very positive. Many of them have sent their friends because Rolfing works and they are feeling healthier.

Rolfing a mountain lion

Briah Anson

A few months ago I had the opportunity to Rolf a mountain lion. This full grown two-year-old male weighed approximately 185 pounds. I was curious as to how he would respond to a Rolfer's touch. Would he be calmer as I worked? What would be the short and long term effects?

Brent had been raised by his owner, Pete, since he was a small cub. When Brent was close to a year old, he became quite destructive inside the house, as well as a bit dangerous to Pete and his family. Occasionally he would take Pete by surprise, slap his head and knock him across the room. It was at this time that Pete realized it was time to build Brent a large room of his own outside. The cute, playful cub was now a growing mountain lion who could inadvertently cause quite a lot of damage.

The prospect of even being close to an animal of this type appealed to me, so I ventured out with an attitude of, "Well, let's see what happens." Pete didn't know anything about Rolfing and seemed pretty skeptical about any changes occurring.

About a year ago Pete had taken Brent out of his large cage to have some photographs taken with him. Brent would have nothing to do with this event. He kept lunging at the photographer and was determined to get him. Pete put Brent back in his cage and had not worked with him at all since then.

Pete remarks, "Before Brent was Rolfed he would always want to grab you. He would hiss and growl and show his aggressive nature. If you would walk up to his cage, he would slap at you through the cage. You were definitely live prey. If a stranger came around, he would be bouncing off the walls. He was always wanting to get someone."

Session One was conducted with great care and some quick jumps away from Brent. The Rolfing work started with his hind quarters as this seemed like the safest place to begin. However, Pete and his wife warned me that he "absolutely hated having anyone mess with his hindquarters as he was very touchy and sensitive there." Nevertheless, I wasn't going to get any closer to that ferocious, growling mouth of his so I opted to just take my time and do little bits of work as Brent permitted.

Brent awaits more Rolfing

The session was touch-and-go for about the first hour and a half. After that Brent was so relaxed and in such an altered state that I was able to work around his head and jaws. There were even a few moments when I was able to lie on Brent and he seemed to be just fine with that. It wasn't until someone walked behind us that he quickly turned his head and was back on full alert. It was then that I realized that Brent was fully accepting the Rolfing work and me. There was definitely a bond of connection that had been established.

Two weeks later I returned and Pete reported that Brent was a different cat. He remarked that the day he was Rolfed he was so mellow that Pete just kept going out to the cage and hanging out with him. "I wanted to take full advantage of this time with him as I figured it would wear off by the next day." The surprise continued as Brent remained very calm and mellow all week. Pete said, "It's like you took the aggression out of him." His appetite increased dramatically, by two thirds his normal intake for a couple of weeks, and then leveled off.

I was curious as to whether Brent would recognize me when I returned for my second visit. I came with three other friends who

Working together with mutual trust

approached the cage, and Brent just remained in a crouched watchful posture. A few minutes later I approached the cage. He instantly jumped up at the cage and greeted me with a half-hearted growl/hiss. He then proceeded to throw himself down on the ground and rolled over on his back. He definitely remembered me and the reaction was positive.

Session Two proceeded as if Brent was good and ready. He just crouched down and started chewing on the lead rope that Pete had around his neck like a dog busy chewing on a bone. Within 30 minutes, Brent was definitely in an altered state and extremely relaxed. Within an hour's time, I was literally holding his head and opened his lips just to see if I could Rolf his gums. Much to my surprise he responded as if I had administered an anesthetic. I was holding his head at that point and he simply dropped the full weight of it into my hands. And so concluded the second session.

I did not return to see Brent again for another six weeks. I couldn't believe my eyes. Brent, already fully grown, was longer in length by about two inches and overall larger in body size. Pete had managed to give him a bath earlier in the day. This task took some assistance and quite some time. Pete said it left Brent on the mad side. Pete was a little apprehensive as to how Brent might respond to the Rolfing this time. He was a little frisky and there were certainly some moments of caution, but once again there was a welcoming acceptance of me and of the Rolfing work.

There was a professional photographer along on this trip, and he made some very interesting observations. He reported that he was fascinated watching Brent's eyes as I Rolfed him. He described it this way: "Amphibians have a transparent second eyelid and one stays open and the other closes while they swim underwater. It seemed as though Brent had a similar phenomenon occurring; the outer eye would remain open and stationary and then there would be an internal blink behind the eye—like a shutter that would open and close for about a tenth of a second. His eyes looked very filmy and would become more moist as Briah continued Rolfing him. The blinks ceased as he got more relaxed and the pupils continued to dilate. He would just get a blank stare. This would remain for a period of time and every once in a while he would come out of this trance state and look around and be focused once again."

The happy part of this lion adventure is that Pete is once again able to have contact with Brent and is now planning on building a larger cage where he can start working with and training Brent.

After his second Rolfing session, Pete took Brent to his nephew's school and the seventh grade class was able to be close to Brent. Of course, Pete had Brent in a small traveling cage and the children were able to pet him on his back through the bars. Brent seemed to be at ease with this encounter, and needless to say, the children were thrilled.

It seems as though the possibilities for Brent's future and Pete's interaction with him have been facilitated in such a way as to provide more joy for both of them.

In terms of the Rolfing process, I worked with him in much the same way as I would a human body, facilitating balance and finding the line. The difference is that, being a four-legged creature, Brent has two vertical lines. The fascial tissue responded similarly to human fascia. After the Rolfing he appeared longer, more balanced, was walking and moving more easily and rhythmically. I hope this experience can be one of many more for me and for the animals that live with us and are willing to teach us about themselves.

So many therapists are striking at the pattern of disease instead of supporting the pattern of health. Rolfers are not practitioners curing disease; they are specialists in health. They are giving their attention to the better working of people's minds and bodies.

—Ida Rolf

Chapter 15

Putting It Together: The Body-Mind Connection

Jude La Claire, PhD

Psychotherapist

There is much discussion these days about the interconnectedness of the mental, physical, and emotional dimensions of our lives. Practitioners and researchers, particularly in the mental health field, are focusing on the effect that the mind has on the body. There is power and practicality in the application of these findings in physical and mental health settings. It is surprising that so few therapists do look at the effect of the biological process on the emotions or psychological well-being of the individual. Many of those favoring this theoretical framework tend to believe that the primary or only cause of emotional or psychological problems is physical: biological, chemical, organic. Hence, the only solution is physical intervention, usually psychotropic drugs. Whole health approaches will be achieved by understanding the effect of the body on the psychological/emotional processes and the effects of the different parts of our brain/mind on the body. In other words we need to understand and integrate the synergistic interaction of the body and mind.

Our challenge is to work for balance in the quest of wholeness. To do this we must learn, re-learn, and teach connections. The key word here is connection. When anyone is in the healing process they are reconnecting with lost or misplaced parts of themselves, connecting with new parts of themselves, making connections between past and present, and dreaming the connection to their future. Hopefully the person is doing this in the context of knowing that their body and mind are inextricably connected and that they are moving and being in a universe that is part of the fibre of their being. Doing all this in the milieu of today's culture amidst the cacophony of the societal chaos is a task that at first seems overwhelming.

Somehow in the actual day-to-day living process, the wholeness of our being is with us at all times. We don't walk around as a dissected mess of parts—brain in one place, nerves somewhere else, heart tucked away in a drawer, feelings sitting on the shelf, while we study the separate functions of the interrelation of two parts. We function as a whole organism with all our "parts" relating to each other in the context of our physical and relational environment.

What does happen is that we can become disintegrated and fragmented in the functioning of all of our "parts" and their connection to each other. We can also easily become disengaged from our environment in ways that can be detrimental to us. We can be unmindful of our physical environment, the living beings in that environment and become seriously out of harmony with this life around us. We can become ungrounded as we lose touch with the earth under our feet and the air around us. This disharmony with oneself and with the environment causes disease and disconnection. Our challenge, living in a culture that has no unifying set of values or beliefs, no single way to approach physical, mental, family, or community health, is to find our own path to wellness, balance, and health.

To me, the therapeutic challenge is to find forms for balance and healing on emotional, spiritual, physical, and environmental levels of life for ourselves and our clients. I spoke about a part of the process of my own search in the chapter on Mothers, Babies and Children. I have to say that the process of putting together various approaches and integrating different theories in practice has always begun in the experience of my own life. As I integrate these things for myself, I am able to work more synergistically with clients.

As therapists, we can fall into the trap of thinking that "we are all that there is" and that our mode of working is "better than" or "more important than" any other approach. It is easy to become insulated and narrow in our focus. Another pitfall is to try to do it all ourselves. We become the "Renaissance" therapist doing psychotherapy, body work, being the support system, etc. I am always cautious about people who do it all. To know about approaches and integrate them in a way that is not fragmenting to the client is helpful. Sometimes, even if we have the skills to do many things, it is better to have other people involved in the group healing process since our clients need different role models and personalities to guide them through their process.

The underlying, sometimes unconscious, process of many health practitioners is to be possessive of their clients. We may suffer from the belief that we should have all the answers, that if we worked hard enough we could solve this person's problems and "help" them or that we are failing by calling on others and other resources. This kind of possessiveness has some basis in different therapeutic modes in the belief that other inputs would contaminate the carefully orchestrated psychotherapeutic process and the therapist would lose "control" of the therapeutic work. As we become more aware of the limitless supply of inner and outer resources for ourselves and can guide our client to theirs, we will not be trapped into those kinds of erroneous thinking.

We can go to another extreme by sending the client to many resources indiscriminately without regard to their compatibility or the client's ability to integrate the different approaches emotionally or physically. Eager, desperate, or compliant clients will willingly run many directions at once which, in the end, invites disaster. I can vividly remember an example given by the mentor in my Gestalt Training Group many years ago. He compared the person to a lawn. A little bit of fertilizer evenly spread around at the right time of the year aids the growth process. Too much fertilizer can drown the new seeds, kill the old growth, and create an awful smell.

The journey to health, like any other, begins with the first step. That first step is desiring change. This may come in the form of escaping pain, eluding suffering, seeking a fix, often thinking the answers are outside of ourselves. This is a beginning and that first step is often a journey of a thousand miles.

This is how the client enters my office. They are hurt, in pain, seeking relief. My first task, after assessing the problem with the client, is to determine what avenue of intervention would be most appropriate. This is where the skill of knowing different points of intervention is helpful. I have had the happy experience of being in practice with a Certified Rolfer for the last twelve years, and we have worked with approximately 150 people together. This has been a successful weaving together of different interventions which facilitated the client's progress more effectively and efficiently.

Diving in

Take the example of Gordon. He was 23 and came to therapy after his previous therapist had moved to another part of the country. He had done some work with her learning to identify and express feelings he had held back for many years. He had made progress in overcoming his long years of depression. There was a bond of trust established which had laid the foundation for our work together. Gordon's early ability to trust was severely impaired. He was second oldest in his family and very early in his life his mother began to experience periods of manic-depression and was hospitalized many times. His father was hard-working, overwhelmed by his wife's illness, and the care of three children. He became uncommunicative, over-bearing, and harsh, and was often absent. Gordon responded by becoming a loner, somewhat introverted, being a "good boy" trying to please those around him. In High School, he became involved in diving and was a state champion.

As we began our work together, it seemed more helpful to focus on finding new places, new connections. My direction is often to pursue strengths rather than dwell on weaknesses. After some months of individual therapy in which Gordon became more confident, I invited him to begin participating in a men's group. He was very reluctant at first but decided to give it a try. He did very well and began interacting with other men in the group dealing especially with issues of trust. At some point in the group process, Gordon decided to go through the Rolfing series. I had talked about it before as a possibility for Gordon, but he had not been ready for the process until then. I asked Gordon for his permission to speak with Briah regarding the interaction of his Rolfing and therapy process. He consented to this. Briah and I discussed how our interventions could be compatible and wondered about how the Rolfing could be a doorway to a new experience for Gordon. He wanted to approach Rolfing much as he had approached therapy, talking about his feelings and fears as Briah worked with him. She had the idea that a good way to change that focus was to direct his attention to a more physical process, i.e., his diving. She suggested that he videotape himself doing his diving routines before Rolfing, during the Rolfing process, and once again at the end of the Rolfing series. He was excited and literally dove into this project.

Finding your line is absolutely essential to a State Champion Diver. "Taking a dive with balance and control is a beautiful sight and brings a great sense of accomplishment," says Gordon.

As his Rolfing progressed, I began to suggest that his often repeated statements of anger towards his father were circular and didn't accurately reflect his true feelings. I suggested that he consider the possibility of looking at his father differently. I had suggested a joint session with Gordon and his father many times. Gordon was opposed to doing this and thought he might never be ready for that session. As I talked about the role his father played, I suggested that though his father wasn't the person he wanted him to be, he was, in fact, there, working, trying to parent, not giving up in circumstances that were painful for him as well as for Gordon and his siblings. Gordon began to cry and said that he loved his dad and missed him. He wanted to know him better and wanted his dad to know him. Gordon's disconnectedness with his family, especially his father, was now incongruous with his new found sense of physical balance. I again suggested the session with his dad.

This time he was eager to do it. We had the session. He and his dad were able to communicate many feelings and thoughts to each other that previously had been locked in painful silence. They decided to see each other once a week. Since that time, they have been doing this. Their relationship is growing and changing. Several months later, Gordon announced that he had met someone he liked and was beginning a relationship. Previously Gordon's relationships lasted two to three weeks at most. He was in this relationship for more than six months.

Most recently, he has connected with his younger brother. They are both going to school and working. The process of connecting and reconnecting continues. He is now working, going to school, and coaching diving part time. He recently made a job move to a smaller company doing more of what he likes to do with possibilities for advancement. In a fairly short period of time (about 18 months), Gordon has made connections with other people, using skills and successes from his past, reaching out to his family, a new relationship, and a different job. My experience as a therapist tells me that this could not have happened with one tool or one kind of intervention. It was a cooperative effort coordinating physical, emotional, behavioral, and social interventions. I believe the Rolfing was a pivotal part of the process.

A dance of life

Another wonderful example of the connecting process happened during the time Briah and I had the rare experience of working with a dance company. It was a small modern dance company with five members and one apprentice. One young woman in the company came to see me because of the trauma she was suffering in an emotionally and physically abusive relationship. Her desire, in the beginning, had nothing to do with her dancing. She was in pain because of a destructive relationship. After several sessions dealing with crisis intervention, I felt strongly that a body process would be more facilitative and strengthening for her. I suggested Rolfing to her, and she immediately chose to do it. We alternated Rolfing and counseling sessions.

Again Briah and I worked together. As the Rolfing process unfolded, she began to feel more centered, stronger in her dancing, and more connected with her body as she moved. In therapy, we were discovering the secrets of abuse in her family, the early perfectionism about every-thing, especially dance. She began to feel more child-like, regaining an innocence she had lost very early in her development. As a result of the counseling and Rolfing, she experienced her body differently and began looking different to others. The choreographer/director of the company stated it this way: "You couldn't ignore it. It was so powerful. You could see it in her expressiveness . . . her ability to connect in a more honest way on the floor with a group of people . . . a growing confidence in her body image as her body, in a sense, matured from that of an adoles-cent ballerina to something much more womanly." She continues, "She started actually having enjoyment in how her body was and that maybe she was an attractive woman."

The next person in the company came to Rolfing first. She came to this process because of a physical problem of pain and discomfort after a cesarean section birth. "I came to Rolfing feeling completely distanced from my body."

As she experienced the fifth session, which works with the abdo-men, much of the physical and emotional trauma of the event returned. During the C-section procedure, the anesthesia had lost its effect, and she was experiencing tremendous physical pain. She tried to tell the attending physician and nurses, but was unable to communicate to them due to the intensity of the pain and the shock her body was experiencing. I happened to be available when Briah was doing the fifth session, so we worked together to help facilitate the release and reframe the traumatic physical and emotional experience. She was able this time to ask for help and to get it, to release the feelings, the physical and emotional pain of that experience.

It is important in the Rolfing process to stay with the primary inten-tion of balancing the body through the manipulation of the fascial tissue. The Rolfer may pause in a session and help guide the person through the emotional experience, help them utilize the images evoked, or to reframe a traumatic memory. Then the Rolfer might assist the person in integrat-ing this with the new feeling of balance and possession of their body.

This differs from body-centered approaches which use a physical intervention for the primary purpose of accessing memories or emo-tions. The person is then encouraged to intensify feelings and experi-ence an emotional catharsis. It does not seem necessary to encourage the heightening of emotional catharsis and release beyond the spontaneous tears, anger, and laughter that come from the person as they begin to experience less inhibited, more flowing emotional experiences of themselves.

It seems, in my experience, that the balancing of the body, combined with utilizing and reframing unconscious images and helping the person with behavioral integration, is all that is necessary for the person to release trauma and begin to experience new behavioral responses.

It was unusual in the case of the woman mentioned earlier that I was there to help facilitate the emotional process as well as the unconscious restructuring of the memory. Ordinarily Briah would have done the session alone, but since I was available, she asked me to assist her. This facilitated the client's easy transition to therapy to continue the process which began in her fifth Rolfing session. She completed the Rolfing series which gave her that underpinning of support and a more balanced physical matrix from which to work.

Her therapy continued for about six months. She took a break and came back about a year later. She said, "It's at this point in my life that I am starting to get to the core issues . . ." It took her some time in individual therapy and group work to get to some inner issues she felt were crucial. "And for me, the Rolfing series and therapy were an introduction. Now I feel I'm ready to move up into a really different level. I'd like to do the Advanced Rolfing now that I'm at this place of discovery."

Her experience speaks to the question, "When is Rolfing the best intervention or when would psychotherapy or some other approach be better?" In the first dancer's case, the person chose therapy because of emotional pain and subsequently experienced Rolfing which facilitated the physical process along with the emotional growth. The second dancer came with a specific physical complaint which was remedied fairly quickly. The work, however, opened up possibilities of emotional and behavioral work which took place slowly over a period of several years. You could say, really, that a person will start where they are ready to begin and move on from that point. Rolfing could predispose one for psychotherapy or vice-versa. The point, I think, is to see the wonderful and dynamic interweaving of the emotional, physical, behavioral, and unconscious threads of a person's reality.

Another dancer, also a masseuse, seemed to focus so much on the body that she often lost perspective of her daily life and her behavior interactionally with others. She began Rolfing and was referred to psychotherapy. Her then chaotic inner process and strained relationships with others began to find some form, as she began to look at herself and her behavior in the context of her intergenerational family history. She had a very fluid and creative imagination. Working with dreams and guided imagery, she found the scared child, the controlling parent, the wild, playful, animal-like self who is fierce, powerful, and demands respect. She has continued the process of unfolding with the Advanced Rolfing series, alternating individual and couples therapy. She has recently been participating in an Art Therapy group facilitated by another therapist for persons who have been sexually abused. All this work has been done gradually over a period of several years with time in between where no particular interventions are occurring. The secret is to use what works when a person is ready and to guide them to their own rich resources, or encourage them to find the resources in their environment that are helpful.

Another of the dancers came to therapy at the suggestion of the director of the dance company. He was struggling with the disassociative way he related to the other dancers in improvisations. He was not sensitive to their presence or energy, though he was a skilled dancer. I had a men's group at the time and he opted for that therapeutic mode after several individual sessions. This seemed appropriate since his main issue was in the relationship area. This was to be the tip of the iceberg as we were all to discover in the following months. His initial time in the group met with slow progress, with doubting and questioning on his part, trying to sort out why he was there and what he wanted to do to change. He had begun his Rolfing several months before he came to the group. He went through the Rolfing series with some changes, the beginnings of a connection with himself emotionally and physically. He was disappointed that his changes had not been as dramatic as some of the other dancers. After about eight months in group, he participated in a weekend workshop with a group of men and made a significant breakthrough in terms of owning his gay lifestyle and manifesting more emotional and intuitive aspects of himself. This was an important step in his journey. He continued in group with more

Karin R. dancing with joy

Steven Johnson

enthusiasm and consistency. Four months after that weekend, he called me and said he needed to see me individually as soon as possible. He came in and spilled his story of years of drug and alcohol abuse. His pattern was that of a binge addict, and he had successfully hidden his addiction from the dance company and even close friends. He had made the decision after eighteen months of work to be sober and to work on his recovery. He began attending AA and NA meetings along with the men's group sessions.

Emotional clarity came quickly along with the physical responsiveness in his dancing. After the dance company performed its final concert and disbanded, he continued to dance with another group. He got some Advanced Rolfing Sessions, the first in his sobriety period. After about six months of sobriety, he decided to go back to school, completing his undergraduate work in dance in preparation for a graduate program. He not only returned to school, but also went back to his hometown, living with his dad during this time.

His last dance performance before his move was exciting to watch. His ability to be present, move fluidly with awareness of his body and of others was very apparent. All this had taken place in less than two years. When I last saw him, he was enjoying his school work and told me that his dad, who was a practicing alcoholic, had decided to stop drinking. His cousin, who was also abusing drugs and alcohol, lived with him during the period of time that he began his 12-Step Program. His cousin took the step to participate in a drug rehabilitation program and is now sober and working his program. It would seem that the re-connecting and healing had come full circle in his life and that of his family.

When a person is numb and frozen physically and emotionally, the process is often slow, or so it seems on the surface. His temperament was very introverted and so his process was also very subterranean. Some work is done in the cave, without light. Then we look for small signals of growth, clues to the inner workings. Encouragement and consistent boundaries, structure in his daily life, and commitment to his process were the important factors, as he approached the breakthrough to these hidden parts of himself and the subsequent ability to overcome the addictions which had controlled him for so long. His journey started almost literally bumping into other people with little awareness of himself and his surroundings. As his defenses and masks fell, replaced by growing parts of himself, he moved and connected differently, with awareness of himself and others.

In time, all the members of the dance company completed the Rolfing series. All of them participated in a therapy process at some point. One member came to only a few sessions for clarifying relationships and work issues. Others spent some amount of time in individual, couple and group counseling. The timing for each person was so different. Some began with counseling, others with Rolfing. Several came to counseling nearly a year after the Rolfing series. Each person's timing was unique and came from their own relationship to their emotional, physical, and intuitive processes. Rolfing may impact each person differently, depending on where they are developmentally and where they are in their evolution.

One might think that the end result was that this dance company stayed together and lived happily ever after. Not so. Actually the process of growth for all the members led them all in different directions. Two are now furthering their education in dance. One is in New York working in the field. One took a faculty position teaching dance at the university level. Two others are dancing/performing and working at other jobs as they spend time on their personal lives. The director/choreographer is taking a sabbatical, spending time with her partner and her small daughter, tending to her own life apart from dance. Their paths separated as they each became more whole. Their last dance concert together was very creative and bold, just as their individual journeys now continue to be.

Emilie's story

Physical pain can come in all sorts of packages. Emilie's story is one of acute physical trauma inflicted on her several years ago. She was assaulted repeatedly over a period of several hours by an intruder who had broken into her home. She sustained severe injuries. There was neurological damage, tissue damage, and much bruising and swelling. She had reconstructive surgery on her face and was hospitalized for ten days. Needless to say, she also experienced severe emotional trauma and shock on both physical and psychological levels. She had some physical therapy following the assault. She was evaluated by a neuro-psychologist who recommended therapy, both physical therapy and psychotherapy. The health care group supervising her recovery did not authorize any psychotherapy until two years after the assault. It was at this time that she came to me for therapy. In addition to the physical and occupational therapy, she received chiropractic treatments. She has continued the chiropractic treatment intermittently since then.

Two years after the assault, she was still suffering from some memory loss, chronic pain, nightmares, anxiety attacks, chronic fatigue, and a constant high level of stress. "Stress tended to just shut me down. I was still stressed by a lot of things at random." Any small stressor could precipitate irrational fears, the onset of a headache, or severe nightmares. She would be incapacitated for a period of time. She had not been working full-time since the assault but was preparing to teach full-time as a Special Education Teacher in the fall. She was concerned that she would not have the energy or the patience to do the work since school was only about a month away. We knew we had a lot of work to do.

Emilie's goals were to be able to go to sleep normally and not awaken with nightmares, and to stop obsessing about small things. She wanted to deal with the anger she felt towards her assailant, the insurance company, and other systems involved in creating a "bureaucratic headache" for her. She wanted to be more focused and confident. She also wanted to control or totally eliminate her chronic pain, particularly the headaches. The overall feeling was one of being victimized. Emilie had an unswerving dedication to fairness in her life, her work, and her political activity, so the assault and its unfairness coupled with the injustice of the systems she had to deal with following the assault was difficult to accept.

We set to work. I suggested a program for Emilie using imagery, visualization, dream work, and relaxation techniques. We also spent time dealing with feelings of anger and helplessness that were always just below the surface. Some exploration of family history helped us understand some of her control, trust, and bonding issues.

It seemed to me that Rolfing would be helpful as soon as Emilie agreed and an appointment was available. She was enthusiastic about the Rolfing sessions and began seeing Briah six weeks after she first came in. During her first session of Rolfing, she had feelings of being back in the hospital and felt disoriented. She slept deeply that night and felt better.

"I think I was having more dreams during the time I was being Rolfed, more that l remembered, anyway." One dream was of a man chasing her through a long tunnel. We worked together with this and other dreams, helping her to call on help, take her time, and feel powerful in the dream or in the recalled memory. We worked through some of the powerful dream and memory sequences in this way. During this time, I did a guided imagery to assist her in finding a safe place and in connecting with a guide who would assist her and protect her. Using the images from this session, I made a tape for her with a relaxation progression and a time of peace and connection in her safe place with the powerful and wise guide. She began using this tape on a regular basis. I recommended that she use it several times a day. She commented several months later, "I've had some hard days at work. One thing that's been real good is knowing that I can have those images, I can create peace. And just knowing that I can helps. I put myself on pause a little more often, and I'm telling my students, too, to stop, take a breath, think about how you need to handle this."

Emilie noticed that her balance was better. "Before the Rolfing, one of the things that had me really disturbed and concerned, and something I had to think about a lot, was my balance." Three months after she completed the Rolfing series she remarked, "I feel more balanced and more grounded, in a sense. And people have noticed that I'm walking better, that I look healthier."

Emilie's comments made me want to explore a book recommended at one of the workshops I attended at the Rolf Institute's annual meeting last year. In *Sensory Integration and the Child,* A. Jean Ayres, an occupational therapist, talks so clearly about the force of gravity and sensory integration. She describes the labyrinth in the inner ear which has two types of vestibular receptors. One of these responds to gravity. She states "Because gravity is always present on this planet, the gravity receptors send a perpetual stream of vestibular messages throughout our entire life (p.35)." In Emilie's case, there was serious disturbance in the vestibular functioning. Her neural system and the tactile sense were seriously assaulted. The continuous beating damaged skin, tissue, neural, and vestibular systems. Thus, she was experiencing "overstimulation," lack of balance, loss of memory, numbness, and chronic pain as a result. Ayres explains, "Vestibular input seems to 'prime' the entire nervous system to function effectively. When the vestibular system does not function in a consistent and accurate way, the interpretation of other sensations will be inconsistent and inaccurate, and the nervous system will have trouble 'getting started." She further states, "Since both our nervous system and our skin come from the same origin, tactile stimuli have a primal role in neural organization (p.39)."

This makes so much sense to me as I observe Emilie and many others who have been Rolfed. They are beginning to feel more balanced, more grounded, often more present. One woman, an incest survivor from an alcoholic home, stated, "I feel more whole and more real, integrated now."

Ayres describes the first sensory integration experiences as happening in the womb (p.36). As the mother's body moves, this stimulates the vestibular functioning. In the beginning, we are literally connected to our mothers, one with her body, experiencing those first sensations of connection on a very real biological level. Our developing sensations and neural functioning are being stimulated. The early experience of being rocked in someone's arms or in a cradle help to organize the brain (p.16). The newborn baby is responding "to the sensations of gravity and movement that come from their inner ears (p.16)."

It would follow that when our bodies are being stimulated in a tactile mode and being restructured to be more vertical in the field of gravity, we begin to feel the comfort, security, confidence, and sense of well-being we experienced in the womb or as infants. If those processes were disturbed early on, it would seem that the Rolfing process would give the person an experience they never had but desperately needed for integrated sensory functioning and integrated emotional functioning.

Emilie's experience of feeling more balanced, more whole, seems to demonstrate this. She has continued to feel better emotionally and physically. She is no longer plagued by nightmares, flashbacks, or anxiety episodes. She experiences headaches periodically, but is able to control them fairly well. She taught full-time at a juvenile facility this year in addition to taking a graduate class in night school. She was married in May and is feeling more content and happy with her life. The sense of constant fatigue does not plague her. There are still physical and emotional manifestations of her trauma, but they are not overwhelming or debilitating. She feels as if she has tools to deal with the problems and has power in her life to take charge of whatever might happen. She received a settlement from the insurance company and is definitely moving on with her life.

Wholeness in recovery

Another woman who had been seriously traumatized growing up, experiencing physical, sexual, and emotional abuse, told her story to me. She was working with another therapist and came to Briah for Rolfing. She was fifty years old and had spent many years coping with the consequences of her early abuse. She had one period of agoraphobia which she overcame through her own efforts and working in a 12-Step Program. She had participated in a therapy group at one time and more recently had gone back to therapy to look at her family issues. After a period of fairly intensive work in which she uncovered some early memories of sexual abuse, she "discovered" Rolfing and began the series. She explained that while she was having an incest memory, she was able to breathe through it and it was "like those people shrunk and disappeared." As she experienced "a very deep level of sadness and needing to be nurtured" she says, "I was able to ask to be held, and I was just amazed at how open my body felt. That was a big breakthrough for me, and I'm really being able to fully trust the Rolfing process. I've felt a tremendous amount of wholeness and recovery since that time, and I think it's just all coming together finally."

It would seem that the process of Rolfing was contributing to a new sense of physical self, less disassociation from the body, more connectedness to the self, and the ability to touch and be touched by others. Perhaps the metaphor of Mother Earth is more than just a metaphor. As we experience or reexperience sensory integration, as we become more vertical in the field of gravity, we begin to feel more connected, grounded, and whole. The sense of being held and supported by the field of gravity is nurturing and protective. Our new sense of well-being and confidence opens the door for connection with ourselves and others.

Another important aspect of this process is that the individual feels more powerful, in charge, and less a victim. The previous client continues, "I have a real clear sense of . . . this is helping me. That's another part of this wholeness that I have. Briah is a facilitator or a catalyst or a supplier in that process and that's real different. I think early on I used to think, help me, fix me, which is what all my clients are doing, too."

This makes me reflect on what Ida Rolf reiterated constantly, "Gravity is the therapist." I also believe that in good therapy, the therapist is a facilitator to help put the person in touch with his or her own inner network of resources. As a therapist, it has been vital to me to have a clear sense of a form for change that would facilitate people in this process of healing and growth. There are really a few basic beliefs that comprise this form or matrix.

They are an integration of principles I have learned from Gestalt psychology, Senoi Dreamwork, the therapeutic approaches of Milton Erickson, Family Systems theory, and Buddhist philosophy. I believe and encourage others to consider the possibility of these truths:

1. You can always call on whatever help you need.
2. You can take all the time you need.
3. Your physical, emotional, spiritual selves are all interrelated.
4. You and your environment are reflections of each other.
5. Every problem has the solution within it.
6. All parts of our reality are resources for growth and healing (ourselves, others, nature, dreams . . . anything in the universe).
7. You can trust yourself; you have the answers.
8. You are responsible for your life, health, and happiness.
9. Finding the gift of compassion for ourselves and others is an essential aspect of growth.
10. Anything is possible.

This is a partial list. Certainly much could be said about each one and how it can be implemented specifically. Suffice it to say that in working with people, I think that the belief system we have is the foundation and form which influences our clients' journeys. If we are clear about our beliefs, we can help our clients know and follow theirs more healthily. It is essential to know what our beliefs are and begin to acknowledge them to ourselves. I am certain that our system affects others whether we ever articulate these beliefs and attitudes or not.

The rhythm of life

About ten years ago I met Necia. She came to a training group I was doing for people in the helping professions. At that time she was working with women teaching them about self-health care and reproductive issues. She came to the training group to help her with her work and to learn more about herself. The group was both educational and experiential, and I encouraged participants to explore themselves.

Necia had been raised in an extended family network. Her great-grandmother, Mama Katie, and her mother were especially important people to her growing up. Necia never knew her father who was a university music professor and a jazz trumpeter. She met him when she was 16, but never really had the opportunity to know him. Growing up, Necia had many difficulties to deal with as she watched her mother struggle with bouts of alcoholism and mental illness. One of the things she learned from her mother was to face the struggle, to never give up, and to overcome the problems. She saw her mother, over a period of many years, overcome her alcoholism and mental problems, and develop herself as an accomplished jazz pianist, earning a degree in music therapy. Necia's models taught her by their example to never give up, to find the resources in yourself and in the community of people around you.

She expressed her early learnings from the training/therapy group in this way, "I received affirmation for that part of me that's real psychic and doesn't appear to be normal. And then the courage to just follow myself, you know, just the courage to follow myself."

In looking back over her experience of group therapy, Rolfing, and family therapy, she could see the rhythm of her life being more attuned to healthier patterns through these therapeutic modes. She expressed it this way, "It's like breaking out of a shell . . . I think becoming is what happens. There are systems that do facilitate that in a clear, rhythmical manner. I'm into tones and rhythms and stuff like that . . . that's real basic to me. It's like a drum rhythm. It's something you can trust and there's real consistency to it. In jazz you can hear the melody. You can always go back to it. You can scat up above it or go under it, but the line is always there. It's the same thing with a bass. That's why bass is so important in the jazz combo." The consistent pattern of each of these approaches was helping her establish this "bass" line in her life.

Her pacing in choosing what instrument of change was helpful at a particular time in her life was something that came from within her. Necia felt that the dream and imagery work, the group work, the systemic family work she did with another therapist, and the Rolfing were all basic rhythms that were helping her to be in touch with her own innate rhythm. "Intrinsic integrity to me is as old as the sound of your mother's heartbeat, and that's all that matters. And your own life has it's own heartbeat and you're either with it or not with it and you can feel it either way. You have options. You can stay stuck and out of whack with yourself or you can find things that help you navigate your world."

She talked about the interface of Rolfing and her therapy work, "I got into Rolfing and it felt good. I felt like I was a little kid a lot of the time. It felt like there were places inside of me that hadn't ever been touched, you know, and it was deep. I was very much aware of the emotional . . . psychological and physical tie-in. The guided imagery and dreamwork I had done, and the other experiences in therapy, helped me get more out of the sessions because I knew where to go with it."

Necia made me think about a question that has been with me so much as I have worked to write this chapter. I know what the external form of Rolfing is. There are ten sessions that deal with balancing the body in relationship to itself and within the field of gravity. Though the external, physical process is not all that happens, it is the matrix, or origin of the changes precipitated. The structure is clear. My question is, "What is my structure of working with dreams, images, memories; the chaotic complexity of the unconscious, and the behavioral and relational aspects of the outer world? Is there some consistent form that guides me in this daily work with people?" Though I had studied several approaches in depth and learned much in my twenty years of experience, I had not really looked recently at what forms I had internalized in working with clients.

She reminded me, as others have recently, that the system of working with dreams taught by the Senoi Indians (a tribe living in the upper Malaysian peninsula) was consistently and powerfully helpful to her as she met different sorts of problems in both her "inner" and "outer" worlds. In this educational system, the Senoi teach their children from the time they are very young to call on whatever help they need and take all the time they need. They are then instructed to approach or confront the powerful figure in the dream and go to the source of their power. They ask for a gift for themselves and the community that represents that power and their alliance with the figure. A quest is embarked upon for the gift, making it tangible in the waking state. (*Creative Dreaming*, by Partricia Garfield)

Necia said, "In the Senoi Dreamwork, you can get completions. Even if you use a piece of it—like go for the power. That's completion. Each stage is complete. It's just always more . . . a different level of enhance-ment. Then finally you go on the quest and you've actualized it."

I realized that this is a nearly archetypal form that is found in elements of hypnosis, Ericksonian work, NLP, Gestalt, and Jungian approaches, and in systemic family therapy work. In my many years of practice I have internalized this form and, now that I'm more aware of it, see that I use it in some way in all my work with individuals, families, and groups.

Many people talked about memories or images coming up in the Rolfing process. If the person has a form for working with those images, then the work can be facilitated fairly quickly. The power of the physical and sensory changes happening while images of the unconscious are also being facilitated deepens and widens the effectiveness of the healing process. The other most important aspect is that people know that it is their process and that they are in charge. Any therapeutic process which empowers people and enables them to feel more in charge of their lives, i.e., emotions, bodies, actions, is more compatible with the form and energy of the Rolfing work.

Necia's sense of being in charge and taking her time is a good exam-ple of following one's own internal rhythm. She began with the group work. Two years later she began Rolfing. Her Rolfing series took place over a year's time. During this period she gave birth to her son, Jamal, now ten years old. She also changed her career direction by becoming a massage practitioner. She went to family therapy later as relation-ship and parent issues came more to the foreground. She has received Advanced Rolfing work and Jamal has also been Rolfed. (See Chapter One: Mothers, Babies and Children.) Her quest continues as her pro-cess unfolds. She has taught me to respect each person's own unique rhythm of 'becoming.

Coming home: healing sexual abuse

The issue of incest and other forms of physical, sexual, and emotional abuse is of concern to any therapist or person doing body work. I have worked for fifteen years with persons who have been sexually abused. Like many counselors, I spent years not really paying attention to what people may have said about this topic, if it ever even came up. My con-sciousness was raised as I listened to myself as a woman, to my feelings, my body, and my sexuality. I began doing women's therapy groups and training groups. The issue of sexual abuse surfaced quite naturally as women were in safe spaces with each other. The journey of one young woman with whom I worked is particularly inspiring and taught me once again how fluid and powerful the human spirit is.

About three- and one-half years ago a very depressed, detached young woman, about 23 years old, came into my office. She came to therapy because she was suffering periods of severe depression. She was also experiencing dramatic mood swings. She would act out self-destructively using sex and alcohol to numb her pain and panic. She was tired of this behavior and frightened by it as well.

In taking her history, it was clear why she felt so overwhelmed and fearful. She had been sadistically abused sexually and physically by her alcoholic stepfather from the time she was nine until age fourteen. Her mother was also abused by him. Her mother, too, was an alcoholic. Her father was not available for her after her parent's divorce and eventually moved from the small town where she lived. Her stepfather was responsible for the "disappearance" of several of her pets. She knew he had killed them. Life for her was unbearable. He committed suicide when she was fourteen. The chaos in her family continued and the pain she carried with her daily haunted her. She ran away several times and hid herself in drugs, alcohol, and acting out sexually.

She had many strengths and resources and, together, we looked for these. She had connected with one high school teacher in particular and had even lived with her briefly during one of the times she ran away. She knew this teacher cared about her and was always there for her. Her grandmother was also a person who loved her and wanted to be there for her, though it was difficult for her to interfere with her daughter's life. She identified these people early in therapy as helpers and loving people in her life.

Another resource for her were her pets, particularly her horse. She lived in a small town and had always had a horse, riding in rodeos and other competitions. I'm sure in many ways her animals, especially her horses, saved her life. She loved the out-of-doors and was at home with the physical world around her.

We talked about her interest in art and drawing. She brought in a pencil drawing of a horse that was magnificent. She, of course, didn't see it as good at all. I could see that there were many resources for her to use.

The initial sessions were around building trust and helping her see the difference between her self-destructive and constructive behaviors. She expressed it in this way, "First, therapy taught me how not to live, and then taught me how to live. It taught me what kinds of things you do in certain situations. It gave me the tools to build the kind of life I wanted."

There were many struggles as she fought with her depression. Her support system was very limited, except for her relationship with her primary partner whom she had been with for about five years. For that reason, I suggested that she become part of a women's therapy group about six months after she began individual therapy. She continued individual therapy bi-weekly for part of the time she was in group therapy.

It became clearer that she still had a substance abuse problem. With the support of the group and my continued insistence on the need for sobriety, she discontinued the use of alcohol as a way to numb herself. During the process of the group, she was able to begin to listen to herself, her feelings, and her dreams. She was able to relate to people in the group, though she was very guarded at times. She was still disassociated at times from her body. This was a normal consequence of the physical and sexual abuse she experienced.

After about a year in the women's group, she decided to do a weekend workshop where music, guided imagery, dreamwork principles, art, and group process were used to facilitate inner work. She had a very impactful experience. A woman guide was showing her the way through many of her life experiences in a metaphoric journey. She saw a white horse wounded and dying. A wolf led her through the dark and showed her a ball of fire. She could use this fire to protect herself, throwing it to ward off danger. At one point, her mother crumbled into a pile of dust which she put into a little pouch and placed inside a hollow in her arm. She was struggling to climb up a mountain, trying to avoid falling into a chasm. She kept floating to the top of the chasm with a turtle on her chest. At another time, she was in the woods beating on a drum. This would keep the bear away and she would be safe. Through the journey, the woman was there to guide her and show her the way.

After the experience of these images, she drew many pictures and was able to share with the group how she could, time after time, call on help and escape danger. She was able to mourn the loss of the self that had died in the abusive part of her life. Her mother was with her and very much a part of her, though not able to help her. She had a new light in her eyes and a new lightness to her I had not seen before.

Briah and I co-facilitated the workshop. This, I think, gave her a way to meet Briah and begin a relationship which would make it safe for her to consider the Rolfing process. Some of the other members of the group had been Rolfed and had shared their experiences with the group. She decided to begin the Rolfing series.

This was a breakthrough for her. "I'm looking back at the one point that I felt was the major turning point of my therapy, and it was right during the time I was being Rolfed."

She experienced the Rolfing in a very concrete way. "Physically the Rolfing was an incredible experience. It was emotionally helpful as well, but it was intensely physical. I felt better, I looked better, my balance was better. I could physically balance my body better, in my riding and everything." She added, "I experienced the physical feeling that I had, I think, during the time when I had been sexually abused, sick, and awful sensations in the gut. Briah had told me sometimes things would come up and to call her if I needed my next session sooner. I called her and asked if I could come in a few days earlier. I did come in for my next session early."

She moved through the physical discomfort and heeded Briah's advice to take care of herself. "Following Briah's advice to drink lots of water and eat the right food, I learned how to start taking care of myself, physically. And I, amazingly, started feeling so much better and more in control of me. I didn't have any guilt for taking care of myself."

As she completed the Rolfing series, she quit a part-time job which was in a very unhealthy environment. She went to school full-time at a junior college, preparing to be a draftsperson. There was a noticeable difference in her ability to deal with other people in the group, at work, and at school. This was the first time I had seen her begin to believe she could really make it. She seemed to be more in charge of herself, her body, her behavior, and her life.

She talked about the difference for her in how she related to her mind and her body. "I had been tuning my body out for so long. My mind and body were two separate entities, unless I wanted them to be the same. If I didn't want to get sick, I didn't get sick. I got very sick after I was Rolfed. I didn't try to stop it. I took care of myself. I didn't vacate. I was more present." She talked about how she would try to disassociate, "I've tried to get back to the old mode. I need some space. Let me close down. And I'm not able to do it. Vacate mode is broken."

She began to notice differences emotionally as well. "I think the Rolfing pulled me together emotionally. It made me want to be more aware of my body." She felt that the strongest release of the emotions around the sexual abuse occurred a number of months following the Rolfing during a very intense therapy session. (She had worked on images, dreams, and memories around the abuse at different times in her individual and group work.) As I recall, there were no specific images of the abuse but a more diffuse, overwhelming sense of pain. She was in a trance state and needed grounding and support. I reminded her of all those people and resources she could call on. She was able to release the feeling and has not experienced that negatively charged emotional state since then.

When she took a full-time drafting job after one semester in school and was also taking evening classes, it was impossible for her to come to therapy. She stopped for about six months. She came to group during the summer and had individual sessions intermittently for about six months. She had the Advanced Rolfing Series about a year after her initial ten sessions. She is not in therapy at the present time. She just went through the breakup of the primary relationship she had been in for eight years. It was a difficult time, but she asked for help from friends and other support people. She has reconnected with her dad. He has visited her here once and she traveled to Alaska to see him. When she was experiencing the trauma of her relationship loss, she looked up the teacher who had been so instrumental in helping her in high school. She has had several phone conversations with her and feels that the relationship is still valuable and supportive for her.

When asked what had changed because of the Rolfing and her therapy process, she responded, "Everything. I learned to like myself. I began to recognize that if I would take care of myself and like myself and other people, they would like me. I stopped being so paranoid all the time. Although I'm still not very good about asking for help, I try to do that. I learned how important it is. I'm not the same person I was." She continues, "I think over a period of time, I learned my patterns. I learned what my red flags are. Sooner and sooner before I start the downward slide into crisis, I recognize my behaviors and can take control."

She summarized her belief about the healing process, "I think once you've gotten the major tools—your screwdriver and your pliers and your hammer and the main tools you need to build that house—then you can leave therapy. You can go back if you run into a detail job or something, that needs another specific kind of tool."

One of the things I have learned in my years of experience in working with abuse survivors, and especially my work with this courageous young woman, is that we can overcome great pain and wounding. I also learned that it is not important to talk about all the details of the abuse. It can be retraumatizing and counter-productive unless reframing forms are used. It is clearly important to move beyond denial to ownership of the reality of the abuse. Every individual is very different in this healing process, so listening to each person's needs is extremely important.

The turning points for this young woman seemed to center on a very physical experience and metaphoric experiences relating to the process of the wounding. She knows her journey is not over, and that she will use what she has learned, reaching out for help when it is necessary as she moves on . . . or into her life more fully.

Combining Rolfing, therapy modes which access the unconscious, using imagery and dreamwork, group work, and family systems approaches—which help us to connect and reconnect with our family and extended family in our outer world—seem to give people a powerful matrix of healing and tools to navigate in the inner and outer worlds.

We have so much to learn in our individual journeys towards our own wholeness. As a therapist, I know I have changed and evolved continuously in my twenty years of work in the mental health field. I know we will all continue to evolve and grow as we learn from each other, from other disciplines, and from our clients.

In using the powerful tools of Rolfing and psychotherapy we can keep in mind thoughts expressed by Edward Whitmont in *Psyche and Substance,* "We are not merely free floating minds but minds embodied. A genuinely holistic viewpoint cannot but see the body as the visibility of the mind and the mind as the expression of the particular individual self's way of embodiment (p.9)."

We are all a microcosmic weaving of many threads of spiritual and material reality living in relationship to ourselves and our total environment. The challenge is to continue discovering individually and collectively the paths to connection and wholeness.

References

Ayres, PhD, A. Jean, *Sensory Integration and the Child*. Western Psychological Services, 1989.

Garfield, PhD, Patricia L., *Creative Dreaming*. Ballantine Books, 1974.

Whitmont, Edward C., *Psyche and Substance*. North Atlantic Books, 1980.

==

"Whatever you can do or dream you can, begin it.
Boldness has genius, power,
and magic in it. Begin it now."

—*Johann Wolfgang von Goethe*

==

Your Personal Rolfing Journey

Getting more from your Rolfing

by Julie Naidich

Your Personal Rolfing Journal

Getting more from your Rolfing

by Julie Naidich

I have just been through the ten sessions of Rolfing! The experience has been an interesting and exhilarating one: it's been a time of rebirth and rediscovery for myself. As a person who had always lived much more in my head than in my body, I would like to share with any readers who are planning to get Rolfed some suggestions for approaching the Rolfing process. They represent a combination of my own discoveries and experiences and things my Rolfer, Megan Gilchrist of Berkeley, has pointed out to me.

1. Park your car several blocks from your Rolfer's house or office. The several block walk immediately after Rolfing will give your body a very nice chance to feel some of the changes it's just experienced. Also, your head may want a little space to work out any emotions or just to experience the wonder of what's happening before you get down to the business of driving.

2. Your body will want you to use it more—you will feel more energy (sometimes restlessness) and a desire to move. Go with it: dance (it's an excellent way for letting your body discover itself), stretch, or do whatever it seems to want. Break up long sitting-still periods with a little movement. Your body will invent things; it knows what it wants, so listen to it and give in to its cravings. You'll probably be pleasantly surprised to feel how good it feels to move, and how graceful and fluid your movements have become. (By the way, if you think you "can't dance," try again: you may have a surprise!)

3. It's often nice to take a warm bath on the evenings after a Rolfing session.

4. You may sometimes feel some odd emotions for a day or two after the sessions. Just accept them and let them happen; it's a normal part of the process of having things released.

5. Don't impose a "head trip," a mental image of what your body should be like. As you go through changes and have old chronic postures and ways of moving released, there may be a temptation to try to hold yourself in accord with your ideas of "good posture." This will only create new strains. Instead, just let your body be its new way—it

has a wisdom all its own, obeying the laws of its physical nature; it doesn't need your head to tell it what to do. My Rolfer has often pointed this out to me; it's been a very nice discovery and has allowed me to see my body in an entirely new light.

6. But do remain sensitive to what your body is feeling and doing. If you find yourself holding—tightening your shoulders, pelvis, etc.—(you'll recognize these tightenings easily after they've been released by Rolfing); just allow them to drop back into the position that seems most natural and comfortable now. Your body may still be used to holding itself in the old habits, so be gently aware of it. What you'll find is that you now have a new alternative way of carrying yourself, and that this alternative, even though it may sometimes feel a little strange at first, is also the more comfortable, natural, and easy way to be.

This also goes for more complex movements. One example comes from a session in which my legs were Rolfed. Several hours after this session, I was walking along when I suddenly became aware of my walking. I realized I was holding something in my walking movements, my leg muscles. So I just let my legs feel the new changes that were in them and move in the way that Rolfing had just made possible. There was no intellectual analysis at all—I hardly knew what was different, I just let my body do it (it knew), and I was walking completely differently. Generally I have found myself going back and forth between the old and the new, but now the new is much more habitual.

Of course, there will be some changes that just happen automatically and stay there without any attention or awareness on your part, and others that are so subtle that while you will be aware that you can "let something go," you'll hardly be aware, on the articulate level, of what it is. It's good to remember that all of these changes will still be there in the fascial structure of your body, even if you don't always let go into them.

Another kind of message your body will give you now that Rolfing has made you more sensitive and in tune with it, and you're not shutting off its signals, is when you're using it in a way that's not comfortable. Sometimes this will communicate itself to you quietly, like a desire to straighten up instead of bending over the sink. Other times it will come in the form of a pulled muscle that hadn't bothered you before (no, Rolfing's not making you worse; your body's just going through adjustments and/or giving you a message to stop using it in a way that has actually never been too good for it). If it's the latter, watch yourself—are you twisting as you reach for something on a shelf for example? And be creative in making adjustments in your movements or your environment.

Rolfing movement integration sessions will be important in your process as you are Rolfed. If you decide to do this, ask a patterner when is the best time to begin lessons—Rolfing and Rolfing movement work well together.

7. You may expect that the changes that you felt so aware of during the first few days after a session will often seem to grow less pronounced towards the end of the week. They're still there! It's just that your body has become more used to them and integrated them. The ten sessions are very carefully worked out in a sequence that is designed to prevent you from regressing. Actually your body will continue to make positive changes in the direction of the Rolfing ideal for at least a year after the last session: six months after the tenth session you'll look different than you do immediately after. I've found that after getting deeply relaxed, or when dancing or doing other exercises, or even getting into a radically different environment such as a vacation in the mountains, I become aware again of changes—new fluidities and possibilities for movements—that I had taken for granted during my more regular activities. I stress this point because it is a common experience for people who have been Rolfed to go through periods of thinking nothing's happening and they've wasted their time. Ain't so!

8. Try not to resist your Rolfer. You'll make more progress by "letting her in." It is common for people to react to pain by tightening against it, or by "running away"—putting the mind and attention someplace else. Your Rolfer will probably make it clear that they won't do anything that is more than you can handle. They can tell by the way your body reacts, and besides you can always tell them how you're feeling—the feedback is good for both of you. So you are in control of the situation and safe. Essentially it's a cooperative effort.

People have different ways of opening up the part of the body that's being worked on. It's voluntary but subtle—again, it's letting your body's wisdom work for you. Basically you are keeping your attention in that area, and accepting the Rolfer's pressure. I like to think of the Rolfer's hand as a trusted friend whom I am welcoming in to help me.

Sometimes I just focus on the area and relax. At times when the pain has been intense, I've sometimes found some sort of a visual image like a flower opening (that one occurred to me spontaneously once) or a field of color that's conducive to relaxing or softening to be helpful. Others have imagined breathing into an area, or lighting it up with a flashlight; the point is that somehow just bringing your attention to that place instead of leaving the scene allows the work to go better.

9. And finally, look in the mirror a lot. Be narcissistic! You'll like the changes.

*It is very important to make the person being Rolfed realize
s/he is the one who can do the feeling about what has happened
to him/her. 'What should I feel?' Well, who the heck knows
what you should feel except yourself.*

—Ida Rolf

Your Personal Rolfing Journal

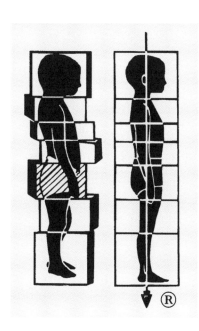

This Journal is intended as a tool to help you take note of the sensations, awarenesses, and changes you experience as you go through your Rolfing process. Even though the medium in Rolfing is a physical approach, when you change the outside you simultaneously change the inside.

Approach your experience as an experiment without judgement and have fun noting all the sensations, thoughts, memories, connections, and revelations you may have as you go through this process week after week.

Since you are engaged in a process of rapid change, I encourage you to make comments in the journal as you think of them. You will find that what felt significant at one moment in time may fade into the background as the next intense awareness comes.

I think you will find this useful in helping you to process your own experience later on, long after you have completed your Rolfing sessions.

Quotes throughout this journal are from *Ida Rolf Talks About Rolfing and Physical Reality* by Rosemary Feitis, published by the Rolf Institute, Boulder, Colorado.

Questions to consider

What am I aware of in my body? (Before, during, and after Rolfing)

What is comfortable or uncomfortable? What are the tension patterns or pain patterns? How do I look? How do I feel in my body? Are there changes in my temperature and breathing?

What am I feeling? (Before, during, and after Rolfing)

What feels good to me about myself? What doesn't feel good? What do I want to change? What feels outside my control? When? Why? Am I depressed/sad/angry? Am I experiencing mood swings or attitude changes? What are my responses to situations?

What's happening to my energy level? (Before, during, and after Rolfing)

What changes are there in my energy, either in quantity or quality? Am I more or less active? How am I spending my time?

What are my dreams?

Are they oriented in the past, present, or future? What themes occur? Are any dreams recurring? What feels significant about my dreams?

What are my dietary habits?

What shifts are occurring in my consumption of alcohol, drugs, sugar, coffee, and foods? What am I decreasing or increasing? What am I eliminating, adding, or substituting?

Session 1

"We are all looking for a way to evoke human potential. We are all looking for a way to establish greater physical and mental vitality."

Session 2

"When the tone of the soft tissue is balanced, there is a sensation of lightness in the body."

Session 3

"We are not truly upright, we are only on our way to being upright. This is metaphysical consideration. One of the jobs of a Rolfer is to speed that process along. We want to get a man out of the place where gravity is his enemy. We want to get him in the place where gravity reinforces him and is a friend, a nourishing force."

Session 4

"If you want a different conclusion, start with a different premise."

Session 5

"All we are doing is directing the flow of gravity by virtue of organizing the body as though it were an electric wire so that gravity can flow through it."

Session 6

"Bodies need to lengthen and be balanced, and a balanced body will give rise to a better human being."

Session 7

"The body process is not linear, it's circular; always it is circular. One thing goes awry and its effects go on and on. A body is a web, connecting everything with everything."

Session 8

"To me, strength is balance. Maximum strength exists in terms of muscles that are balanced."

Session 9

"Rolfing has to do with gravity. Not chemistry, not medicine, not the idea of individually fixing this and that gone wrong. Gravity is the one and only tool that we use. I think my experience justifies making this very broad assumption: gravity is the only tool that deals with chronic situations in the body."

Session 10

"Over and over again, people come to me, and they tell me, 'You just don't know how strong I am.' They say 'strength' and I want to hear 'balance.' The strength idea has effort in it: this is not what I am looking for. Strength that has effort in it is not what you need; you need the strength that is the result of ease."

Acknowledgments

ACKNOWLEDGMENTS FOR SECOND EDITION 2023

First of all, I want to acknowledge all my clients and parents who so generously shared their personal journeys with Rolfing, and who gave written permission to use their stories as well as the before and after Rolfing photos for this book.

The following people had a big hand in upgrading all aspects of this book: Susan Hoffman, editing; Arlene Appelbaum, editing and proofreading; Jillian Platt, original cover illustration; Diane Waller, cover design; Jill Rivard, art consulting; and Carrie Voyles, editing corrections and book support services.

ACKNOWLEDGMENTS FOR FIRST EDITION 1991

This book owes its existence to the generosity of many people. I am grateful to all of them.

This book would not have been possible without the many clients who made valuable contributions during the process. In particular I wish to thank all the individuals whose stories appear in this book. I equally appreciate those people whose stories do not appear.

I would like to thank Nancy Wells, the primary editor, with whom I have worked most closely over the past five years. Without her constant effort and loyalty, this book would still be a someday project.

Charlotte O'Hara deserves many thanks for spending countless hours interviewing people. Her enthusiasm and love for Rolfing is contagious.

I would especially like to thank Jude La Claire, my friend and colleague. For fourteen years we have journeyed together in the work of facilitating people in the process of self-healing. I am also grateful for her many contributions.

Linda Thweatt was responsible for the final design and production of the first edition. She went above and beyond the call of duty, contributing a positive attitude and hard work in the critical final hours before publication.

A note about the author

Peter Koeleman

Throughout Briah Anson's life she has been a leader and an innovator. Her key strength is her breadth of experience with integrated care modalities coupled with her commitment to enriching every client, be it a person or animal with whom she works.

This calling began in Costa Rica where Briah grew up pursuing and becoming a highly trained athlete, ballet dancer, member of the national swim team, tennis player, and golfer (four-time Junior National Golf Champion of Costa Rica). At age seventeen, she set the Costa Rican women's Olympic javelin record. In college, Briah continued to compete in swimming and tennis, playing on the men's varsity tennis team.

Briah received her BA degree from Oakland University and an MA in Counseling and College Student Personnel from Penn State University. She was a member of the Dean of Students' staff at Penn State University, Colorado College, and the University of Minnesota, Morris.

Today, Briah is a Certified Advanced Rolfer® and a Certified Rolf Movement® Practitioner with over forty years of experience. She is the author of *Rolfing®: Stories of Personal Empowerment* (1991) and its second edition, Indie published by Heartland Personal Growth Press in 2023. She also published *Animal Healing: The Power of Rolfing® Structural Integration* (2011), and produced a children's video, *Growing Right with Rolfing®* (1996).

Continuing her evolution as a healer, Briah completed her academic training in Classical Homeopathy at the Northwestern Academy of Homeopathy in Minnesota (2019). This homeopathic training deeply informs her Rolfing work. Briah also incorporates a variety of other healing modalities including Rolfing scar tissue work, Frequencies of Brilliance energetic work, and the Erchonia® Low-Level Laser Therapy (LLLT) into her practice.

Briah has also been a mentor for new Rolfers. She is a member of the Dr. Ida Rolf Institute® and the International Association of Structural Integrators®.

Briah has a private practice in Minneapolis, Minnesota.

"This is the gospel of Rolfing;
when the body gets working appropriately,
the force of gravity can flow through.
Then, spontaneously, the body heals itself."

—*Ida Rolf*